The Unfinished
Health Agenda

The Unfinished Health Agenda

Lessons from Hawai'i

Edited by Bob Grossmann
and Jim Shon

Hawai'i State Primary Care Association

HONOLULU

This book is printed on acid-free paper and
meets the guidelines for permanence and
durability of the Council on Library Resources

*Copy editing, book design,
and camera-ready
pages by Jan Ferris Koltun*

Distributed by
University of Hawaii Press
Order Department
2840 Kolowalu Street
Honolulu, Hawai'i 96822

Contents

Preface

This book provides some of the missing pieces to the puzzle of health-care reform. Its editors and contributors contend that the national and local debate, as well as the proposals, are incomplete. We invite you to explore the hidden *facets* of the system, as well as many of the hidden *clients*. We offer differing perspectives of the strengths, weaknesses, structure and political forces driving health care in Hawai'i. Each author writes from years of specialization.

The section, **No Room On The Bus for Us**, examines three groups who seem to be always left out. Jon Martell, Susan Chandler and Mark O'Donnell powerfully portray the plight of Hawai'i's homeless and those suffering from mental-health problems. Jeanette Takamura and Marilyn Seely explore the dynamics of long-term care financing, and the dangers of letting this issue slide too long.

From clients left out, we move to the big picture: **Myths, Money and Medicine**. Deane Neubauer reconstructs the context for an overall analysis of health-care finance and reform in Hawai'i. Few doubt that the flow of cash ultimately sets the rules of who pays or who plays. Hank Foley explores Hawai'i's much touted Prepaid Health Care Act, the only employer-based mandate in the United States. Bob Grossmann argues that Hawai'i has lost its health-care reform edge and that some of its strengths are being eroded. Jim Shon gives us a guided tour of the system's fragmented structure.

In Section Three, **Who Dares To Care?**, we look at the persistent debate over who will deliver primary care and under what circumstances. To say there is competition for the health-care dollar among professionals is putting it mildly. Bob Hollison provides an insight into just how specialist-conscious our medical schools have become. Greg Loos, Jan Pryor and Daniel Domizio examine the need for mid-level practitioners such as Physician Assistants and Certified Nurse Midwives. Nancy McGuckin-Smith launches us head-on into the legislative debate over whether nurses should be allowed to prescribe drugs.

Section Four, **Harm Reduction and Other Heresies**, takes a close look at some tough policy questions. Health care is more than just money, global budgets and government pigeonholes. It is values, and how to move beyond our cherished myths and prejudices to make a real impact on the lives of our people. The conventional wisdom of the day is challenged in three chapters. Don Topping gives us an insight into the raging debate over legalization of drugs. Scott Whitney and Joyce Ingram-Chinn follow up with an in-depth review of how the chemically-dependent client is an unwanted element in the system. Finally, Pam Lichty, describes Hawai'i's heroic efforts to stem the growth of the AIDS epidemic among populations such as intravenous drug users.

No serious analysis of current health care would be complete without a hard look at managed care and how it really affects people. Section Five, **Managed Care or Damaged Care?** begins with Kathryn Smith-Ripper's placement of the QUEST experiment into the larger debate over the use of managed care as a model. Geri Marullo and Chenoa Farnsworth discuss the impacts of managed care on women and children, giving a way to measure its effectiveness. Frank Chong writes from the perspective of community health centers.

Finally, in the hope that reading any part of this book will make you want to learn more, University of Hawai'i School of Public Health Librarian Ginny Tanji has compiled a Bibliography of useful resources.

These chapters were designed to foster a broad debate. The authors volunteered all efforts, to help us to meet our inherent responsibility to question the cornerstones of whatever is being proposed to restructure national and state health-care systems. Because Hawai'i's plans may be preempted by the Clinton program, understanding the relationships between Hawai'i's strengths and weaknesses and the national plan is important.

If the other states are watching, and if Congress and the President care to look beyond Hawai'i's employer mandate, there are lessons to be learned. Coverage is not care. Medical care is not health care. One cookie-cutter approach does not necessarily do the job for all segments of the population. We hope this volume contributes to a fuller understanding of the Health State.

PART ONE
No Room on the Bus for Us

CHAPTER ONE
Another Day for You and Me in Paradise
Health Care for the Homeless

JON MARTELL

She calls out to the man on the street
"Sir, can you help me?
I'm cold and I've nowhere to sleep,
Is there somewhere you can tell me?"
He walks on, doesn't look back
He pretends he can't hear her . . .
Seems embarassed to be there.
Oh, think twice, it's another day for you and me in paradise.

Phil Collins, But Seriously

The Institute for Human Services (IHS), the major emergency shelter for the homeless of urban Honolulu, is a nondescript cinder-block building relegated to the city's historically-disreputable warehouse district. It is situated, with apt though accidental irony, between the Salvation Army Rehabilitation Center and the City Morgue. During the day, people passing on the way to the K-Mart across the street probably notice nothing unusual: a few vagrants sleep in the bushes in front or loiter in the side parking lot. The day here is quiet.

In the evening, after the shoppers and workers are mostly gone, the scene changes. Gradually as twilight deepens, the homeless straggle in from the rest of the city, drawn by the prospect of a hot meal and a place to sleep. They come singly or in small groups, silently or talking either to themselves or others. You might not notice the first few but they gather to become a group, a throng, and eventually, a crowd. Every night, 200 to 300 people lay out thin mats, one next to the other, and sleep in ranks on the floor. They choose the fitful slumber in the crowded, noisy shelter to the insecurity of night on the streets.

The respite is not long. In the morning, the shelter duty managers awaken the sleepers early. At 5:30 exactly, the lights

3

are turned on and guests must get up, get dressed, eat breakfast and move back onto the streets. In the half-light they go out to day labor, appointments at social-service agencies, or to hours of idleness in the streets, parks, or malls.

Not everyone eats and moves on: every morning a queue forms in front of the shelter medical clinic waiting for 6:30 when the doors open. The clinic, part of Kalihi Palama Health Care for the Homeless Project, occupies two small rooms down a narrow hallway on the first floor of the shelter. In the first hour and a half every morning, 40 patients crowd in to receive care. Every weekday, opening before dawn and closing after sunset, the clinic provides services for 80 clients or more. Some patients are acutely sick, many are chronically ill, and most cannot or do not receive health care elsewhere.

Were you to take the time to sit in the clinic for a morning, little would impress you. You might remark on how small the main clinic area is, barely 15 feet square, or how crowded and noisy it becomes as a half-dozen clients or more squeeze in for attention. The medical care, however, would seem mundane. Clients crowd in for trivial problems: some to have minor wounds cleaned and bandaged, some for vitamins or packets of their prescription medications. People wander in for colds, coughs, or fevers or just to sit and have their blistered feet soaked in antiseptic solution. Occasionally a psychotic patient, agitated and talking to himself or herself, wanders in, complains to no one in particular, and wanders out without waiting for help. Although nothing dramatic happens, the seeming triviality of the complaints conceals the seriousness of the reality.

These people, superficially healthy, receiving simple care for minor problems, are part of what is arguably the most unhealthy population in the country (Brickner, 1986; Bowdler, 1989; Breaky, 1989). Serious illness, hospitalization and premature death are as characteristic of the homeless as the more obvious poverty and lack of housing (Cohen, 1988; Martell, 1992). If you compare them to the general population, these clients will be admitted six times more often to community hospitals and 100 times as often to the state psychiatric hospital (Martell, 1992). They die at a rate six times higher than average, at a median age of 47, in a state where the average life expectancy is 79 years (Martell, unpublished data). If you were to compare them to populations in the Third World, their death rate, 32 per thousand persons each year, exceeds that of the poorest countries.[1] That hospitalization and death rates this high occur in a state with near-universal medical insurance suggests that this problem is not remediable through medical insurance alone.

The issue of homelessness and health is complex. Discussions of homelessness and health-care access often focus on willful behavior and personality flaws in this population. It is common to hear about how the homeless "refuse to take care of themselves" and how they "abuse the system." Such abstract explanations are easy to formulate and justify when setting health-care policy: these individuals do not take care of themselves and they do not use the health-care system as we would wish (Morris, 1989; Wlodarczyk, 1988). Although these constructs appear valid, they fail to grasp the profundity of difficulties that come with homelessness: they assume that the homeless actually have control of their lives. Homelessness, however, is not usually a lifestyle by choice, nor can it be easily unchosen. The homeless condition is not merely lack of adequate housing but a set of concurrent conditions: poor health, social isolation, poverty, impaired social and cognitive skills and despondency.[2]

A personal glimpse into life on the streets is needed to gain an adequate picture of how health and homelessness are interlinked. The following case studies are drawn from clients at the Kalihi-Palama Health Care for the Homeless Project. They have been selected to provide insight into the homeless condition by focusing on the complex interaction of physical health, mental health and social services.

Case 1. Mrs. M.

Mrs. M. was a 56-year old woman of part-Hawai'ian ancestry who had been a client at IHS practically since it was founded as a storefront mission 15 years ago. In appearance, she seemed a typical bag lady: a slight woman, unkept with bedraggled clothes, hair unwashed and out of place and teeth missing. She usually kept to herself, was often noncommunicative and was sometimes hostile, prone to outbursts of temper or to sulking. Her story was difficult to obtain.

Mrs. M, it turned out, was severely intellectually impaired. Though we did not have test results, she had an IQ no greater than 60 and the temperament, in keeping with her mental age, of a four-year-old child: impatient and impulsive. Because of this developmental disability, most of her early life was spent in Waimano Home, an institution for the mentally retarded. Due to her infantile personality and her institutionalization, she never learned basic social skills. When she was moved from Waimano Home to a community group-home in the 1970's, she was unable to adapt. She developed behavioral problems that resulted in a steady downward progression of care homes and residential settings that culminated in her life on the streets and in shelters.

While at the shelter, she married a homeless alcoholic man 15 years her junior. A few months after the wedding her husband was hit by a car while crossing the highway and suffered multiple injuries. After a prolonged hospital stay he was placed in a care home, brain-damaged and immobile. She remained devoted to him and visited him frequently.

Attempts by her state guardian to find a place for her to live were invariably frustrated by Mrs. M.'s insistence that she must be close to her husband and by her inability to interact with other people. Placement in care homes, when one could be arranged, always resulted in temper tantrums, shouting fits and eviction. Eventually she became unplaceable.

Medically, she suffered from diabetes and severe arteriosclerosis. These conditions were worsened by the uncontrolled diet at the shelter, cigarette smoking, occasional binges of alcohol and her sporadic health care. Because of her disabilities, she received medical coverage through Medicaid and Medicare, which her state guardian conscientiously kept active. Ability to pay for office visits and medication was not a problem.

For Mrs. M. having insurance was not enough. Her private physician became frustrated by the difficulties in caring for her. She often forgot appointments and, because of her personality, was impatient and disruptive when she did keep them. What care he could provide was limited by her inability to understand diet and her incapacity to comprehend or undertake more complicated treatment for her diabetes. Although her disease was not controlled by pills, insulin therapy was not possible as she seemingly could not learn to administer it herself. The result was two hospitalizations for hyperosmolar coma[3] and the loss of several finger tips because of gangrene.

After her second hospitalization in coma, the Health Care for the Homeless Project decided to manage her care aggressively. She was switched from pills to supervised insulin therapy. Every morning she came to the clinic to get her insulin injected and her blood sugar checked. Reluctant at first, she gradually learned the routine. Once, when in an exercise of willfulness, she stopped coming, arrangements were made through her guardian to make her weekly allowance contingent on her receiving medication. After three months she began giving her own shots; within six months she was able to give her own insulin without supervision.

Once she was capable of self-care and her diabetes was stabilized, her guardian was able to place her in a single-room apartment close to her husband. The entire process took more than six months but at the end, the hospitalization ceased and Mrs. M. was suitably housed. She continues to live independently and has not returned to the streets in the more than two years since her placement.

Case 2. Mr. S.
On the day the Health Care for the Homeless Project opened in May, 1988, Mr. S. was there at the shelter. He was pointed out by a psychiatrist from the State Division of Mental Health who was concerned because he was severely psychotic, unapproachable, and had a face swollen by an abscessed tooth. Attempts to start him on antibiotics had been unsuccessful because of his suspicion of medication and medical personnel. This paranoia kept him from coming to the clinic for help so the medical staff, concerned that the infection might become serious, would seek him out behind the shelter to offer him Tylenol and antibiotics.

A week passed before he accepted any medication but this was the crucial first step. With the medicine, his pain decreased and he came to trust the clinic staff. He started coming to the clinic spontaneously to ask for Tylenol or to just sit in the waiting area and ramble incoherently to himself. He was allowed to come in and sit as part of a process of engagement.[4] Each time he came, the clinic staff would try to make contact: give him coffee, or talk to him. One staff member made an extra effort by sitting with him to talk and sing songs. This probably made all the difference.

It took a year before he was ready for the next step. After six months of these daily visits we began to offer him Thorazine, a medication for schizophrenia, every time he came to the clinic.

It took another six months before he agreed. Once he started medication, the results were gradual but dramatic. Over the next few months, the paranoia decreased and then disappeared. Thoughts that had been rambling and incoherent became organized and understandable; intelligible conversations became possible; and he began to interact with people. Things that had been impossible before were accomplished: obtaining identification, signing up for food stamps and Medicaid, getting dental and medical care, and getting him interested in a place to live. After two years of effort he was placed in a transitional housing program. Three years later he continues to live independently and receive regular psychiatric and medical care.

Case 3. Mr. P.

Mr. P. was a 56-year-old alcoholic, though he liked to call himself a drunk. He grew up fast in west-side Chicago: started working at age 10, dropped out of school and started drinking at age 12. The forty years that followed consisted of a series of dead-end jobs that he left, a marriage that failed and excessive drinking that became constant. Over time the alcohol took its toll on his body and spirit. He severed all his social ties to became a loner: socially isolated and aloof.

As he grew more distant from other people, his life became progressively more intertwined with the medical world. Alcohol led to nerve damage and seizures. Trauma, mostly while he was drunk, led to many broken bones, most of which he refused to have repaired. He had repeated emergency-room visits and hospital admissions for seizures, for infections and for alcohol withdrawal. Eventually he was being hospitalized once a month or more; ambulance crews knew him by name; and emergency rooms knew his history by heart.

Mr. P. was a classic "abuser" of a medical system that was not set up to deal with him. The problem was not access to health care: he had medical coverage that allowed him to get care and medication if he wished. The problem was that he did not want treatment. He disdained regular medical care, saying that all doctors are "quacks" and that none of them could help him. He was, ultimately, largely right. Because his drinking and his independence were non-negotiable, there was little that could be done for him medically. If Mr. P. were to receive appropriate medical care, it would have to be against his desires. It was on this basis that intervention was undertaken.

The first step in the rehabilitation of Mr. P. was to request that his Supplemental Security Income be assigned to a representative payee so that he would not have direct access to money. A standing account was set up at a restaurant where he could eat; a daily monetary allowance was established. A contract was drawn up requiring that Mr. P. go to the clinic for his medication each day before he collected his allowance.

For six months this contract worked. He came every day to get his thiamine (a vitamin that prevents nerve damage from alcohol), his seizure medicine and, when necessary, his antibiotics. Hospitalization stopped and ambulance trips decreased. The solution was effective but proved temporary. Eventually his need for independence became more important than his health or money. He stopped coming to the clinic, stopped taking medication, and stopped collecting his allowance. Efforts were made to get him back into supervision but he refused. He remained a loner, scrounging money for drink, and his health deteriorated. One day after breakfast Mr. P. stood up, walked over to the dumpster behind the shelter, collapsed and died.

Although these case studies are drawn from individuals with markedly different backgrounds, common themes in their stories illustrate why this population is so unhealthy and why the traditional medical system is not able to reach them. The central idea is that availability of medical insurance alone is not enough. The reasons for this are: 1) those who need medical insurance the most may have the hardest time getting it; 2) providing medical care for the cognitively-impaired takes incredible patience; 3) medical needs must be met in a context that deals with the patients' other needs; and 4) sometimes nothing works. These themes should be explored in depth to understand their implications for health care delivery and reform.

Difficulty Obtaining Medical Insurance

> The law, in its infinite wisdom, prevents the rich as well as the poor from stealing bread and sleeping under bridges.
>
> *Anatole France*

Seventy percent of the urban homeless population in Hawai'i has no medical coverage (Martell, 1992). These uninsured homeless are a heterogeneous group comprising able-bodied young men who work part-time or 'under the table'; illegal immigrants for whom health insurance is not available; minimum-wage earners who need the money more than the insurance; and the cognitively impaired.[5] All court financial disaster through serious illness. All court medical disaster by delaying their care because they cannot afford to pay. Most of these uninsured individuals qualify for health insurance. The functionally-capable choose it; the mentally-ill, the mentally retarded, and the demented—those who need help the most—are without insurance because they are incapable of understanding the need or completing the necessary paper work.

Forty percent of the homeless population is seriously mentally ill, mentally retarded or demented (Fischer, 1986; Breakey, 1989). These individuals are so impaired that they have become isolated from friends and family, have stopped medication and are lost to state and Federal support services. Driven by their needs, their fears and their delusions, they live chaotic lives on the streets. They live a perilous life of exploitation, violence and incarceration. Most of their encounters with authority come in entanglements with the legal system, most of their medical care occurs in visits to the emergency room. Neither experience is pleasant for them, so they become distrustful of establishment, government, and medicine. These patients, because of their disability, are entitled to social assistance and medical coverage through Medicaid, Medicare, or both. They cannot obtain this help for many reasons. Often they have no personal identification and cannot or will not give the background information needed to obtain duplicates. If identification is obtained, clients often refuse to sign forms because of their paranoia or previous bad experiences with government. After the forms are signed, there are still difficulties. A series of appointments follows, for intake, for review, and for exams. All must be kept without fail but the clients are too impaired to get their mail or remember dates, so frequent absences occur. The bureaucracy is most unforgiving of missed appointments.

The system has few options for the individual incapable of completing the paperwork or keeping appointments. Guardianship for the demented or mentally-retarded can take six months to establish;[6] involuntary commitment for the mentally ill can only be obtained if the person is an immediate danger to themselves or others. Often the only way to obtain assistance for these clients is by working outside the system: stabilizing them first, then leading them step-by-step through the appointments and paperwork. For Mr. S. stabilization took a year and a half of intensive work. Very few agencies can commit that much time and effort.

A Lengthy Process

The cases of Mrs. M. and Mr. S. are examples of the persistence needed to care for persons with cognitive impairment. This process—making contact, gaining trust, initiating therapy, and stabilization—can take a year or more. Over that time, daily contact and special attention are required. Mrs. M. had well over 500 clinic visits prior to placement and Mr. S. over 700. Some clients still active with the project have had a thousand encounters with clinic personnel. Some require long periods or continued contact after placement to be able to maintain their stability.

Community clinics and medical offices are not able to work with patients in this way. Not only are they incapable of providing daily attention, there is no financial incentive to do so. Nearly all of the encounters during the stabilization process are not reimbursable through insurance and there is no alternate way to recover the cost.

Contextual Treatment

I often do six impossible things before breakfast.
Red Queen in Lewis Carroll's Through the Looking Glass

Health-care providers are more accustomed to viewing medical care in isolation than in the context of other needs. To them medical care is *the* priority, rather than one of several conflicting needs and priorities. This attitude works well in general but causes difficulties when working with members of disadvantaged populations such as the homeless. In the hierarchy of needs for these individuals, medical care has a low priority, falling after food, shelter, money, and companionship unless there is pain or severe illness.[7] Indeed, the cognitively impaired patient may not perceive the need for medical care even when seriously ill. Health maintenance and preventive care carry trivial importance to someone who is hungry, or broke, or mentally ill.

This conflict of priorities more than anything else explains the perception by health-care providers that the homeless individuals abuse the medical system. That they do not keep appointments, do not follow through on treatment, and that they neglect illness until they are seriously ill is undeniable. That the burden of caring for these neglected illnesses falls disproportionately on the emergency rooms and hospitals is also undeniable. To understand this as willful abuse, however, is to misunderstand the context of their lives. They are noncompliant because other priorities intervene or because they cannot understand the need for adherence. They neglect illness or fail to follow-up because services are not available in a location, at a time, or in an acceptable non-threatening environment.

The inconvenient locations and operating hours of the Health Care for the Homeless project are intentional. To provide for homeless patients, services must be available when their priority conflicts are minimal: before and after work, before government offices open, and before they have sorted out social groups or plans for the day. This means offering care at the shelters and soup kitchens in early morning and late evening and in the parks during the day.

Traditional medical providers are not set up to provide care in this way (Torrey, 1990). The days of the mobile physician providing house calls and services outside the office are long gone, replaced by large multi-practitioner offices and health centers. Even community health centers now function this way. Outreach programs, when they exist, are usually for health education or to bring individuals back to the clinics for care. This is not an issue of neglect by health care providers but of financial necessity. The economic and technologic imperatives of medical care require centralized services. Health-care reform may accelerate the proces, leading to increased isolation from health services of special needs groups such as the homeless .

Sometimes Nothing Works

Reasonable expectations must be set for projects working with populations such as these. None will solve homelessness, none will do more than reduce hospitalization and death rates, and gains may be off-set by growth in the population or change in disease patterns. Tuberculosis and HIV disease have had a major impact on the health of homeless populations on the East Coast but not yet inHawai 'i. This kind of change in underlying patterns of illness can make effective programs look ineffectual when it occurs.

On an individual basis, the case of Mr. P. illustrates this final principle. With patience and determination, success is possible with many but not all homeless persons. Some will remain unapproachable due to mental illness, dementia, addiction or personal choice. The inability to a few does not negate the value of projects both to those it helps and the community at large.

The Cost of Doing Nothing

The problems of medical care for the homeless population cannot be ignored. A study conducted in Honolulu suggests that the excess expense of hospitalization alone cost $3.2 million for each thousand homeless persons over one year's time (Martell, 1992). With an estimated 4,000 urban homeless individuals in Hawai'i at any given time,[8] the projected expense is in excess of $12 million annually. This does not include emergency room and ambulance charges. One way or another the cost of these excess health-care services will be recovered, through higher charges, higher insurance rates, or taxes to cover excess Medicaid expenditures. If adequate care is not provided at shelters and in the parks, the homeless will come to the emergency rooms and hospitals and the bill will have to be paid.

The problems will not be solved by instituting universal medical insurance on a national level. In Hawai'i, substantial barriers to medical care continue to exist for this population despite Hawai'i's near-universal medical insurance. There is every reason to belive that these institutional and personal barriers would persist despite a National Health Insurance Program.

Indeed, the homeless problem cannot be solved through any amount of medical intervention alone. The situation, as illustrated above, is a complex social and medical issue and needs to be addressed by social and economic means. This does not mean, however that the situation cannot be ameliorated. Intensive case management is effective in other populations analogous to the homeless. Effective intervention is not, however, inexpensive. In a study of the severely mentally-ill, case management reduced exacerbations of illness and hospital admissions, but the cost was roughly equivalent to the expense that would have been incurred if no intervention been undertaken (Borland, 1989). There was, however, a gain: the improvement in quality of patients' lives. No data exists but a similar outcome might be anticipated for the homeless population. In other words, to reduce the excess cost of medical illness by half, $6 million each year, might require a program that costs a similar $6 million annually. It is, however, an outcome that would be satisfactory: it may well cost no more to improve the quality people's lives than to do nothing.

Conclusion

In Hawai'i, much is already being done to provide medical and psychiatric services for the homeless. The Wai'anae Coast Comprehensive Health Center, Waikiki Health Center, and Kalihi-Palama Health Clinic all have active programs for this population. Funding for these programs comes from Federal McKinney Block Grants, Hawai'i State Primary Care Funds, Hawai'i Division of Mental Health, Aloha United Way, and various private agencies.

From 1988 to 1993 the Kalihi-Palama Health Care for the Homeless project has seen patient encounters triple from 8,000 annually to 24,000 annually. Despite this growth, funding from many sources has been reduced.[9] Every year during the Federal and State legislative sessions there is uncertainty about funding, an insecurity that makes it hard to build a stable and high quality program. The long-term commitment on a local and national level is unclear, particularly with the projected expense of a National Health Insurance Program.

The lesson to be drawn from the homeless is not limited to that population alone. Universal health insurance will never be sufficient to meet all the medical needs of our diverse society. Special populations, such as homeless and migrant workers, will require additional initiatives that do not rely on traditional health-care providers and medical insurance. These projects will need independent and stable funding and will need to co-exist with insurance providers and managed health-care systems. To be effective, these programs will have to be designed along the principles outlined above and staffed by dedicated professionals. Projects such as these will not be cheap but, if well-designed, may well pay for themselves through reducing the demand on expensive tertiary-care medical services.

References

1. The United Nations reports the crude death rate in Ethiopia and Somalia as 21.3 and 23.4 deaths per thousand individuals during the drought year of 1989. These are the highest recorded anywhere during that year but are less than the documentable death rate in the homeless population in the same period. These data are useful for comparison purposes but do not mean the basic causes of death are the same.
2. The complex relationship between medical and social factors in creating and perpetuating the homeless condition are discussed at length in *A Nation in Denial—The Truth About Homelessness* (Baum,1993). It is probable that homelessness is not the primary condition but the end result of medical illness and social isolation. This book makes a compelling case for eliminating the term "homeless" from the discussion.
3. Hyperosmolar coma is the result of neglected diabetes and any concurrent problem that prevents the person from drinking adequate water. The resulting severe dehydration often causes coma and possibly death. In both cases Mrs. M. was found unconscious in the shelter. The fact that she was in a place where someone would notice her probably saved her life.
4. The engagement process is a way of gaining the trust of clients through comfort with the staff and the facility. Individuals needing medical or psychiatric help are often approached with non-threatening, non-directed contact–a greeting, a cup of coffee or conversation. Once trust is established, other issues can be addressed.
5. The group of cognitively-impaired individuals incudes those with significant problems with content or organization of thought. This includes people with mental retardation who have intellectual impairment, with dementia who have impaired memory, and with psychosis who have disorganized thought.
6. Involuntary guardianship for mentally-impaired individuals is a complex process. The individual must first be identified as impaired and a health-care worker must take enough interest in the patient to initiate proceedings. The client must have a competency exam, usually by a psychiatrist, and a formal report must be filed with the Office of the Public Guardian. The mandatory judicial hearing may not take place for six months or more from the time the papers are filed. Even then, significantly impaired individuals can often appear competent enough in court to get the petition for guardianship denied.
7. See Maslow's Hierarchy of Needs for a discussion of the prioritization of needs and how that effects behavior (Maslow,1968).
8. Exact numbers of homeless individuals are difficult to obtain. One study estimated between 6,400 -7,000 individuals are homeless each week

on O'ahu (SMS 1990). Agencies providing services to this population generally thought this estimate too low. Kalihi-Palama Clinic,
which provided services to 1,500 individuals that year, was not included in the count. An estimate of 4,000 urban homeless is a reasonable estimate and may well be low.

9. In 1990, the Kalihi-Palama Health Care for the Homeless Project had 12,315
patient encounters; in 1993, these increased to 24,000. Simultaneously,
Federal McKinney funds have decreased from $116,000 to $110,000
annually; Hawai'i Primary Health Care Funds have decreased from
$135,000 to $122,000 yearly; funding that the Hawai'i Department of
Human Services provides for case management through the shelter
has decreased from $75,000 to $33,000 annually and will be termi-
nated this year. Only funding from the state Department of Health,
Mental Health Division, has increased over this period.

Bibliography

Baum AS, and Burnes, DW. *A Nation in Denial—The Truth About Homelessness.*
1993. Westview Press, Boulder, Colorado.

Borland A, McRae J, Lycan C. Outcomes of five years of intensive case management. *Hospital and Community Psychiatry.* 1989; 40: 369-76.

Bowdler JE. Health problems of the homeless in America. *Nurse Practice,* 1989;
14: 44, 47, 50-1.

Breakey WR, Fischer P, Kramer M, et al. Health and mental health problems of
homeless men and women in Baltimore. *Journal of the American Medical Association,* 1989; 62: 1352-7.

Brickner PW, Scanlan BC, Conanan B, et al. Health problems of the homeless
in America. *Annals of Internal Medicine,* 1986; 104: 405-9.

Cohen CI, Teresi JA, and Holmes D. The physical well-being of old homeless
men. *Journal of Gerontology,* 1989; 43: S121-8.

Demographic Yearbook. United Nations Press. New York 1990.

Fischer PJ, Shapiro S, Breakey WR, *et al.* Mental health and social characteristics of the homeless: a survey of mission users. *American Journal of
Public Health.* 1986; 76: 519-24.

Martell JV, Seitz RS, Harada J, et al. Hospitalization in an urban homeless
population: the Honolulu urban homeless project. *Annals of Internal
Medicine,* 1992; 116: 299-303.

Martell JV. Mortality in an Urban Homeless Population: the Honolulu urban
homeless project. Unpublished. Available on request.

Maslow A. *Toward a Psychology of Being,* New York, 1968.

Morris W, Crystal S. Diagnostic patterns of hospital use by an urban homeless
population. *Western Journal of Medicine.* 1989; 151: 472-6.

SMS Research and Marketing Services. *Hawai'i's Homeless.* Published by SMS
Research and Marketing, Inc. 1042 Fort Street Mall, Suite 200, Honolulu, Hawai'i. 1990.

Torrey EF. Economic barriers to widespread implementation of model programs for the seriously mentally ill. Hospital and *Community Psychiatry.* 1990; 41: 526-31.

Wlodarczyk D, Prentice R. Health issues of homeless persons. *Western Journal
of Medicine.* 1988; 148: 717-9.

CHAPTER TWO

Beyond Mirrors and Smoke
The Challenge of Longevity
and Long-Term Care

JEANETTE TAKAMURA AND MARILYN SEELY

In early April, 1994, a panel of 50 Americans from across the country traveled to Washington, DC, to share their health care concerns with First Lady Hillary Clinton. Toshi Nakasone from Hawai'i brought a poignant personal message which was prophetic of what the American family will face in increasing numbers. Beseeching her to continue the fight to include long-term care provisions in a national health-care reform program, he told Mrs. Clinton that he:

> . . . never dreamed that someone in his family might need long-term care. Then his sister suffered a massive heart attack and had to go to the hospital, ICU and a rehab facility. She exhausted her savings of more than $250,000. Three months later, [other relatives], 85 and 96 years old . . . were diagnosed as having "gradual degeneration of brain functioning" and would do things like leave pots on the hot stove for hours. Mr. Nakasone and his wife were enjoying their retirement when they had to devote their lives to caring for their relatives around the clock. After 13 challenging months, the Nakasones put their kin in a residential care home at the price of $3,600 a month for both . . . (*Health Right*, 1994).

For many, the issue of long-term care seems neither exotic nor immediately compelling enough to capture and hold the public's interest. Instead it is widely seen as a downright depressing subject, best left in the private domain of the family, most particularly its older members. Because long-term caregiving can test and exhaust even the most loving and dedicated of families, the issue will not remain confined to the privacy of the family home.

In July, 1993, Margaret O'Brownlee, by her son's description "very loving and caring, just like any other mom . . . got herself in a situation she could not handle anymore." O'Brownlee, a sole caregiver who had once worked in a gerontology program, broke under the strain and strangled and suffocated her abusive Alzheimer's afflicted mother. Sadly, many caregivers understood her distress.

Pili Gonsalves, a Baby Boomer and a caregiver to her mother, knows all too well the dimensions of despair:

> [She] hasn't sold the Hawai'ian quilts that have been in her family for more than 100 years. But . . .she has sold family jewelry, put her house up for sale and is looking for a second job to cover . . . costs for her mother. Gonsalves, 46, is one of the state's thousands of residents struggling to make ends meet as they pay for expensive care for ill parents, children or other relatives. Instead of staying in the shadows, like many of her friends, she went to the Legislature to ask for a mandatory long-term care program. . . .Gonsalves, who wants to minimize the emotional and financial drain for others, said people won't save on their own and insurance is too expensive. "People don't think about tomorrow," she said. "As it is, they have to work two jobs to pay their bills." [Her mother is] in a residential care home, which costs about $1,500 a month. She said her paycheck and her mother's retirement and Social Security checks don't cover the mortgage on her mother's house. She withdraws from her savings, watching the illness eat up what the family has squirreled away (*Hosek, 1994*).

Because of her experience, Pili pleaded at a legislative hearing for the passage of a mandatory long-term care financing proposal: the Family Hope Program. Had it passed, it would have constituted a public policy breakthrough.

Ambivalence or Care?

Toshi Nakasone, Margaret O'Brownlee, and Pili Gonsalves are among thousands of family members who have experienced the heartbreak of long-term care. But unlike other family dilemmas, long-term care has not yet been fully eased out of the closet into the realm of every-day conversation. The reasons are understandable. The issues are complex, with an alphabet soup of their own to describe levels of disability, care alternatives, financing streams, and more. Many persons extrapolate inaccurately from acute health care. Typically, for example, newcomers to the issue assume that long-term care is provided by physicians using state-of-the-art technology to sustain life in hospital settings.[1] They are grossly mistaken.

But misconceptions abound. One University of Hawai'i gerontologist tells about her own father's erroneous insistence that Medicare provides reimbursement for long-term care. Other professionals admit to advising clients afraid of long-term care costs to transfer their assets to children to qualify for Medicaid, the welfare program funded with matching Federal and state dollars.[2] In so doing, they disregard the fate of non-institutionalized spouses who must then live out their lives in an era of human longevity with limited incomes and very limited assets.[3]

In many regards, long-term care issues are colored by widespread ambivalence about aging, old people, disease and disability, and notions of societal responsibility for those who no longer work at paid jobs—even if they may be productive volunteers or caregivers to grandchildren. They are also colored by ambivalence about the "senior lobby"—sometimes disparagingly called "greedy geezers"—and the emergent role of women. Unfortunately, the ambivalence is borne out of the acceptance of stereotypes. While older persons are faring far better economically because of Social Security and other retirement provisions, there is nearly universal ignorance about longevity's impact upon fixed retirement incomes. Adequate or generous at the time of retirement, such incomes quickly become insufficient when the compound effects of inflation eat away year after year.

Although long-term care is generally thought to be an "old folks" issue, young and old alike are affected by it, as care recipients or as caregivers. Indeed many contend that those truly at risk, "are [mostly] middle-aged people" (Ball, 1989). But young and middle-aged adults who have an interest in seeing long-term care protection established are reluctant to speak about family matters at community forums and legislative hearings. They are not alone. One legislator, in a moment of candor, shared that he "didn't want to have to take care of my parents."

Faced with the day-to-day ramifications of public policy gaps and shortcomings, both care recipients and caregivers are susceptible to being viewed as having planned poorly or as lacking sufficient forbearance or filial piety in dealing with the sometimes unrelenting social, psychological, and economic strains tied to long-term care. For example, 21 percent of informal caregivers studied by Stone, et al, reported concomitantly bearing child care responsibilities, 9 percent quit their jobs because of the demands of long-term caregiving, and 20 percent reported experiencing other forms of work conflict (Stone, Cafferata, and Sangl, 1987). Yet, Americans, who do not as a rule plan and save adequately for their children's college expenses, are rarely subjected to moral judgments about these patterns of behavior. Can everyday people be expected to interact with the threat of long-term care extraordinarily—i.e., planning wisely, saving for retirement, accumulating far greater sums for long-term care, and securing guarantees from loved ones for help if care is needed in the home? Can Baby Boomers save $500,000 apiece to cover their own nursing-home care for two and a half years?

Fox posits an explanation for the American policy-maker's ambivalence toward chronic illness and disability issues. He believes that chronic illness and disability have never caught the fancy of policy-makers because the management of chronic illness and disability is seen "mainly as a problem for people with the lowest incomes" and as a private matter, rather than a public responsibility (Fox, 1993). Whether one agrees with him or not, there is ample evidence of ambivalence in American public policy.

In current times, Clinton's Health Security Act is among one of two national health-care reform proposals to acknowledge the importance of addressing the growing long-term care needs of America's families.[4] While Clinton has called for new home and community care benefits for those unable to perform at least three activities of daily living,[5] most other Congressional proposals have been silent about long-term care or have recommended that its costs be jettisoned to the states.[6]

Policy ambivalence in Hawai'i is exacerbated by the stereotype-driven assumption that Asian and Pacific Islander Americans (APIAs) view long-term care as belonging strictly in the domain of the family. Astute observers would probably argue otherwise: that APIA notions of filial piety and of family responsibility are either eroding or are emerging in new forms much more tolerant of assistance from non-familial sources. At least one recent mainland study has noted that some APIAs would prefer to receive formal institutional care to avoid burdening their children (Yu, Kim, Liu, and Wong, 1993). Indeed, Toshi Nakasone and others caution against assuming that the family, regardless of its ethnic background, can carry long-term care responsibilities and costs unassisted.

In some instances, policy ambivalence is driven by a fear of sacrificing children and child care for elders and long-term care. After more than a quarter century of unrelenting work by child welfare advocates, one bold step by Lt. Governor Ben Cayetano to establish the A+ Afterschool Care Program cut through decades of incremental tinkering in child care. While the work in child care is not complete, it is still possible to note that "child care is an issue we are growing out of and long-term care is an issue we are growing into" (Waihee, 1994). Certainly, long-term care giving tends to be years longer in duration and tends to cost significantly more.

That the public policy agendas for child care and long-term care need not be pitted against each other—one human service need against another—is clear. As in child care, the vast majority—three quarters—of all caregivers are women and a sizeable number of them (approximately two out of three) between the ages of 25 and 64 are also in the workforce (GAO, 1994; The Urban Institute, 1993). It is not surprising that women are beginning to understand the ramifications of long-term care for their families and for their own long-term quality of life. Some are also beginning to consider their life experiences against observations such as that offered by Hartman and Walker:

> ... "family" is a euphemism for women, and community care for the elderly depends primarily on. . . female family members to provide that care (1990).

Here to Stay: The Demographic Realities

This is not to say that men are not familiar with the dilemmas of long-term care and caregiving. Straw (1991) reports that two out of five Americans 45 and older can claim some personal experience with long-term care. Put another way, Stone and Kemper (1989) have noted that nearly 13.3 million Americans have a disabled parent or spouse who may need long-term care.

Like it or not, long-term care as an issue is here to stay. e demographic realities of population aging will ensure this. At the turn of the century, Americans had an average life expectancy of 47 years, with those over age 65 representing a minuscule 4 percent of the U.S. population. By 1990, the average life span had increased to 75.6 years for Americans with adults 65 years of age and older representing about 12.5 percent of the population. While the growth in the older adult population to date has been significant, its future growth will be astounding. By 2030, older Baby Boomers will have doubled the size of the 65+ age segment to about 65.6 million elders, accounting for 22 percent of the U.S. population (DHHS, 1991).

As America "grays" rapidly, the need for nursing-home and home care will rise accordingly. Kemper and Murtaugh estimate that 43 percent of all Americans now turning 65 will use nursing-home services before they die, 21 percent of these requiring nursing-home care for 5 or more years (Kemper and Murtaugh, 1991). Moreover, an AARP report issued in 1988 found that almost one-quarter of those 65 years of age and older and almost one-half of those over age 85 need help with at least one activity of daily living.

Hawai'i's rising long-term care needs are hardly a surprise, given the growth of the elderly population over the last decade. Between 1980 and 1990, this segment grew dramatically (52.4 percent) from 113,944 to 173,733 persons 60+. The 85+ population registered an astonishing 87 percent growth rate, all in comparison to the 14 percent rate of growth in the general population up to 1,108,229 during the last decade (Executive Office on Aging, 1992). By the year 2010, 18.9 percent of Hawai'i's people will be 60 years of age and older, accounting for a 133 percent increase among elders by 2010 (EOA, 1992).

In the context of Hawai'i's remarkable longevity, approximately 17,000 persons are afflicted with Alzheimer's disease and still others suffer from chronic illnesses or injuries that impair physical or mental functioning. Unfortunately, there is a severe shortage of nursing-home beds and of home and community-based services. While the U.S. average was 52.8 beds per 1,000 persons 65+, Hawai'i's nursing-home bed ratio per 1,000 persons 65 years of age and older was 14.4 beds in 1989 (SMG Marketing Group, Inc., 1989). This amounted in 1993 to an inventory of 3,490 nursing-home beds with hundreds of persons spilling over into acute-care beds. Although the State Health Planning and Development Agency (SHPDA) has approved certificates of need for building nearly 1,000 more beds, there are questions as to whether these will be built (SHPDA, 1993; SHPDA, 1994).

A woefully low supply of community-based resources is also a reality in Hawai'i. At the start of the decade, 16 adult day care programs had 563 licensed slots for eligible clients and six adult day health or day hospital programs which had 119 licensed slots. In 1991, 494 Type I adult residential care homes (ARCHs)—which accommodate no more than five residents— offered 2159 beds and 14 Type II ARCHs accommodating six or more residents offered 450 beds to persons needing long-term custodial care (Executive Office on Aging, 1992).

The formal home-care industry in Hawai'i serves approximately 5,000 individuals through 12 home health agencies, licensed by the Joint Commission on Accreditation of Healthcare Organizations, which upholds clearly defined levels of quality. Not all home care is provided by licensed agencies. An unknown number of independent contractors of variable backgrounds and capabilities also offer home care, generally charging less than do licensed agencies. The debate already brewing around the legitimacy, quality, safety, and affordability of care by licensed providers as compared to independent contractors may be expected to heighten in the years ahead.[7]

Long-term care financing options are limited primarily to paying out-of-pocket, depending upon Medicaid, or counting upon private long-term care insurance. While sources of financing are limited, nursing-home care averages $54,000 per year. Such costs must be considered against a two and a half year average length of stay in a nursing facility, usually following years of care in the community or in the home. Small wonder that SHPDA noted that 90-95 percent of Hawai'i's long-term care patients in 1992 were dependent upon Medicaid (SHPDA, 1994).

The future offers little hope under the current financing scenario. Projections by the Executive Office on Aging (EOA) suggest that one year of nursing-home care will cost Baby Boomers more than $200,000 before 2020. In fact, cash outlays by Hawai'i's families for nursing-home care will grow by more than 1,100 percent by 2020 (EOA, 1991).

Hawai'i's Long-Term Care Initiatives
In 1988, the Hawai'i State Legislature adopted the *Long-term care Plan for Hawaii's Older Adults,* the outcome of deliberations by nearly 100 persons from various sectors of the community. The Plan called for action in three basic areas: long-term care services and system development, quality of care, and long-term care financing. Since its enactment, a number of major program initiatives have been instituted by the State (See Table 1.)

Of all the initiatives, the proposed Hawai'i Family Hope Program has been the most complex and the most controversial. Through it, the State sought to protect families against impoverishment, prevent elder abuse and caregiver burnout, meet mounting demographic realities, facilitate manageable individual savings for long-term care, avoid sacrificing other important public policy priorities, institute long-term care service system reform, stimulate the role of private long-term care service providers, establish clear criteria for benefit eligibility, compel service system coordination, and encourage quality of care and cost containment.

The Hawai'i Family Hope Program[8]
By the mid-1980's, rising Medicaid costs and escalating service needs impelled a small handful of states to stretch beyond incremental approaches reliant upon Medicaid waivers and other adjustments to explore the feasibility of developing their own long-term care financing strategies. Hawai'i was one such state.

By 1988, the Robert Wood Johnson Foundation (RWJ) was inviting states to participate in a private long-term care insurance demonstration project. After attending an invitational RWJ project meeting, the State of Hawai'i through the EOA, decided to forge its own way without prematurely committing to a specific financing approach.

The EOA Project Team believed at the outset that Hawai'i's state long-term care financing proposal would be heavily private insurance-based with some public sector components. To avoid begging the question, nonetheless, the Office utilized an analytic design schema to facilitate comparative analyses of different options. The criteria and the factors considered included access/availability, affordability, comprehensiveness of benefit coverage, reliability of benefit pay-out, adequacy of benefits over

Table 1. Major Long-Term Care Program Initiatives Instituted in Hawai'i Since 1988

Information, Access, and Coordination:
- **LTC: Let's Take Charge!:** a long-term care public information program offered through community forums, a long-term care television series, a community college based caregiver training program, and the dissemination of caregiving and other informational guides
- **SAGEline:** a statewide multilingual information telephone access line
- **SAGE Plus:** a health insurance benefits counseling program
- **SAGE Care:** a multilingual Alzheimers information and service project
- **Operation Assist:** a case management research and demonstration project[9]

Home and Community-Based Service Options:
- **CHOICES (Community and Home Options for Independence and Care for Elders through Services):** entrepreneur training, business grants and loans, and technical assistance. Twenty-two new for-fee home and community-based long-term care services were launched.
- **Adult Day Care Development:** a strategic planning and implementation project aimed at developing adult day care as a major long-term care resource
- **Long-Term Care Workforce Development:** an initiative to develop policy and program interventions to build an adequate supply of workers and to assure quality of care

Reliable Reimbursement:
- **The Hawai'i Family Hope Program proposal:** a mandatory state long-term care financing program which would provide in-home, community-based, and nursing-home care

time, the extent to which private long-term care services would be stimulated so that government would not need to become a service provider, client choice of care provider, quality of care, level of asset and income protection, cost containment orientation, Medicaid spend-down, Hawai'i State Medicaid cost savings, Medicaid offsets, the durability of the program through various economic scenarios, and opportunities for the private long-term care insurance industry. Other important considerations included the extent to which a financing strategy might be seen by non-Hawai'i residents as a reason to move to the islands, intergenerational equity, the administrative structure of a program, its fiduciary standards, and others.

More than 100 financing options ranging from private long-term care insurance, social insurance alternatives, government entitlement programs, and to the continuance of the status quo (inaction) were analyzed. Ultimately, the Team believed that policy-makers would appreciate receiving state-of-the-art, multidimensional comparative analyses employing a long-range perspective. It was hoped that this would help them select a "best" alternative through which a "good society" can be pursued by persons of all ages.

The Hawai'i/Brookings/ICF Long-Term Care Simulation Model and actuarial analyses were among the basic analytical tools upon which the Team relied. The Hawai'i/Brookings/ICF Long-Term Care Simulation Model used microeconomic computer simulation techniques on a sample of 28,000 individuals to project the number of persons who would consume specific home and community-based and institutional long-term care services in Hawai'i from now through the year 2020. The financing of such usage through a range of public and private payment sources was also projected over time.

In order to ensure analytical accuracy, the Brookings/ICF Model had to be modified by the EOA project team to reflect such local realities as population distribution patterns by age, sex, marital status, employment status, income, institutional and noninstitutional service utilization rates, and living cost. The EOA team also modified the Model by developing a module to permit the simulation of funding and benefit provisions for long-term care financing options, and enhanced the Model to reflect the participation in a long-term care financing program of all age groups.[10]

The Hawai'i Family Hope Program proposal which was put before the 1993 Legislature detailed a comprehensive mandatory State long-term care financing program for bona fide Hawai'i residents, regardless of health status.[11] Although the Project Team had anticipated that their proposal would rely heavily upon a private insurance base, the outcomes of the analyses pointed out that this would not be most advantageous or helpful to Hawai'i's families. Program benefits included coverage of both home and community-based and institutional care —respite, home care, home health care, adult day care and day health, care in adult residential care homes and in nursing homes, and alternative care. Access to such benefits was to be phased-in and benefit vesting was a feature of the proposal.[12] When fully vested, the insured would have access to 80 percent coverage for long-term care services for life. The EOA anticipated that most participants would subscribe to a supplemental private insurance plan to cover the 20 percent copayment.

Funds were to be administered by a State Long-Term Care Fund, for which fiduciary responsibilities and investment guidelines were explicitly detailed. It was anticipated that the actual insurance operations of the program would be contracted out to the private sector.

A mandatory contribution or a tax was not cause for jubilation in the Project Team, the Waihee Administration, or among interested legislators. All parties subjected the proposal to innumerable challenges, seeking reassurances that there was not any other, more palatable means of financing. In the end, there could be no integrity without presenting the recommendations and findings straightaway.

Support for the proposed program came from senior citizen, social welfare, health, and labor organizations state-wide as well as from a number of local and national organizations, such as the American Association of Retired Persons and the National Association of Retired Federal Employees. Many of the Hawaii groups subsequently organized themselves into The Coalition for Affordable Long-Term Care and engaged in letter writing, lobbying, developing petitions, and other grassroots organizing activities. By 1993, 32,000 petitioners of all ages had signed on in support of the Family Hope Program.

Opposition to the proposed program came primarily from the Chamber of Commerce—opposed in principle to any mandatory program—and from parts of the life and health insurance industry. The Chamber's stance followed its 1970s opposition to the Prepaid Health Care Act and its early 1990s rebuff of dependent care legislation. It lobbied vigorously, relying upon its "Monday Report," radio spots, and meetings with the Health Care Association, the life and the health underwriters associations, at least two private long-term care insurance companies, private sector lobbyists, and government representatives.

Active insurance opposition came generally from companies and agents who did not understand the societal consequences of private insurance's shortcomings or the potential of the supplemental insurance market created by the proposed program. Regrettably, insurance groups that understood both chose to refrain from expressing their support publicly.

There were other complications during both the 1993 and 1994 sessions. Nationwide, government as an institution was under attack, with the public's confidence undermined first by a faltering economy and also by a series of fiascos ranging from Iran-Contra to the savings and loan scandals and the misuse of the U.S. House Bank. Taxes were a major issue, exacerbated by Bush's "read my lips" promise which sounded even more disingenuous over time.

The Hawai'i scenario was no less complex. The State's economy was registering all-time lows, turning the price of living in "paradise" into a popular topic. The Waihee Administration was winding to a close with public approval ratings falling far short of those received in its initial years. And the kinds of hard-hitting assessments generally put into play in the last years of any administration as a prelude to a new gubernatorial election fanned the mood of the day. As was the case nation-wide, the reinvention and "right sizing" of government was on everyone's agenda, without consideration of the requisite infrastructure, given the public's expectations of services and programs or of the net economic impact of such restructuring upon the State and upon families with unemployed members.

Hawai'i legislators were understandably hesitant to act in such a context. Questions were raised and answered in legislative hearings, briefings, and interim meetings about the actuarial figures, the Trust Fund, in-migration of persons interested in long-term care protection, whether the program needed to be mandatory, whether a program could be constructed to cover a smaller population, whether the financing mechanism could be a sales or a general excise or an employer tax or anything else, whether the 0.4 percent tax was too high or too low, the stance of the Administration, and whether a State program would be premature in light of the Clinton Administration's efforts to adopt a national health-care reform package. After the 1994 Session had concluded, more than one member of the leadership of the Legislature stated, however:

> It wasn't the numbers. We didn't really have any questions about the work. It was a political decision. We've got to do something. We may have to raise a tax. We just couldn't do it this year.

Indeed, decisions about proposals such as the Health Security Act and the Family Hope Program are political and differences of opinions about them are essentially ideologically based.

Beyond Mirrors and Smoke

The convergence of a number of factors—longevity, female labor force participation, the evolving structure of the family, the effects of long-term care upon productivity in the workplace and the quality of family life, diminishing family resources for long-term care,[13] the rising cost of long-term care, the short supply of long-term care services, among others—will heighten the need for social policy interventions in the future, particularly if national health-care reform legislation passes without substantial new long-term care provisions.

There is much to be learned from Hawai'i's own history about the dangers of waiting for national health-care reform, which may or may not occur and which may or may not cover long-term care. Since 1937, the United States has been "on the verge" of establishing a national health care program. Vision and courage were all that a few Hawai'i legislators and the labor community had in 1974 when they succeeded in engineering the passage of the Prepaid Health Care Act. The opposition then to a state health insurance program was considerable and from nearly the same groups, as it is now to a state long-term care financing program.

The impact of a public policy of inaction or of incremental action will mean that the threat of impoverishment will continue to loom over our families. It will mean delays in the development of a sorely-needed long-term care infrastructure. Years of planning and preparation are needed to build nursing homes, to develop more community-based programs, to recruit and train needed workers.

Wiener has asserted:

Although it is fashionable to argue that the problems of long-term care are insolvable, its financing is actually one of the more tractable social problems. Unlike crime, poverty, teen-age pregnancy or racism, we do in fact know how to solve it. The answer is to raise. . .money. The question is whether we as a society are smart enough and have enough political will to do so (1991).

Mirrors and smoke will not hide the everyday challenges of long-term care. It is a matter of time before the family threshold is unable to contain the burden, strain, and fears of those receiving and providing long-term care. Few are likely to be exempt from grappling with the thorny issues it presents. Baby Boomers will be the most hard pressed as they find themselves dealing with their parents' and their own long-term care needs and as they begin to join the ranks of our senior population. But the challenges presented by longevity and long-term care also offer opportunities, if Hawai'i rejects a course of benign neglect. The opportunities which are within the grasp of Hawai'i's people are opportunities to be prepared for one's own advanced years; to live free from the fear of disability, impoverishment, and of burdening family members when they cannot serve as caregivers; to have a good supply of home- and community-based services and of nursing-home beds; to receive quality care; to ensure that all persons of all ages will "have room on the bus" to live lives of dignity. None of this will evolve on its own. Families and individuals young and old can ill afford to turn away from engagement in the creation of public policy directions which must be taken by the state. Without this, there will be no cause for family hope now or in the new century to come.

References

1.   Long-term care can be defined as "a wide variety of ongoing health and social services provided for individuals who need assistance on a continuing basis because of physical or mental disability. Services can be provided in an institution, the home, or the community, and include informal services provided by family or friends as well as

formal services provided by professionals and agencies" (Executive Office on Aging, 1991, p. D-6). For the most part, long-term care is custodial care provided primarily by the family or by nurse aides.

2. Currently, persons who transfer their assets, within a 36-month period, for the purpose of qualifying for Medicaid assistance are held liable for their own long-term care costs. The 1994 Legislature passed HB 3323, SD 2, CD 1, Relating to Recovery of Payments, to facilitate the State's recovery of assets from persons who intentionally transfer assets for the sole purpose of becoming eligible for medical assistance. The legislation provides for placement of a lien against property owned by an institutionalized patient, if such person cannot return home.

3. Under existing provisions, a married individual receiving Medicaid assistance with long-term care costs may not have a monthly income or assets exceeding acertain amount. This means that the surviving spouse must live with limited resources.

4. The Clinton Health Security Act (S. 1757/H.R. 3600) calls for new home and community care benefits with $4.5 billion in new Federal spending in 1996, phasing up to $35.5 billion in 2002. The state-administered home and community care program is to serve persons, irrespective of age and income limits, who are unable to perform three ADLs (See Footnote 5, below). Each eligible individual is entitled to an assessment, a care plan, and personal care, the latter as defined by the state. Under the Clinton proposal, Medicaid continues with some changes. Uniform national standards and tax deductions are proposed for private long-term care insurance.

In comparison, the single payer McDermott/Wellstone proposal (H.R. 1200/S. 491) includes home and community-based long-term care and nursing-home care for all ages and income. Eligibility, as in the Clinton Health Security Act, is based upon physical, cognitive, or mental impairment. McDermott/Wellstone would repeal Medicaid and prohibit the sale of insurance that duplicates coverage under the basic national health-care plan.

The Cooper/Grandy (H.R. 3222) and the Breaux/Durenberger (S. 1579) proposals do not include any long-term care benefit. Instead, Medicaid is repealed and Federal funding for long-term care would be phased out by 1999, with long-term care costs becoming the responsibility of the states.

5. Activities of daily living or ADLs are "basic self-care activities, including eating, bathing, dressing, transferring from bed to chair, bowel and bladder control, and independent ambulation, which are widely used to assess individual functional status" (EOA, 1991, D-1).

6. The U.S. Bipartisan Commission on Comprehensive Health Care, otherwise known as the Pepper Commission, issued a report in December, 1990, which set the standard and the stage for the inclusion of long-term care provisions in the Clinton Health Security Act. Despite the enlistment of two key members of the Pepper Commission staff into leadership positions on the Clinton health-care reform team, Title II B —Long-Term Care, Part 1—State Programs for Home and Community-Based Services for Individuals with Disabilities, gained a place in the bill only after a long uphill battle.

7. Licensed care providers point to such standard practices as criminal background checks, training, and monitoring and supervision to argue that their services are much more likely to assure quality, despite their higher cost. Independent contractors argue that their services are much less expensive and are responsive to the needs of their clients.

8. The Hawai'i team which planned, designed, and analyzed the proposed Hawaii Family Hope Program included Dr. Melvin Sakurai, Marilyn Seely, Dr. Lawrence Nitz, Bradley Mossman, and the author. Dr. Ping Sun Leung completed a preliminary actuarial analysis. John Wilkin of the Actuarial Research Corporation's Maryland office served as the actuarial consultant, with assistance from Ed King. David Kennell, John Sheils, Lisa Alecxih, and Peter Robertshaw of Lewin/ICF, Washington, DC assisted with simulation and modeling. Phyllis Thompson of Covington and Burling, Washington, DC, served as external legal counsel. Other external consultants included Dr. Judith Feder (Washington, DC), Virginia Felice (Massachusetts), Edward Howard, J.D. (Washington, DC), and Dr. Kevin Mahoney (Connecticut).

9. A number of different case-management programs concentrate on serving older adults and their families. Following assessments by national experts of the existing array of options, the Office initiated work toward development of a standardized case-management program which utilizes bachelors instead of masters level workers, a client-empowerment approach, and other features aimed at such outcomes as appropriate use, cost-effectiveness, and quality assurance.

10. Prior to the Project Team's modification of the Brookings/ICF Model, the Model used a simulation protocol which was limited only to the consideration of older adults. The modification was deemed essential since long-term care needs are not limited to older persons and since the Team wished to examine the effects upon all ages of a full range of financing strategies, including those which would call for program participation by younger persons.

11. The 1991 Legislature received EOA's massive *Financing Long-term care* report and decided to call for the appointment of a Long-term care Financing Advisory Board to review the recommendations presented. Because the Gulf War threatened to impact upon the State's economy, the Administration decided not to introduce a legislative proposal in 1992. Instead, the Legislature considered a proposal calling for the enactment of the Family Hope Program which was introduced at the request of advocates. In 1993 the first fully detailed proposal was introduced with modifications recommended by the Long-term care Financing Advisory Board established under Act 333, SLH 1991, and as a consequence of community, interagency, and Legislative input.

12. The reader is advised to examine the Executive Office on Aging's *Financing Long-term Care: A Report to the Hawai'i State Legislature* for full proposed details of program benefits and the vesting system.

13. Stone and Kemper caution that there is a need to consider the current and future availability of children and spouses to serve as informal caregivers (Stone and Kemper, 1989).

CHAPTER THREE

Mental-Health Services in Hawai'i
Time to Reform

SUSAN CHANDLER AND MARK O'DONNELL

Hawai'i, frankly, has been cruelly indifferent to the pathetic human problems of all too many of her mentally ill. The Territory's set-up for the care of these sufferers has been altogether inadequate; in many instances, antiquated and inefficient.

Sherwood Lowrey, President,
Chamber of Commerce, January 19, 1939

The whole mental-health system in Hawai'i is in serious need of attention. . . The Waihee administration seriously intends to change Hawai'i's ranking in care for the seriously mentally ill from last to first among the states. [The state was rated worst in the nation—three times—by the Public Citizen's Health Research Group and the National Alliance for the Mentally Ill.]

John Lewin, M.D. Director of Health,
State of Hawai'i, May 12, 1987

It is apparent that as early as 1939, grave concerns were being expressed about mental-health services in Hawai'i. It is equally apparent that in the intervening period Hawai'i has made insufficient progress in creating a mental-health system that adequately meets the needs of its citizens with serious mental illness. It remains a source of tremendous stigma both in our state and nation despite the fact that mental and emotional disorders occur in one out of five individuals (Gerhart, 1990; Talbot, 1987). Few families are immune, as seen from a national perspective:

   • 27 million adults (15 percent of our population) currently experience a mental disorder;

• 40 million adults (22 percent of the population) have a mental disorder at some time during their lives;

• 3-4 million children and adolescents (1.7-2.2 percent of our population) suffer from mental health problems that are severely emotionally disabling;

• 7.5 million children and adolescents (4.2 percent of the population) have a diagnosable mental or emotional disorder. (National Mental Health Association Statistics)

The Parameters of The Problem

Mental illness is not rare and it doesn't only happen to others. People with mental illness are our family members, our friends and our neighbors. Mental illness costs billions each year in health insurance, treatment, training, construction, and research as well as in lost employment, reduced productivity, absenteeism, and premature death (Chandler, 1990). Mental illness has been treated differently from other illnesses throughout history. People with mental illness have been ostracized, abused, ignored, and segregated, expected to make it on their own, and blamed when they can't.

During the last decade however, there has been an explosion of knowledge about the causes and progression of serious mental illness, as well as an explosion of knowledge about effective treatments (Hargreaves and Shumway, 1989; Liberman, 1993). New medication and treatment techniques are helping people who previously would have been confined for life to a state hospital or an institution (Reid, 1990). While better treatment and services are now available, poorly organized service systems and insufficient funds make these services inaccessible to most of this vulnerable population. This chapter will outline the persistent problems in the mental-health care system in Hawai'i and suggest some system level reforms that would provide comprehensive, publicly-funded, high-quality services.

Government Irresponsibility

Across the United States, there has been little consistent leadership or support given by the Federal, state or county governments to provide comprehensive, publicly-funded services to persons with mental illness (Hudson and Cox, 1991). In 1854, President Franklin Pierce vetoed legislation to establish an asylum on Federal lands stating that it was "not the government's responsibility to assist mentally ill persons." Ever since, the government's response and leadership in developing mental health policy has evolved very slowly. The Federal government created policies that encouraged people with mental illnesses to live in their communities, but too little money was provided to help them remain there.

Between 1960-1975, a deinstitutionalization movement relocated hundreds of thousands of mentally ill persons out of inadequately-funded and poorly-staffed state hospitals nationwide (Kiesler and Simpkins, 1993). These initiatives assumed that the states and counties would design and fund community-based treatment programs with dollars flowing from the hospitals and following those former patients into their communities. This never happened and this policy failure has resulted in a tragic irony. The number of persons living in state hospitals decreased significantly, but now, due to insufficient leadership to design the community-based programs and insufficient budget commitments, persons with mental illnesses find it both extremely difficult to access community-based programs and even more difficult to get admitted into a hospital program even for short treatment stays. Historically, once admitted to a mental hospital it was difficult to get released. Now seriously mentally ill persons are often quickly discharged, not necessarily when therapy succeeds, but when an individual's health insurance runs out, or when the state can't pay anymore. Consequently, many still-sick people move onto the streets rather than into community-based programs. Appropriate programs are not available.

Today, more individuals with mental illness reside in jails than in mental health facilities (Teplin, 1993), and huge numbers live unaccounted for as the ranks of the homeless continue to surge. The dollars that once were used to treat, protect and house individuals with mental illnesses in state hospitals haven't followed patients into the communities. They have instead funded mental-health professionals, physicians, insurance companies and bureaucracies that simply are not doing the job.

tuation in Hawai'i

Although Hawai'i has been called the "Health State," it
er been a leader in the provision or delivery of mental-
health services (Torrey, 1990). Recently, the Legislature has begun directing more dollars towards improving the system. But,
after decades of neglect, there is still very little, sustained, administrative, political or public commitment to community-based
mental-health services. Hawai'i continues to spend money on
large institutional-based care(such as the state hospital, prisons,
and jails) for its severely mentally ill, when common sense, state-
of-the art treatment, and cost effectiveness all should lead policy
makers toward the development of diverse, community-based
treatment programs. And now, in the face of the recent economic
downturn in Hawai'i, the Legislature is recommending cuts in
the Community Mental Health Centers' (CMHC) budgets which
will in turn further reduce the services available to individuals
with serious mental illnesses. Limited private mental-health insurance coverage exacerbates this problem, leaving many low-
income persons in need of services, but unable to access them.

In Hawai'i, the bottom line is that we need a new mental-health system. There is no shortage of models to improve
the situation here dramatically.

Hawai'i's 'Miracle'

We're about to perform a miracle and
move up to the top ten states in the next two to
five years, thanks to Governor Waihee and this
year's Legislature.

State Director of Health John Lewin, MD,
September 13, 1988

Unlike any other state, Hawai'i's mental-health system
is, in the main, publicly run. Among its other chores, like planning services for developmentally disabled citizens, promoting
Hawai'ian health care, preventing HIV infection, and ensuring
a safe environment, the State's Department of Health (DOH) runs
the Adult Mental Health Division, the Child and Adolescent Division and the Alcohol and Drug Division. The state purchases
services through contracts (some $28,022,000 worth of services
in 1993) with a variety of private agencies and providers to
supplement its own direct services. However, the bulk of the

mental-health dollars are controlled by the DOH and spent on the salaries of personnel and civil service positions.

Hawai'i delivers its public mental-health programs through nine distinct, geographically-bound, diverse, service areas, each with its own CMHC. All but one are state-run. Though the communities are diverse, the funding, programs, resources and personnel in these centers are remarkably standardized and quite inflexible. The services that the state provides are often difficult to access and are considered by most consumers with mental illness and their families to be inadequate in meeting their diverse needs. Because of the state's centralized structure and organization, it is not surprising that several studies, including the National Alliance for the Mentally Ill and The Public Citizen's Health Research Group since 1986 have rated Hawai'i at the very bottom of the states in its provision of services to adults and children with serious mental illnesses.

Prodded by citizen outrage and the threat of lawsuits, Hawai'i spent over $32 million to build a new state mental hospital which opened in 1993. This expenditure was necessary because the state hospital had not been accredited since 1972 and U.S. Department of Justice (DOJ) charged the state with multiple civil rights violations. But now, in order to satisfy the DOJ mandates, funds are being drained away from the CMHCs in order to adequately operate the State Hospital. Again, we are insufficiently supporting the community-based programs that most effectively and efficiently serve the severely mentally-ill.

Our entire mental-health system needs to be reformed. The following case studies illustrate some common problems and issues. The chapter will close with recommendations for Hawai'i as it attempts to improve its mental-health services.

> While there are some excellent services, some very good people delivering [mental-health] services, the service system is a fragmented and inadequate system of care. Community programs are inadequate in number, there are some very important programs that are not present at all; and the programs that are present are not very well coordinated with one another.
>
> *Leonard Stein, MD, Professor of Psychiatry,*
> *University of Wisconsin, February, 1987*

Ms. M.: A Case Study

Ms. M., 22, was diagnosed by a private psychiatrist in Honolulu as suffering from paranoid schizophrenia. Having trouble in school, she eventually quit to look for work, but was unable to find a job. Her parents were very concerned about her changing behavior and tried to arrange for a psychiatrist to treat their daughter. Since Ms. M. wasn't covered under her parents' health insurance policy, and because she had no coverage of her own, no psychiatrist would accept her. Ms. M. had received prescription medications at the time of the diagnosis, but couldn't tolerate the side effects and stopped taking them. She began to hear voices and experience extreme sleep disorders. She returned to her parents' home to live. Occasionally, after an argument with her parents, she would sleep on the streets. Once she was picked up by the police for disorderly conduct and spent the night in a cell block. Due to staff shortages, the local CMHC was unable to provide outreach to Ms. M.

Because her behavior was extremely unpredictable and her whereabouts often unknown, Ms. M.'s frantic parents called the local CMHC to inquire about what Mental-health services might be available and to ask if her daughter was being seen by their staff. Since Ms. M. is not a minor, no information about her can be shared with her parents without her consent.

Eventually, Ms. M. was picked up for shoplifting food and put into jail. There she met a member of the DOH Jail Diversion Team who tried to link her with a CMHC. With strong efforts by one dedicated worker, Ms. M. got an appointment to see a case manager at a CMHC. Perseverance was required since the CMHC wouldn't "accept" her since she didn't have an "address" and thus didn't "live" in any known service area.

Ms. M. talked to her assigned case manager at the CMHC who gave her a card with a phone number to call if she needed help (between the hours of 7:45 AM and 4:30 PM Monday through Friday). The case manager set up an appointment with a psychiatrist for two weeks later. However, when Ms. M. called two days later, she was told that her case manager had quit and nobody was assigned to her case. She tried a second time but this time was referred to the crisis team since the clinic was closed. Not wanting to talk to another stranger, Ms. M. stopped calling and with no job, no place to live, no help, and an increasing sense of hopelessness, met a friend at Institute of Human Services who introduced her to drugs such as crystal meth (ice). Her parents haven't heard from her in six months. Neither has the CMCH.

Reforms to Benefit Severely-Ill Adults

If Ms. M. and her family were living on the Wai'anae Coast, it is likely that her experience with the Mental-health system would be quite different. In 1988, the Wai'anae Coast CMHC (WCCMHC) successfully separated itself from the state bureaucracy. It is a non-profit organization that contracts with the DOH to provide a comprehensive, innovative, culturally-competent array of Mental-health services for individuals with serious mental illnesses on the Coast. The WCCMHC is able to hire the staff they wish; to design, organize and implement the services that are most appropriate to the community's needs; and has budget flexibility to spend as they see fit on mental-health services. Wai'anae is able to provide cost-efficient, culturally sensitive, community-based alternatives rather than costly hospitalization for their clients, and can return those savings into the development of additional services. This has resulted in Wai'anae having the lowest rate of hospitalization in the state. The WCCMHC is run by a Governing Board made up of local citizens. Flexible outreach services have been designed by the WCCMHC to prevent clients like Ms. M. from getting lost among the system units.

WCCMHC was initally funded to be a demonstration project for the other centers to follow. But, even after it demonstrated its effectiveness and efficiency, no other state run center followed. Even though the Robert Wood Johnson Foundation gave $2.5 million to the DOH to innovate and try different models of care, not much innovation is apparent, aside from Wai'anae.

The state Community Mental Health Centers have described a superb array of case management services in their policy manuals. These policies define a comprehensive package of services, including outreach activities, employment and skill training, educational or training referrals, medication management, entitlement assessments (Social Security or welfare) and housing supports. Case managers are supposed to provide the services crossing the boundaries between DOH, Department of Human Services, Social Security Administration, Hawai'i Housing Authority, doctors, social workers and psychologists. But a case-management system has not been successful in any of the community mental-health clinics. Difficulties in recruiting and maintaining workers makes it even more unlikely in the future.

Tragically, the services for Hawai'i's children and adolescents are even worse than those for our adults. The case of Roy K. described below, outlines some of the system problems that must be addressed to help our children.

> The conditions in the [Hawai'i] Adolescent Services Program were simply abhorrent. There was no identifiable therapeutic programs of any type in place. Most frightening of all was the terribly unsafe manner in which adolescents were placed into restraints.
> *Civil Rights Division, Dept. of Justice, May, 1992*

Roy K.: A Case Study

Roy K., age 16, was abused by his uncle at age four. Shortly thereafter, he began to act out, especially after he entered school. Because of disruptive behavior, Roy was suspended several times over the next couple of years. He was said to be a "naughty boy" who required discipline. Although his parents consulted with his teachers, nothing seemed to work. Roy's parents were aware that his behavior was becoming increasingly wild and unpredictable.

Though they were concerned, they did not know what to do. They felt isolated and it was insinuated by their son's educators that Roy's problems were their fault, something they could correct. One of his teachers suggested that Roy be tested. He was evaluated for learning disabilities, but found ineligible for services. At age ten, his parents were notified that he had been accused of abusing another child. While no charges were brought, the principal and others put the blame squarely on the shoulders of his parents. One teacher suggested that he be tested again. He was eventually found to have minimal learning delays in several areas as well as a severe emotional handicap. His parents were informed that he was eligible to receive special education services. No psychological services were recommended, in part because none were available at the school.

At 14, Roy began to hang out with adolescents who had histories of behavioral problems including criminal activities.

He was involved in a car theft, placed on probation and later was sent back to school. By chance, Roy's parents heard about a non-profit agency that might help parents like them. They asked for another Individualized Educational Plan (IEP) meeting, at the suggestion of the agency. With support, they were able to ask for an independent clinical evaluation to determine his emotional needs. They received opposition from the school as to who would pay. After several meetings and continued disruptions in school and violations against other children, the school authorities agreed to pay for the evaluation. It was determined that he would need intense mental-health counseling and an aide to work independently with him. Who would provide these services and pay for them is still a point of debate between DOE and DOH. Roy is now sixteen and still struggling, as are his parents as they wonder what will happen to their son.

Special Needs of Children and Adolescents

Roy and his parents are not alone in Hawai'i. At least 35,400 children, or 12 percent of our state's 295,000 children under age 18 suffer from mental health problems severe enough to require professional treatment. Between 3-8 percent of all children experience more severe emotional disturbances (Tuma, 1989). The Department of Health's Child and Adolescent Mental Health Division (CAMHD) serves approximately 1,600 of these children, that is, less than 8 percent of those in need (Mazer and O'Donnell, 1993).

Reforms for Children and Adolescents

Emotionally-disturbed children and adolescents like Roy need a full range of well-integrated services provided by well-trained professionals and staff, accessible in their home communities. Not only is community-based prevention and treatment more effective, it is often cheaper and more cost efficient than long-term residential care (which has cost the state up to $200,000 per year per individual for some emotionally handicapped children). The ideal system of services for emotionally disturbed children and adolescents is comprehensive, and includes not only mental health care, but also social, educational, vocational and support services for the child and family. Both residential and non-residential mental-health services are a vital component of such a comprehensive system. The non-residential services needed by emotionally-disturbed children and adolescents include prevention, early identification and intervention, assessment, respite and after-school care, out-patient treatment, home-based services, day treatment, and crisis and emergency services (Mazer and O'Donnell, 1993).

All too often, families like Roy's are not made aware of the range of services which should be available to them. And too often, our state systems intentionally do not reach out to those who need their services (for cost-saving, personnel or personal/arbitrary reasons). For example, though all children are entitled by law to appropriate education regardless of their disability, many parents are not made aware of the process through which they can obtain special educational services by the Department of Education (DOE). Parents also have been discouraged from requesting those services by DOE personnel. And unlike the DOE, the DOH's CAMHD has no mandate to serve all children and adolescents in need of its services. This problem is further complicated by conflict between state and Federal laws. Federal law focuses on the DOE and mandates care for a child whose needs interfere with his or her receiving a free and appropriate education. State law indicates that the DOH should take care of emotionally handicapped children, if funding is available. This allows each system to blame the other. Unfortunately, the only people who suffer in this situation are the parents and their emotionally handicapped children.

In addition, most of the services needed in Hawai'i are simply not available because they have never been developed. Even if they are available on a limited basis on Oahu, they are almost wholly non-existent on neighbor islands. The current patchwork of fragmented services in Hawai'i provided by several large systems too often results in a lack of appropriate care and education for the children and youth who most need them.

Needed: Coordination and Accountability

Hawai'i needs a comprehensive, coordinated mental-health system. This system should provide a comprehensive set of treatment services for emotionally-disturbed children and adults. It would incorporate four basic features:

• a clearly defined target population, particularly focusing on persons with serious emotional disturbances who are at greatest risk of incurring substantial long-term public sector costs (a target population definition was created in 1993 and is still in the process of being refined in Hawai'i);

• an interagency staff network to coordinate and effectively provide services across agencies under formal interagency agreements;

• a continuum of mental-health services delivered in community-based, interagency settings (which are the most appropriate for delivering a range of services);

• a system for tracking clients served by many agencies and for evaluating overall system outcomes, not just the typical counting of clients served and dollars spent.

For the past two decades, policies underlying mental-health services for emotionally-disturbed children and adolescents and adults in Hawai'i have not proven effective, either from a cost or human perspective. Today, lawmakers can choose to either create an appropriate system of care which saves both money and human lives, or they can continue to react to crises and pay the high costs of repeated institutionalization and other social consequences. There is a choice.

Many sectors of the community—the public, the Legislature, the Governor, the state bureaucracies, as well as private-mental health providers—need to come together to develop a coordinated, comprehensive, high quality mental-health system that is consumer-driven, community-based, culturally competent and adequately funded. Many other states and communities are making substantial progress in developing such a system, but Hawai'i is not yet on the right track.

Community Control: Dr. David Goodrick, a frequent consultant to the state, says that Hawai'i's communities do not have sufficient planning authority and fiscal responsibility for mental-health services. This is clear. CMHCs do not have sufficient control over their budget; nor the hiring of their personnel; nor sufficient data about their clientele; nor can they reinvest money that they might save into additional programs and services for their clinics. Yearly, they must plead for funds at the Legislature and then fight among DOH's many other priorities to get and keep their allocations throughout the year. Since 1988, the DOH has been promising that the CMHCs would be released from the stifling constraints of the state bureaucracy and would obtain fiscal control of their budgets. This would halt the current arrangement of having a separate, totally distinct, uncontrollable, state hospital budget. Currently, there are very few incentives for the CMHCs to promote cost-effective, community-based services. The CMHCs have very little role in determining how long their clients will remain in the state hospital and they have no fiscal control over when and where their own clients who need hospitalization will go. Until recently, the CMHC's weren't even informed when one of their clients had been hospitalized or was about to be discharged. Since patient hospitalization is much more expensive than community-level care, giving incentives to the CMHCs to encourage development of high quality, equally effective alternatives is essential, but it is not happening.

Staff Training With the explosion of knowledge about the brain, neuroleptic drugs and new treatments, staff members need continuous updating of their knowledge and skills. Spurred on by the DOJ Settlement Agreement, the DOH hired a training coordinator at the Hawai'i State Hospital. In collaboration with the University of Hawai'i, training programs have been established for the hospital personnel and now are being offered to community mental-health center staff. However, the DOH budget has no line item for a community training coordinator and thus, there is no permanently-funded training position to design on-the-job training to upgrade texisting skills or train new staff. Staff turnover is extremely high, often leaving the seriously mentally ill to untrainedmental-health workers.

Citizen participation Citizen input, a measure of success in most of the states with good systems of care, is haphazard in Hawai'i. The DOH has given inadequate staff support and very little access to information to its advisory boards and councils. While citizen groups and advisory boards have made hundreds of recommendations over the years, even bringing in (at their own expense) national experts to consult with the state, few of their suggestions have ever been implemented.

What Should We Do?

It is already apparent that the solution will not be easy to implement. The solution is not, however, difficult to identify and there is, in fact, a great deal of information that points in the appropriate direction. Over the past couple of decades, organizations such as the Mental Health Association in Hawai'i, the Alliance for the Mentally Ill, Hawai'i Advocates for Children and Youth, United Self Help and others have attempted to bring that information to the implementing authorities. The State of Hawai'i has chosen not to pay much attention to the evidence.

One strategy which has worked very well in other states is a system which allows money to follow the clients (Stein and Test, 1985; Stein, 1989). The principle here is that funding stays with the individual wherever s/he goes (hospital, community mental health center, residential program) rather than to a large, expensive bureaucratic structure where overhead eats away at the actual provision of services. This system would allow community-based programs to control their own budgets and to design appropriate services for their own communities based on the needs of their consumers. This concept is practiced by the states leading the nation in mental-health care (e.g. Vermont, New Hampshire, Rhode Island, Connecticut, Ohio, and Colorado).

It can be done in Hawai'i. But first we will need to attack some systemic difficulties that will not easily go away. Some of these difficulties are represented by very powerful interest groups in our state—for example, the civil-service system, politically appointed staffs, and state bureaucrats. As they fight to protect their own turf, these entities tie the hands of the entire system, reducing the innovation and flexibility needed to respond in a timely fashion to the needs of mental health consumers. When it takes six months to get a check cut in the state system; when it takes a year to find office space; when it takes 18 months to recruit and hire qualified individuals into the system; when contractors are required to do the work but are not paid for six or more months; when it takes the DOH over six years to establish a new classification of case managers, we have a system that is self-centered, not client-centered. When community mental health center hours of operation are set according to the prevailing union contract rather than the needs of the consumers, we have a system that is staff-centered, not client-centered. Someone must be accountable for the sorry state of mental-health services. There is clearly a lack of leadership in Hawai'i that permits this situation to remain, with only sporadic progress.

Necessary Reinventions

In a major study three years ago, the American Public Health Association recommended that it was in the best interest of states to limit their roles to funding and monitoring. State departments of health would maintain oversight for services and would plan, assess, evaluate and fund programs, but all direct services would be provided by community-based non-profit or for-profit organizations. A similar set of recommendations was presented in a report funded by the Legislative Reference Bureau called, "Reinventing" Governance of Hawai'i's Public Mental Health Delivery System—Problems, Options, and Possibilities" (Gochros, 1994): 1) Clear separation of the policy-making and regulatory functions from those functions related to the management and administration of direct provision of services; 2) A substantial degree of decentralized, community-based control; 3) A service delivery structure which promotes competition between service providers.

The report suggests that the State create a "Mental Health Corporation" (or Mental Health Authority) which assumes the following responsibilities: 1) receives all funds, including state, Medicaid, charitable and Federal block grants, 2) directly manages the provision of all services; 3) directly employs service providers and support staff; 4) contracts for mental-health services by private providers through purchases of service when appropriate or necessary; 5) screens, assesses, and develops service plans for clients.

Under this model, the DOH has the responsibility for policy-making and regulatory functions which would be carried out by the existing Adult, Child and Adolescent, and Alcohol and Drug Abuse Divisions. The DOH has been meeting to discuss the feasibility of implementing such a plan.

A New Approach for Hawai'i

Building from the knowledge and experiences of other states and the Gochros "Governance" report, the Mental Health Association of Hawai'i has introduced legislation to establish a Mental Health Public Benefit Corporation (MHPBC) for Hawai'i. This body would be authorized under statute and would have the relative flexibility of a non-profit organization. It would not be bound by restrictive Civil Service rules nor the cumbersome contracting procedures of the State's Department of Accounting and General Services. While monitoring and quality control would remain within the DOH as suggested above, all direct services would be provided under contract through the MHPBC on either a state or regional basis. (The WCCMHC discussed earlier would fit nicely into this model as they are already prepared to contract for all of their existing services with a Regional or State Mental Health Public Benefit Corporation).

This concept is already being successfully used in states such as Georgia, Oregon, North Carolina, Ohio and Texas. If such a corporation were in place, the outcomes of the case studies described earlier could have been quite different. In a system designed (and contracted) to provide continuous care, Ms. M. would not have been lost between the cracks. She would have been provided a continuous-care team that would have assertively reached out to her and maintained contact until the appropriate services had been provided in her community. Roy K. would also have been helped much sooner. The corporation would take responsibility for all of Roy's mental health care needs and coordinate these or other relevant services with the DOE.

We are optimistic that this new approach would provide Hawai'i with an innovative organizational and administrative structure that will locate the source of service accountability; will clarify the benefit package of services that a mentally-ill person can expect to receive, will establish an information system that accurately provides data about the services being provided and their effectiveness and, finally, will reform the services for persons with mental illness.

The Clinton Health Care Plan / Health QUEST

Much of what is suggested above will be moot, however, with the passage and implementation of the Clinton Health-care reform or the state's Medicaid initiative, Hawai'i's Quality care, Universal access, Efficient Utilization, Stabilizing Costs, Transforming, health care provision (QUEST). The aim of both of these plans is cost containment as well as universal coverage. Both programs offer great hope for broader and more comprehensive coverage for individuals with serious long-term and other shorter-term mental illnesses than ever before.

In the Clinton Plan, mental health would not achieve parity with physical illness until the year 2001. Meanwhile, limited in-patient hospitalization and out-patient psychotherapeutic services would be available. The Plan's inclusion of community-based services—partial hospitalization, day treatment, psychosocial rehabilitation, home-based services and behavioral aides for children—is a breakthrough in that most private insurance plans do not cover them. But 2001 is far off and broad-based mental health parity could be delayed or even deleted.

Critics of the Clinton Plan say that the entire mental-health benefit is an expensive "frill" except as applied to individuals with serious mental illnesses. We believe that, it is an integral component of health care which has the potential to favorably impact the bottom line that concerns businesses. Large and small businesses lose money through employee absenteeism, reduced productivity while on the job and turnover. It is estimated that mental illnesses cost the U.S. some $74.9 billion annually in lost productivity and earnings according to the U.S. Department of Health and Human Services. Current data from many states and from Fortune 500 companies—representing millions of Americans with insurance coverage—demonstrate that mental health coverage is cost-effective and controllable. For example, in 1989, McDonnell Douglas Helicopter Company introduced a managed mental health employee assistance plan which focused on individualized patient care planning, with no constraints on treatment. One result was that psychiatric inpatient cost decreased by 50 percent while the average length-of-stay declined 47 percent (NMHA, 1993).

Health QUEST covers most of the same services as the Clinton Plan though more extensively and it will impact Hawai'i's adult mental-health consumers much sooner, with implementation scheduled for September, 1994. Health QUEST's mental-health coverage has the potential both to set a standard for care that will be a drive for the improvement of the services provided by the DOH and serve as a working model for the Clinton Plan. Health QUEST may also force change on the DOH in that a proposed expansion of QUEST to include the aged, blind and disabled populations in the second year of the project, in combination with the general assistance Medicaid, State Health Insurance Program and Aid to Families Dependent Children populations, will effectively deprive DOH of most of their clientele. DOH may be in the position of changing themselves or be-ing changed by others. This initiative would have a major im-pact on the proposed Hawai'i MHPBC, perhaps making it un-necessary given the duplication of the population covered.

Clearly, it is time to reform the system of mental-health care in Hawai'i. There are many dedicated mental-health work-ers in the state hospital and in the CMHCs who are committed to providing high-quality services. Many of these individuals seem to be thwarted by the very systems designed to organize the delivery of their skills. Nonetheless, thousands of mentally-ill persons and their families wait patiently for Hawai'i's system to significantly improve. It must happen now.

Policy Recommendations

The following policy recommendations are offered to reform Hawai'i's mental-health system and guide in the deci-sion-making:

• Remove DOH from the role of providing direct services.
• Establish a Mental Health Public Benefit Corporation.
• Privatize all mental-health services in Hawai'i.
• Establish non-profit community mental-health centers with fiscal control over all of their service-delivery system.
• Establish a single budget stream for a coordinated hospi-tal and community mental-health system.
• Require ongoing and regular staff training.
• Require the DOH to monitor the mental-health services with appropriate outcome measures.
• Ensure that there is sufficient consumer participation in-cluding primary consumers, family members and advo-cates in the needs assessment, planning and evaluation activities of the state.

Tough decisions must be made in order for Hawai'i to take advantage of the opportunities that will present themselves with health-care reform. Tough decisions must be made now in order for Hawai'i to deliver appropriate, high quality services in a timely and humane way to children, adolescents and adults in our state who have an emotional disability or mental illness. While most of the staff and leadership within the state DOH agree with these principles, we all are still waiting for action and implementation.

Bibliography

Chandler, S.M. (1990). *Competing Realities: The Contested Terrain of Mental Health Advocacy*. New York: Praeger Press.

Gochros, Susan L. (1994). *'Reinventing' Governance of Hawai'i's Public Mental Health Delivery system-Problems, Options, and Possibilities*. Legislative Reference Bureau.

Goodrick, D. (1992). *Designing Client-Centered and Responsive Community Support Systems*. Washington, DC: Cosmos.

Hargreaves, W. and Shumway, M. (1989). Effectiveness of Services for the Severely Mentally Ill, in Taube, C., Mechanic, D., and Hohmanis, H. (eds.) *The Future of Mental Health Services Research*. National Institute of Mental Health Publication No. (ADM) 89-1600.

Hatfield, A. and Lefley, H. (eds.) (1987). *Families of the Mentally Ill. Coping and Adaption*. New York: Guilford Press.

Hudson, C. and Cox, A. (1991). *Dimensions of State Mental Health Policy*. (eds.). New York: Praeger Press.

Kielser, C. and Simpkins, C. (1993) *The Unnoticed Majority in Psychiatric Inpatient Care*. New York: Plenum Press.

Liberman, R.P. (1993). *Handbook of Psychiatric Rehabilitation*. Allyn and Bacon.

Mazer, N. and O'Donnell, M. (1993) *The Future of Child and Adolescent Mental Health in Hawai'i*. Mental Health Association in Hawai'i.

National Mental Health Association (1993) *Health Care Reform* Access Legislative Alert.

Reid, W. (1990). Access to Care: Clozapine in the Public Sector." *Hospital and Community Psychiatry*, 41(8).

Stein, L. (1989). *Wisconsin's System of Mental Health Financing in New Directions for Mental Health Services*, No. 43. San Francisco: Jossey-Bass.

Stein, L. and Test, M. (eds.) (1985). Training in the Community Living Model: A Decade of Experience in New Directions for Mental Health Services, No. 26. San Francisco: Jossey-Bass.

Talbott, J. (1987). The Chronic Mentally Ill: What Do We Now Know And Why Aren't We Implementing What We Know?" in Menniger, W. and Menniger, G. (eds.). *The Chronic Mental Patient*. Washington, DC: American Psychiatric Press, Inc.

Teplin, L. (1993). Psychiatric and Substance Abuse Disorders Among Male Urban Jail Detainees. *American Journal of Public Health* (in press).

Tuma, J.M. (February 1989) "Mental Health Services for Children:The State of the Art" *American Psychologist*, **44** (2): p. 190.

Torrey, F,. et al. (1990). *Care of the Seriously Mentally Ill: A Rating of State Programs*. Public Citizen Research Group and National Alliance for the Mentally Ill. Washington, DC.

U.S. Congress, Office of Technology Assessment (December 1986), *Children's Mental Health: Problems and Services*. Washington DC: U.S. Government Printing Office.

PART TWO
Myths, Money, and Medicine

CHAPTER FOUR

Health Care and Money
Perspective in the Policy
Debate Over Cost Control

DEANE NEUBAUER

Americans have a profound ambivalence about health care and the costs associated with it. On some dimensions they are concerned with the high costs of health care, recognize that something akin to a "crisis" exists within health care, and that reform is necessary. On other dimensions they desire high-tech, high-quality care, profess to be willing to pay for it, and see that having this kind of care separates them from others in the world who are less fortunate.

For some, the crisis in health care takes the outlines given to it by President Clinton in his address to the nation in late September, 1993. Thirty-five to forty million Americans live without medical insurance coverage and lack adequate access to care; two million Americans lose their health care coverage each month. The major barrier to coverage for this gap group is cost; the relatively high cost of obtaining insurance coverage has driven them out of the market. Many have entered the group as a result of downward employment mobility as the economy experiences "rationalization," losing manufacturing jobs and shifting workers to lower paid, more marginal positions that do not include health care coverage as an employment benefit.

The high cost of health insurance impacts the family budgets of individuals who are often forced into the hard decision of doing without insurance coverage in order to gain other "necessities." Corporations and government each experience higher medical care costs as a drain on resources. Businesses argue that high costs of providing coverage, whether they do that by purchasing coverage in the market or directly covering their own workers, add a charge to goods and services that renders them vulnerable to foreign competitors. Governments find their ever-increasing health-care obligations a threat to other endeavors: funds spent on health care are not available for housing, education, transportation, economic development, or similar ends, all deemed desirable and important by some segment of the population. In this sense health care competes with other social values; as its costs increase, the ability of the public sector to recognize and serve these other values declines. Other, more direct costs include government as an employer that must purchase health care for its employers (in Hawai'i this amounts to 60 percent of health insurance premiums for 40,000 employees); as a Medicaid matcher for mandated programs; as an in-house provider of services, such as public health nurses; and as subsidizer for private non-profits (which in Hawai'i accounts for over $100 million.)

Some do not see a crisis in health care. While they acknowledge problems in providing adequate insurance coverage to all of society's members, they are careful to argue that the urge to do so should not endanger the overall nature and quality of care. Health care in the United States, it is argued, is the best in the world. No other nation enjoys the benefit of so much research, leading edge technology, and high quality care. The cost of care may be high, but that is a necessary cost one must pay to gain this outcome. Indeed, much of the impetus for continued medical innovation comes from the public itself whose demand for high-quality care establishes the context which supports this activity. Misguided efforts to reform health care by controlling costs, in this view, may place damaging constraints on health professionals, from practicing physicians and surgeons to pharmaceutical companies whose efforts in the direction of continual innovation have produced the current system.

For yet others, health-care spending itself is a distinct plus. Health care is a giant industry ranging from huge privately owned hospital chains, to global pharmaceutical and medical supply companies, to HMO's and group practices, to individual proprietorships. Over the past two decades one in six of all new jobs and one-seventh of the GDP have been supplied by the health-care industry. Every dollar spent on health care, and in 1993 that was over $900 billion of them, is income to this industry. While the rest of American industry has staggered under the combined struggles of meeting global competition and restructuring, health care has continued to grow each year, often at twice and three times the rate of the economy itself. From this point/ view, what some have experienced as an unwanted growth and increase in health-care costs is experienced by others as highly desirable economic growth. It is important to note that even when one turns to highly controversial and heated issues concerning the practice of medicine, such as the way medical malpractice occurs and is litigated in the society, these activities contribute significantly to the incomes of individuals who come to high status in the society and serve as role models for others.

Indeed, one part of the construction of Hawai'i as the "Health State" is a focus on health care as a major economic industry, one which can be allied with tourism to diversify the economy while giving it a distinctive stamp. As tourism throughout the world becomes more competitive, the argument goes, it becomes ever more important to differentiate the local environment. Hawai'i, the Health State, can become a focus for bringing health-seeking tourists to the islands (and these are likely to be more upscale tourists) by offering them resort facilities tailored to these activities. The Ihilani Resort at Ko'Olina will provide a spa-based program for $3,646 a week. Department of Business Economic Development and Tourism Director Mufi Hanneman calls this "fitness-related tourism," and Dean Chuck Gee suggests that up to $3 billion in annual revenues could be produced by health-related tourism. State senator Stan Koki speaks of building a "Mayo Clinic of the Pacific," an idea also endorsed by Lt. Governor Cayetano. The Hawai'i Community Development Authority argues that a health-related development in Kakaako could be "a new economic generator for a tropical paradise" (*Honolulu Advertiser*, April 11, 1994). A Wai'anae Coast Comprehensive Health Center goal is to develop Hawai'i as a training ground for health professionals in the Pacific. The Center for Asian Pacific Exchange (CAPE) brings nurses each year (mainly from Korea) for two-week training sessions. St. Francis Medical Center and the University of Hawai'i provide training for foreign nurses. At one time Hawai'i was a Peace Corps training center for health programs. An Aloha Health Corps is on the books, but undeveloped. Also at the University, the Curriculum Research and Development Group has developed materials for health education. The health industry in Hawai'i is broadly based and continues to expand.

There remains the fact that a career in health care, especially in medicine, remains one of the prized objectives for talented young people, even if such careers are marginally less attractive then in the medical-school enrollment heyday of the late 1970's and 1980's. Faced with issues of how to make the economy grow, planners in Hawai'i look to expansion of health care as a viable sector. Some suggest that by 2010 the health-care system could contribute more to the state product than tourism.

How The Money Flows

In the remainder of this paper I want to examine three aspects of how money is generated by and impacts health care in Hawai'i. Table 1 indicates the major sources of payment within the national health-care system and the major recipients of that payment. While the volume of money in this system increases yearly (for much of the past 25 years that rate of increase has been between 5 and 15 percent), the proportioning of these expenditure and income flows has remained fairly constant.[1]

The Prepaid Health Care Act emphasizes employer paid health-care costs. Thus, for Hawai'i one would expect lesser out-of-pocket expenditures and greater contributions from business. As Table 2 suggests, this may not be the case. Individuals in Hawai'i pay 25 percent of their health dollar out-of-pocket, which combined with the 40 percent paid by private health insurance, accounts for most of the system's income. These data suggest a somewhat larger out-of-pocket expenditure for Hawai'i than mainland counterparts. Payments to non-traditional medical practitioners will account for additional out-of-pocket payments. These are thought to be somewhat higher in Hawai'i, reflecting cultural traditions, and are not included in these data.

These data are useful for illustrating a number of points concerning health-care costs. They suggest the relative importance of issues that arise in discussions about costs. For example in Hawai'i as in other states, the money which business has to pay for workers' compensation and temporary disability insurance are frequently identified as particularly onerous for business, and legislatures are impugned to find ways to control these costs, which are often alleged to be 'out of control' or particularly subject to abuse. But these costs as a whole account for only 2.3 percent of expenditures. If we were to assume that 20 percent of such costs were unreasonable and that reforms would

Table 1: Major Sources and Recipients of Health-Care Payments, Nation-Wide

Sources	Recipients	
Households (35%)	Hospitals	39.8%
Ins. premiums (individual and employer sponsored		
6.7%		
Medicare contrib. 2%		
Out of pocket 21.2%		
Government (33.1 %)	Physicians	19.5%
Employee ins.premiums 5.4%		
Federal Programs 16.3%		
State, Local Programs 11.4%		
Business (28.8%)	Nursing Homes	8.2%
Insurance Premiums 21.6%		
Medicare Contributions 4.7%		
Workers Compensation and TDI 2.3%		
	Drugs and Medical	
Industrial in-plant 0.3%	Sundries	8.6%
Non-Patient Revenue 3.1%		
	Dental Care	5.3%
	All Other	18.6%

[1] Data taken from Levit, Katharine R. and Cathy A. Cowan, "Business, House-holds and Governments: Health-Care Costs," *Health Care Financing Review,* Winter 1991, Vol. 13, no. 2. and appear in a technical paper prepared for the Governor's Blue Ribbon Commission on Health-Care Costs, Summer, 1992 by Terresita Rameriz.

eliminate them, such a reform would reduce this item of total spending to about 1.8 percent of expenditures. The point is that most health-care spending (and income) involves two categories: spending on doctors and hospitals.

Second, these data, when converted to aggregate dollar figures make clear how enormous the health-care system has become as a money system. Most estimates suggest that 1993

Table 2: Source of Hawai'i's Health Care Dollars (1988)	
Medicaid	7%
Medicare	11%
Other public	17%
Private health insurance	40%
Out of pocket payments	25 %

expenditures on health care will have run about $950 billion. If so, we would have as a nation spent $378 billion on hospital care, and $186.2 billion on physician care. When numbers get this large, even small increments of change involve huge amounts of money.

Health Expenditures in Hawai'i

Because of the way data are currently collected, or not collected in Hawai'i, one cannot easily model expenditure and income data with much reliability and sophistication. Some relevant data collected from various sources exist, but it is common for various data collectors to employ different and often incompatible methodologies, thereby limiting the use of the data to address common problems. Recently, the Department of Health (DOH) has attempted without success to interest the Legislature in developing a mechanism that would permit the regular and systematic collection of aggregate health-care cost data, an effort that was also recommended by the Governor's Blue Ribbon Commission on Health-Care Costs. The concern of those arguing for such steps is that in the absence of such data, one is limited in the kinds of analysis one can do of cost problems, both in attempting to address where the problems lie and in developing prospective interventions. While it would seem reasonable to many that such data should be readily accessible, this assumption overlooks the fact that often health-care data are regarded as "proprietary," that is, owned by the private firms that produce them. Among firms operating in this way are insurance companies, hospitals, and physicians. These firms, like those in other industries, are not eager to display their inner financial workings to public scrutiny.

In the 1994 Legislature, yet another effort to develop the basis for a comprehensive data system in Hawai'i suffered defeat. Senate Bill 3270 called for the creation of a single claims forms and format for the state to be administered by the Department of Health. In arguing for the form the bill's language emphasized that whereas almost all providers of health care services use the same form, in many cases individual insurance carriers require their own form, leading to confusion and a high rate of rejected claims. SB 3270 would have created a uniform core dataset under the direction of the DOH Director, and in consultation with an organized policy or data advisory group to illuminate public-health programs and consumer cost and quality information for the delivery of health-care services. Virtues attributed to such a data set would be: reduction of administrative complexity; elimination of unnecessary duplication in the collection and reporting of data; facilitating the integration, consistency, and transfer of data among public health and health service programs; and the monitoring of health status, planning, policy development, service coordination, quality assurance and program evaluation for all public health programs. While the Blue Ribbon Commission emphasized the importance of common data to the performance of good public policy in health care, that message has not yet found majority support in the Legislature.

This section presents some illustrative data for Hawai'i drawn from varied current sources. Most are produced by the Health Care Financing Administration, the "official" national source of data on health care expenditures. (Unless indicated otherwise, all data in this section are from HCFA, 1993). Others employ various local sources. There is considerable sentiment within the local health care community that HCFA data are often wrong. As an example, in Fall, 1993, the journal *Health Affairs* published an article drawn from some of the data used in this section which demonstrated that the growth rate in Hawai'i health care expenditures was essentially undifferentiated from those of counterpart states, thereby providing a conflicting interpretation of what is widely believed to be Hawai'i's relatively unique success in controlling health-care costs. I deal with this issue below. My point here is to underscore that made immediately above: the absence of a central health-care data source in

Hawai'i inhibits the growth of a consensus on what might really be happening in the health-care system in cost terms.

I state above that hospital and physician expenditures account for the bulk of spending in health care. Table 3 shows the growth of hospital and physician expenditures in Hawai'i throughout the decade of the 1980's. These local data compare with national trend data for the Eighties which witnessed a slowing of hospital costs from an annual rate of 7.2 percent in the period 1970-1980 to slightly above that rate in the 1980's. From 1980-1985 real hospital expenditures grew at a rate of 4.8 percent; from 1985-1989 at a rate of 4.6 percent (K. Davis, 1993). Table 4 converts these data to display the rate of change in hospital and physician expenditures for Hawai'i in the decade.

These data adhere to the general cost trend identified by Davis, a gradual decline in the rate of spending growth during the 1980's. They are, however, surprisingly "lumpy." It is hard to offer a ready explanation, other than the failings of the survey instrument employed by HCFA, that accounts for such rapid annual peaks and valleys in expenditure patterns. Table 5 compares these Hawai'i expenditures for hospitals and physicians with national expenditures by developing the local data as a ratio of national expenditures. This permits us to put the rapid rise and fall of rates of increase (displayed in Table 4) in the context of similar fluctuations in the country as a whole, thereby factoring into the data a whole variety of things which influence aggregate health-care expenditures. Interestingly, when we compare these cost ratios, the "lumps" disappear, suggesting that national variations are as acute as Hawai'i, or that the survey instrument is consistent in its bias. These data suggest that at the beginning of the decade hospital expenditures were below their mainland counter-parts and rose to be on parity with them, while physician expenditures behaved in just an opposite manner: beginning the decade far in excess of mainland counterparts, but entering the 1990's in relative parity. It is these data on hospital rate increase that have provoked a defensive reaction within the local health care community.

These data are consistent with increases over this period in the average daily hospital census, average length of stay (in days), hospital occupancy rate, and total inpatient days.

As a measure of industry growth, during this period the

Table 3: Hospital, Physician Expenditures (in millions)

Year	Hospital	Physician
1980	360	251
1981	433	308
1982	514	357
1983	550	387
1984	597	389
1985	653	442
1986	716	463
1987	797	508
1988	862	587
1989	967	629
1990	1,161	680
1991	1,287	719

Table 4: Annual Change Expenditures for Hospitals and Physicians, 1980-1991

Year	Hospital	Physicians
80-81	19.0%	22.6%
81-82	16.8%	15.7%
82-83	7.1%	8.4%
83-84	8.6%	.7%
84-85	7.3%	13.5%
85-86	9.6%	4.7%
86-87	11.4%	9.7%
87-88	8.2%	15.7%
88-89	12.1%	7.2%
89-90	20.1%	8.0%
90-91	10.9%	5.8%

Table 5: Annual Change Per Capita, Hospital and Physician Expenditures

Year	Hospitals	Physicians
80-81	19.0%	21.3%
81-82	16.8%	13.9%
82-83	5.1%	6.4%
83-84	7.0%	-0.8%
94-85	8.0%	12.2%
85-86	8.4%	3.5%
86-87	9.8%	8.1%
87-88	7.0%	14.4%
88-89	10.6%	5.7%
89-90	18.1%	6.1%
90-91	8.8%	3.7%

Source (Tables 3, 4, 5): Health Care Financing Administration, 1993

Table 6: Ratio of Hawai'i to National Expenditures on Hospitals, Physicians

Year	Hospitals	Physicians
1980	0.83	1.31
1981	0.86	1.39
1982	0.89	1.44
1983	0.87	1.38
1984	0.88	1.23
1985	0.90	1.20
1986	0.92	1.14
1987	0.94	1.11
1988	0.93	1.14
1989	0.95	1.11
1990	1.02	1.08
1991	1.00	1.06

Table 7: Numbers of Physicians per 10,000 population

Year	No. of physicians
1980	13.1
1981	14.6
1982	15.1
1983	15.5
1984	16.1
1985	16.8
1986	16.4
1987	16.5
1988	16.7
1989	17.0
1990	17.5
1991	17.9

Table 8: Hawai'i Health Care Expenditures as a Percentage of Gross State Product

year	% of GSP
1965	6.0%
1970	7.2%
1975	8.2%
1980	8.7%
1985	10.3%
1986	10.4%
1987	10.9%
1988	10.9%
1989	10.7%
1990	11.0%

Source: Hawai'i DBEDT, Hawai'i Gross State Product Accounts, June, 1989. 1986-90 are estimates.

Source (Tables 6, 7, 8): Health Care Financing Administration, 1993

numbers of persons providing hospital medical and allied services rose from 8, 022 to 13,639 (70.0 percent). The numbers of practicing physicians rose from 1,335 to 2,034 (52.4 percent). Table 7 displays this growth as a measure of number of physicians per 10,000 population, and indicates that growth in the number of physicians exceeds the rate of population growth. In 1980, physician expenditure accounted for by each physician was $188,300. By 1991, that number had grown to $353,600 per physician. These figures compare with averages for the Far West states of $181,600 in 1980 and $431,000 in 1991, supporting the trend suggested in Table 6 of physician costs to decline relative to national averages over the decade.

Another important measure is growth of health-care expenditures relative to that of the whole economy. Dispute existed in the 1980's and early 1990's about the exact level of this spending. Estimates cited here are derived from the Gross State Products Accounts gathered by the Department of Business, Economic Development, and Tourism. Richard Stenson has utilized these data in making the most currently accepted estimate of total aggregate spending (Stenson, 1992). Table 8 indicates the growth of health-care expenditures over the period 1965-1990.

Finally, it is of interest to note that estimates gathered during the late 1980's indicated a shift from public to private sources of funding, as the share of private (out-of-pocket and private health insurance) rose from 56 percent in 1980 to 65 percent in 1990. The crises in Medicaid spending of the past three years suggests that this relationship may have reversed. Data are not readily available to make this comparison.

Summary

•Contrary to some expectations, Hawai'i's out-of-pocket expenditures on health care are slightly higher than the US average.

•Hospital expenditures rose from approximately $360 million in 1980 to $1,277 million in 1991.

•Per capita hospital expenditures rose from $372 in 1980 to $1135 in 1991.

•Hospital expenditures rose at an average rate of 10.78 percent between 1980-1991.

•Hospital expenditures at the beginning of this period,

1980, were significantly below the national average (a ratio of .83). By 1991 they had risen to equal the national average (ratio 1.0).

•During the period the numbers of physicians increased from 1335 in 1980 to 2034 in 1991. By 1991 each physician accounted for an expenditure of $356,600.

•The growth in physician numbers was more rapid than the rate of population growth, 13.8 physicians per 10,000 population in 1980 to 17.9 physicians per 10,000 in 1991.

•Expenditure on physicians grew from $251 million in 1980 to $719 million in 1991, but the rate of increase declined progressively. For the decade as a whole physician expenditures rose at an annual average of 10 percent.

•Measured as a percentage of State Gross Product, the largest rise in health-care costs took place at the beginning of the decade, leveling off at between 10.3 percent and 11.0 percent during the period 1985 and 1990.

Cost Cutting and Policy Implications for Hawai'i

Let me attempt first to make sense of these data in terms of the historic claims made for Hawai'i's health-care system.

First, it has often, and justly, been claimed that Hawai'i's health-care costs are lower than its mainland counterparts. This is variously attributed, but some consensus exists that a primary reason is the Prepaid Health-Care Act which brings more people under the umbrella of insurance coverage, reduces the gap group, and produces less irrational utilization of higher cost health care resources. Another view has it that Hawai'i (for reasons of genetics and climate) is a healthier place than many, and that our data reflect this fact. Some data (generalized longevity) support this view; others (the high incidence of morbidity of the Native Hawai'ian population and its premature mortality) belie that view. John Lewin has accounted for the relative success of Hawai'i's health care system by citing four "lessons" from Hawai'i that are meant to account for lower costs.

First, experience shows that emphasis on primary care produces a healthy population at decreased cost. Hawai'i residents have among the lowest mortality and utilization indicators, which may be explained by ready access to effective care at reasonable costs, and by the fact that Hawai'i's doctors emphasize outpatient care. Second, mandated employer coverage can be an effective tool for universal access. Third, strong insurance reform accompanying the employee mandate can lower costs. In Hawai'i while a mandatory community-rating law does not exist, a form of voluntary rating between the two dominant insurance providers, HMSA and Kaiser, tends to hold insurance costs down. Having fewer players in the insurance market has benefited purchasers. Finally, costs can be controlled through such mechanisms as the Certificate of Need process, managed care, and competition among insurance providers within clearly structured ground rules. (Lewin, n.d.)

Contrasting interpretations of Hawai'i's experience can be drawn from these lessons. One is that intended by Lewin, namely that good public policy can be employed in ways that promote the rational use of resources within the health-care system. When this is done, the aggregate burden on the state is lessened. The implication is also clear in the sense of constituting a lesson for Hawai'i: one good turn deserves another. If Prepaid has made such a significant difference for Hawai'i (the difference between spending roughly 11 percent of Gross State Product on health care vs. the national figure of nearly 15 percent), then other aggressive acts of public policy should be pursued to maintain that advantage. This has been the rationale for the creation of SHIP, and has been incorporated into QUEST, albeit that the impetus for QUEST came from the Department of Human Services and not the Department of Health.

Lewin's notion of a "seamless" health-care system has been in part based on finding ways of maximizing the impact of public funding of health care while holding funding to reasonable levels—defined in practice by what the Legislature has been willing to support. Lewin's intended seamless system is meant to operate at one level as a macro-cost control mechanism: it targets expenditures efficiently and rationally. By squeezing irrational applications out of the system (by having everyone covered by health insurance), the state can maximize its policy position by gaining cost control with a minimal amount of direct regulation. The relative importance of this can be appreciated in the context of the national policy debate where hospitals, insurance companies, and physicians are all enormously resistant to direct acts of governmental regulation in the name of accomplishing a national health-care system (one main goal of which is to provide universal coverage). The genius of Prepaid, given American values about the limits of state regulation of the private sector, is that it accomplishes a significant measure of insurance coverage while leaving the bulk of decisions on the particulars of health coverage in the hands of insurance companies, physicians, hospitals, and consumers operating through their purchasing agents, mainly employers. It is this combination of attributes that the Clinton health reform is seeking in its notion of purchasing cooperatives. It is important to recognize that the primary alternative to this system of private sector arrangements produced by a defining act of state regulation is a much higher level of state regulation across the board which would seek to control costs more directly in their application.

One of the ironies of Lewin's position is the attacks he has borne by conservative physicians in Hawai'i, especially those organized in the Hawai'i Federation. These physicians along with some allies in the hospital association and various members of the Legislature have attacked all Lewin's measures of the past few years to complete Seamless, most particularly the efforts to establish some entity that would be in charge of mandatory data collection, a bill to establish a mandatory community rating, and a bill to establish an alliance framework (the local version of Clinton's purchasing cooperatives). They have also opposed QUEST which attempts to fold Medicaid and SHIP together through the mechanism of private insurance coverage particularly for its managed ccare provisions. These reforms have been opposed in the name of the inroads they make on autonomy of practitioners and other providers in the public sector; all were seen as unwarranted extensions of state power. These characterizations, in my view, are parochial in the sense that they significantly misread the national temper for health-care reform in the country as a whole (into which Hawai'i will be swept unless it takes some action to preempt Federal inclusion), and misguided because by reading Lewin's essentially conservative program to maintain the essentially private sector character of health care coverage as an excessive extension of state control.

A more appropriate critique of Lewin's position and Seamless, and QUEST emerges from another interpretation of his "lessons from Hawai'i" that focuses on the current rate of growth in health-care expenditures. This is the argument that an examination of trend data suggests that Hawai'i may lose whatever advantage it may have enjoyed in the cost realm (as least as expressed by the aggregate amount of spending). Rather, it is argued, what we see currently is a rate of spending growth that is undifferentiated from mainland counterparts (the *Health Affairs* argument). This has been experienced, in part, by the rapid increase in Medicaid and Workers Compensation expenditures. If this is true, then an explanation different from that offered by Lewin's "lessons" is required to characterize Hawai'i, because the cost escalators apparently operating within the current system are producing growth rates equal to the rest of the country. If this is the case, then, it is argued, one needs to look at the factors which are conventionally held to be the source of growth in health-care expenditures and seek to understand why expenditure growth in Hawai'i is no longer differentiated. A standard list of such factors includes demographic trends (growth and changes in population composition), epidemiological and public health factors, use of high-tech medical devices and techniques, coverage and structure of private health insurance, state-mandated insurance benefits, government policies affecting provider reimbursement, medical malpractice and defensive medicine, the rise in consumer expectations, and administrative inefficiencies (*Blue Ribbon Commission Report*, 1992). To these, I would add the phenomenon of medicalization, the tendency of medicine to include a widening number of social processes in its treatment warrant, e.g., aging, violent behavior, genetic modification of behavior. Clearly only some of these factors lie within the boundaries of Lewin's lessons and imply quite different approaches to control the costs associated with these escalators.

A third explanation for the relatively low aggregate expenditure rate in Hawai'i comes from critics of the health care system in general, and especially the state's role in it. Many who subscribe to this critique are represented in this volume; they hold that the society and the state simply do not spend what they should to produce adequate health care for important sectors of the society. Foremost of these is in the area of mental health, the mental health of youth and children in particular. This is seen as a historical failure of public policy in Hawai'i, one which has been admitted repeatedly in public by Lewin who intimates that support for this issue simply does not exist among the public and consequently the Legislature. In this view, mental-health coverage includes funding appropriate interventions for alcohol and other drug abuse; adolescent violence and endemic school failure by significant groups of youth; and family violence. This view takes a broader view of health than that normally associated with the medical model, in effect expanding the boundaries of public health. In this context the notion of "health-care expenditures" has to be disaggregated to differentiate those devoted to support of the medical system and those directed at medically-prior conditions. This critique of current practice argues that social expenditures on both categories for this population is lower than it should be.

Another form of this criticism is to identify groups within the population who lack suitable access to the health-care system, however defined. These listings usually include: Native Hawai'ians, especially in semi-rural areas like Waianae and Waiamanalo on Oahu; recent immigrants; the very poor; the homeless; others in rural areas. The conditions mentioned in the previous paragraph are most prevalent in these groups.

Some, like Jim Shon, one of the primary legislative supporters of SHIP, contend that the administration (read: the DOH) has contributed to this situation by failing to take advantage of provisions within existing state law that would permit more resources to be directed at these populations. SHIP administrators, for example, have failed to provide sufficient funding for health clinics that directly serve these populations. In his view, the state has erred by seeking out ways not to involve itself more directly in supporting those at the bottom of the health care pecking order, leaving this task to the insurance system. Insurance providers, in their turn, have constructed coverage programs which (no matter how costly others think them to be) are not fully effective for the needs of these populations.

Three Positions on Health-Care Expenditures

These disparate views tend to bundle into three modal positions on health-care expenditure in Hawai'i, each viewing the needs of the society quite differently, each interpreting the cost issue differently, and each looking for a different set of approaches (interventions) for "controlling" costs.

One group, which I have identified with the views of medical conservatives, is composed of practitioners who do not want the state—the public sector—to be further involved in the regulation of health care. This approach emphasizes the high quality of the current medical system, the importance of protecting medical judgment in the making of treatment decisions, and the certainty that these valuable qualities can only decline with further state intervention. Robert Alford many years ago termed those who hold this view *vis a vis* reform efforts "professional monopolists;" more recently Paul Starr has called them "health care entrepreneurs." These are providers of medical services, who like other businessmen in the market, want to be left alone to offer their goods free from state intervention. Their views emphasize the right of free choice between those offering the service and those purchasing it; although the facts of the economic exchange are not stressed, their discourse focuses on the importance of individual physician choice to presumptive good medical practice.

This group is likely to discount the so-called "crisis" in health-care funding and favor no intervention at all (unless it is reform of the tort system to constrain medical malpractice suits). Some will respond with the old market response that as suppliers of a good (medical care), they are only giving people what they want. The press of consumer demand is emphasized. To others' claims that cost escalation can be related to over-medication, or excessive technology utilization, or unjustified practice variation among physicians, the reply is likely to be that patients are (and should be) free to choose their own doctors; if they don't like what is going on they can go somewhere else. This is the position of the free marketer unwilling to concede that the market is neither one which maximizes choice for the consumer, nor regulates behavior to produce an ultimate social value. When faced with claims that the aggregate amount spent on medical care is excessive, the response if likely to be, "what makes 12 percent of GNP sacred? or 14 percent or even 20 percent?" Why shouldn't a society spend what it wants on health care? There is no magic number that says we are "overspending." As the health economist Ewe Reinhart continues to point out, whatever other value such blatant free market arguments may have in the health-care debate, when they are made by practitioners and other providers, they are also fundamentally arguments designed to defend these groups' privileged income base.

A second modal position on the cost issue is that of the political center. Both nationally and in Hawai'i that ground is occupied by those who seek reform to rectify identified abuses in the system while seeking to preserve its basic outlines; this is an argument focused on insurance coverage. Currently dubbed "managed competition" to signal the focus on the competitive marketing of health insurance coverage, this position focuses on private health insurance as the basic mechanism for health-care funding. This position is also a market position, but look at the "managed" side. This group emphasizes the barriers that exist when the free market position is applied to health care:

- consumers must have an effective means to make intelligent choices about health care plans (ergo such devices as purchasing cooperatives);
- universal coverage is essential to the rational application of both private and public resources (ergo such devices as community ratings to insure inclusive coverage, a universal standard benefits package, and privatizing Medicaid through private insurance mechanisms);
- purchasers must have good and reliable knowledge of the options available within medical care (ergo such devices as organization of hospitals and physicians in health plans, and creation of outcome measures and data to determine appropriate and comparative levels of medical performance.)

Managed competition advocates also claim that further and important cost control measures can be gained by the rationalization of insurance practices to reduce unnecessary overhead expenditures. (Nationally, some estimates of this cost run as high as 22 percent of expenditures. The claim has been made that Hawai'i's costs on this dimension are far less, a result of its unique two-provider-dominant system.) Members of this persuasion see restricted government intervention as a key to restraining the income aggrandizing potential of unchecked private interests.

The third modal position is occupied on the national health-reform stage by those who favor a single payer system. This view holds that the current system contains within itself the seeds of its own destruction. It is fragmented, dominated by vested interests who seek their advantage at the expense of good public policy, expensive, wasteful, and impossible to regulate effectively. For this group, the worst element of the current system is that what Americans pay for health care does not even begin to meet the needs of over 20 percent of the population.

To advocates of the single payer system, the most important elements of reform are universal coverage and the creation of a standard benefits package. Only the public sector can provide these guarantees. They see managed competition as a gigantic concession to the private insurance industry. Rather, government must ensure to all citizens the right to quality health care, *and* it must do so in a fiscally responsible manner. The key to this outcome is global budgeting in which the public sector through regional health authorities would bargain with providers—hospitals, physicians, health plans, pharmaceutical companies—for the lowest charges. The private insurance health care insurance industry would be abolished. Such a system, it is maintained, would have sufficient market power to match that of the firms currently controlling health care; only such a mechanism can hope to control costs in the long run. This proposal, it is further argued, is consistent with the nature of health care and the need of people for it: health care is a right, a benefit to be gained from social membership. It is not a market commodity that can be traded like any other commodity; to continue to treat health care in this way is inevitably to invite inequality, distortion of application, and social harm. (Stone, 1993)

This position has lacked support within Hawai'i, save some articulate and persistent advocates of more egalitarian solutions to health care such as the well-known Ah Quan McElrath, and a few voices in the union movement. One suggestion is that the Prepaid Health-Care Act brought Hawai'i closer to universal coverage and the standard benefit package than any other state. In current congressional politics, it is argued, resistance to reform by the health-care industry and business is so great that one must propose something as radical as a single-payer system just to make universal coverage and the standard benefit package priority items—circumstances that don't exist in Hawai'i. What does exist is a voice for a far larger role in the provisioning of care to those who currently lack it.

Those who hold this view share some attributes with their single-payer counterparts, with an important difference.

Whereas the single-payer position attributes most of the cost and coverage issues to the industry, in Hawai'i these are shared equally with the Department of Health and state government; on the latter score primarily through its long-term subsidization of hospitals on the neighbor islands. Again, Prepaid is at the core of the argument. Prepaid, it is argued, establishes most of the conditions that would emerge under a national policy of managed competition, and what one sees is that the relationship between providers is not one of effective competition on cost, but rather one of mutual accommodation in the steady rise in costs. Prepaid mandates a large market for the major suppliers in the Hawai'i insurance environment, two of whom dominate their would-be competitors—a scenario single payer advocates predict for the mainland should the Clinton reforms come to pass. No effective competition exists between providers on costs. And, this view would argue, should other local managed competition type reforms come to pay, such as QUEST, the situation would be just more of the same. An additional problem is the DOH itself, perceived as an overly large, out-of-date, out-of-touch bureaucracy that even an activist director such as Lewin had little success reforming. Even when it is given a mandate for reaching needy populations, its conservative instincts keep those reforms from being effective. Lewin's response has been to place an increasing amount of activity, such as the state hospitals, in the private sector where, on his view, they can be subject to the disciplines of the market. The critical view is that the DOH itself needs to be reformed top to bottom by some powerful authoritative agency, itself only possible as a creature of the state. Again, global budgeting is viewed as one such mechanism.

Conclusions

How then, one might ask, should one go about controlling health-care costs in Hawai'i? The burden of the above arguments is that the answer to this question has everything to do with where one stands. Every effort to "control" costs has winners and losers. There are no "technical" answers which magically produce savings for all. Even the issue one might most consensually nominate for this, reform of administrative costs, is complex. This is always the issue first raised in cost-control discussions, in part one suspects, because it is usually called "administrative waste." Physicians and hospital administrators complain about the endless forms they must fill out both for insurance companies and to be in compliance with the forest of governmental regulations. Even the supposed mother's milk of administrative reform, electronic record keeping, is opposed by a substantial portion of physicians who fear the encroachment of state control.

The bottom line on cost control is that it is a zero sum game. Even disease control and health promotion, if very effective, would subtract significant amounts of demand from the health care system and with it withdraw income. So, the question must be changed to: who would propose which cost controls, over what, and for what ends? What one prefers as an intervention to produce control over costs is a direct product of the broader political fabric from which one makes judgments about the world. Cost control is an outcome, not so much a process. It is a set of decisions that deploys values and strategies. This means that needs are to be traded off within the arena of care and the costs associated with it. On every score, some will make arguments that press the value they hold most dear. Not surprisingly, some of those arguments will closely parallel the benefits which their proponents draw from them. And those who have been the beneficiaries of the current system will see every move to rectify existing inequities of the system as a loss.

Every move in public policy to limit aggregate social spending, especially public sector spending, will be seen as a threat to the autonomy of those currently performing these services. Robert Evans, a Canadian political economist specializing in health care, has pointed out the distinct error of arguing that cost control is unachievable. Providers, he maintained, have been very successfully controlling costs for some decade, against the efforts of public authorities to deploy the values which they prefer. This next stage in the drama we have come to call health-care reform promises to feature new actors with new agendas to contest these historically-successful practices of cost control.

Bibliography

Robert Alford, *Health Care Politics*, Chicago, University of Chicago Press, 1975.

Governor's Blue Ribbon Commission on Health-Care Costs, *"Health Care Expenditure Information and Health Policy Directions,"* September, 1992.

Katharine R. Levit, Helen C. Lazenby, Cathy A. Cowan, and Suzanne W. Letsch, "Health Spending by State: New Estimates for Policy-Making," *Health Affairs*, Fall, 1993, 7-26. Data in Part B of this paper are derived from the data set for this article.

John Lewin, "Four Lessons From Hawai'i," State of Hawai'i, Department of Health, xerox paper, no date.

Paul Starr, *The Transformation of American Medicine*, New York, Basic Books, 1982.

Deborah Stone, "When Patients Go To Market: The Working of Managed Competition," *The American Prospect*, Summer 1993, 13.

CHAPTER FIVE

Hawaii's Insurance Strategy
What Are the Facts? Is Prepaid Worth Preserving?

HENRY A. FOLEY

In a 1994 Hawai'i poll,[1] residents ranked health care as their top problem only after the economy and crime. Even though Hawai'i's politicians had labeled it "the health state," its residents were concerned. Their concern is the result of inflated propaganda in the face of harsh realities.

From 1989 through 1992, elected and non-elected state officials proclaimed locally and nationally that Hawai'i's Prepaid Health Care Act (PHCA) and State Health Insurance Plan represented the best approach to assuring universal coverage, low costs, and excellent health status. During the campaigning about the solution, the state's unemployment rate rose to 4.9 percent due to a reduction in tourism, the collapse of the sugar industry, and the resultant closing of many small businesses.

Residents lost their private insurance coverage and either enrolled in Medicaid or the State Health Insurance Program, if eligible, or went without health insurance. Concomitantly, Hawai'i's rapidly increasing rise in health-care costs–greater than on the Mainland–continued unabated despite claims that Hawai'i's insurance approach led to lower costs! By 1993, Hawai'i experienced moderate success in assuring insurance coverage and escalating costs to government and business because its state-mandated insurance approaches lacked cost-containment mechanisms. Inflated claims about Hawai'i's Prepaid Health Care Act had distracted the public from the real danger: that health care's increasing costs to all employers and government were eroding support for coverage in the state. Significant improvements in Hawai'i's insurance approach were warranted.

By 1994, although the rate of health care inflation was decreasing on the Mainland, it was either still increasing or remaining constant on our islands. Those who lived in urban Honolulu in 1993 experienced a rise in the cost of health care at twice the overall inflation rate.[2]

The Claims and The Facts

What have been the political claims, what are the facts about Hawai'i's insurance strategy, and how do we proceed to improve that strategy?

CLAIM: Hawai'i's PHCA resulted in a significant reduction of the percentage of uninsured persons after its passage in 1974.

FACTS: There is no evidence for this claim. No data was collected before or after the passage of Prepaid to substantiate any such claim. The claim was based on guesses made in the Seventies because no systematic analysis was done before and after Prepaid was implemented. The President of HMSA, Marvin Hall, estimated a reduction of 5,000 uninsured persons.

In a very recent scientific study,[3] A.W. Dick determined that there was a reduction of 8-16 percent in the number of uninsured (or 8,000 persons) and not the 66-percent reduction implied by the State Director of Health, John Lewin, and his deputy, Peter Sybinsky.[4] Hawai'i's PHCA had done relatively little to extend insurance to the uninsured. Rather, the labor contracts and ethnic composition of Hawai'i are the basis for Hawai'i's extensive coverage.

Hawai'i's Prepaid Act came into being in a labor environment where the pineapple and sugar industries provided comprehensive medical services to their employees and labor unions negotiated comprehensive health care benefits as a part of collective bargaining contracts. This pattern carried over to many small businesses. As a consequence, mandatory employer contribution to health insurance coverage was not a repugnant requirement for most Hawai'i businesses. Most employers provided health benefits before the mandatory law was passed in 1973 in order to compete for qualified workers in a labor market with a low unemployment rate (below 5 percent in 1993).

A significant fact, overlooked until recently, is that Hawai'i's higher rates of coverage compared to the Mainland appear to be due largely to the ethnic makeup of Hawai'i's population: two-thirds Asian-Americans, who tend to have high rates of insurance throughout the U.S.[5]

Although Hawai'i's Prepaid Act is the only employer mandated insurance program in the United States, it is flawed in its extent of coverage and enforceability. Prepaid is not universally inclusive because it exempts part-time workers, state employees who are categorized as temporary, seasonal agricultural workers, insurance and real estate salespeople working on commission, and individual proprietorship members in small family-run businesses. Prepaid does not require coverage of the employee's dependents.

Employer compliance rests on a weak mechanism: monitoring and enforcement occur only when an eligible employee files a complaint with the state investigative unit of the State Department of Labor and Industrial Relations that he/she has not been covered. Often, an employee who is a recent immigrant will not know that their employer may be required to offer coverage. Prepaid can be viewed as a check on the expansion of the number of uninsured as long as voluntary compliance remains firm.

Given the limits of Prepaid, it is not surprising that 13 years after its passage, Hawai'i's uninsured rate was 11.1 percent, slightly worse than Massachusetts' (10.1 percent) but better than that of California (18.8 percent), New York (13.9 percent) and Texas (23 percent).[6] While Prepaid but marginally reduced the number uninsured, it had become an important symbol to many that Hawai'i was committed to universal coverage.

CLAIM: PHCA led to health-care costs lower than those of the Mainland.

FACTS: Health-care costs in Hawai'i are lower due to a lower cost basis inherited from the period prior to Prepaid and preserved by oligopolistic pricing practices of the state's two dominant insurers, HMSA and Kaiser. Since 1988, however, the rate of growth in the cost of health care services has exceeded the Mainland's; Prepaid has failed to slow the cost increases.

The lower rate of hospitalization costs has been due to factors other than Prepaid. Since 1955, health insurance in Hawai'i has been biased positively toward outpatient care, as opposed to hospitalization, covering the former from the first office visit. Lower secondary and tertiary hospitalization rates for non-Oahu residents have led to lower hospitalization costs than the national average.

Another downward pressure on private sector costs has been the increasing use of Federal dollars to reimburse hospital costs under the disproportionate share program for Medicaid patients which grew from $8 million in fiscal year 1991 to over

$51.3 million in fiscal year 1994.[7] These payments are adjustments made to hospitals serving a large number of Medicaid patients.

Despite these downward pressures on private sector costs, Hawai'i's inflation in health-care costs has accelerated. Between 1980 and 1991 Hawai'i's per capita health expenditures increased at an average rate of 9.8 percent, slightly higher than the national average of 9.4 percent.[8] Hawai'i's increase in hospital administrative costs, in health professional wages and in medical equipment reflected the pattern of the nation.

Since 1991, Hawai'i's health-care inflation has ranged from 10-14 percent per year. In 1991 alone, covered hospital charges rose 30 percent; ancillary charges, 33 percent; and room and board charges, 22 percent. By the end of 1993, Hawai'i's average daily hospital charge—for room, board, and ancillary services—was $2,040, up about 10 percent from the previous year. HMSA premiums rose at 10 percent per year; Kaiser's premiums increased from 14 percent to 22 percent per year. Medicaid's inpatient and outpatient expenditures increased 41.57 percent and 35.78 percent respectively in 1992 alone. In the past three years Hawai'i's average Medicaid cost per recipient has risen between 7 and 9 percent each year. Impacted also has been the workers compensation program which has experienced significant medical care service costs during the past decade.

Given that health care inflation continued unchanged, it is not surprising that the U.S. Government Accounting Office found in 1993 that 56 percent of the state's small businesses surveyed considered health insurance a major cost problem—a higher negative rating than for any other state requirement.[9] By the spring of 1994 HMSA and Kaiser seemed to have become more responsive to the inflation problem. HMSA held its premium increases to less than 3 percent and Kaiser implemented an average 8 percent increase in premiums. Is this the beginning of a lower inflationary trend or a momentary dip?

CLAIM: The State Health Insurance Program covers the remaining uninsured.

FACTS: More than 15 years after the passage of Prepaid, the State of Hawai'i under the Waihee administration established the State Health Insurance Plan (SHIP) to cover the gap group, those not covered by Prepaid or the public insurance programs of Medicare, Medicaid and CHAMPUS. In 1989, the Waihee administration estimated that 5 percent of Hawai'i's population remained without coverage. Not explained was the dramatic 50 percent reduction from 11 percent uninsured in 1987, if such a reduction occurred. During a time of state budget surpluses, the state created SHIP for residents with gross incomes of less than 300 percent of Federal poverty.

SHIP contracted with HMSA and Kaiser to provide primary care benefits including immunization, check-ups and other preventive measures and a minimal number of hospital days. By 1993 SHIP covered 20,000 residents or 1.77 percent of the population.[10] The state also sought to enroll as many as possible in Medicaid, about 101,000 or 9 percent of the population by fiscal year 1993. However, it targeted native Hawai'ians especially for enrollment because statistically they tend to cluster in the lower end of the economic scale and have the poorest health status. Ironically, two years after enactment of SHIP, the Waihee administration chose to veto SHIP coverage for its own uninsured temporary employees, some of whom had been in temporary status for more than five to ten years!

Despite a dedicated effort by state staff to enroll the total gap group, 32 percent of the community health center clients remained uninsured. In response to this situation, the state redirected some of the SHIP appropriation to fund the centers in order to cover the costs of the uninsured. For the period from July 1, 1992 to June 30, 1993, the centers were paid at a level of $56.06 per visit, times 9,642 visits for a total of $539,952.[11] Still, 4.3 percent of the total population remained uninsured.[12] They were composed of immigrants, state temporary employees, self-employed, persons between jobs and without coverage, some dependents and others. However, it shall be noted that at the same time the uninsured on the Mainland rose to 14.7 percent.

CLAIM: Hawai'i's premiums are lower than those of the nation as a whole.

FACT: This claim is true. Hawai'i's premiums are lower by $358 to $396 than the U.S. average cost of $1,604 for comparable coverage. There are two basic reasons for this reality.

First, there is little basis for cost shifting from the public sector to the private sector. Almost everyone is covered where services are available through a comprehensive web of private insurance, Medicaid, Medicare, SHIP, CHAMPUS, and numerous categorical programs sponsored by the Federal and state governments. The insurers use a modified community rating structure, which has spread costs evenly so that businesses can purchase insurance at reasonable rates. Medicaid payments to the providers are 116 percent of Medicare. The fact that Pre-paid prevents employees from dropping health-insurance cov-erage assures that most citizens will have the ability to pay for their health-care services. The 4.3 percent or more of unin-sured have access to public programs although some do occa-sionally receive uncompensated care. Thus, the comprehensive web of coverage and programs leaves precious little reason for providers to cost shift.

Second, with its continued emphasis on primary care through physicians' offices and primary-care clinics, Hawai'i's insured averaged 3.9 to 4 visits per client in 1992, which may provide a partial explanation for Hawai'i's lower inpatient ad-mission rate, lower hospital admission rates, and less hospital cost pressure on premiums.

Hawai'i's experience with extensive private and public insurance coverage has led to several paradoxes:

1) An employer-mandated insurance program and a state sponsored program of gap coverage still leaves approximately 4 percent of the population uncovered at any one moment.

2) The uncovered population may obtain access to ser-vices through publicly and privately sponsored non-profit clinics and state operated programs as long as taxpayers support these endeavors. Many of our tax-payers are unaware of this important infrastructure or safety net. Without it, uncompensated care would dramatically increase and significant cost shifting to the privately insured would follow. Many of our pub-lic policy-makers have yet to consider that the total privatization of health care in Hawai'i will require the integration and ongoing private or public financial support for this culturally-sensitive infrastructure.

3) The lack of long-term care beds, home health pro-grams, and appropriately trained professionals causes usage of hospital beds for long-term and chronic pa-tients. Were alternatives to hospitalization in place or

developed, there would be a downward pressure on hospital costs and the revelation that Hawai'i has an excess of beds on Oahu.

4) Even with an emphasis on primary care providers the inflation in health-care costs continues to absorb a disproportionate share of private and public dollars which are no longer available for business expansion, school improvements, and housing.

Have we begun to examine the inefficiencies and inappropriate utilization which may be driving the inflation in our health care sector? We have the methods to do so. Are enough of us asking the key questions: How can we provide or obtain care more economically? Do we have the will? How can we stay within some overall realistic budget as private citizens and as taxpayers? Do we have the discipline?

None of these questions can be addressed without easy access to information. We cannot stay within an affordable budget if we do not have access to the information base which would allow us to know our expenditure patterns and to question those patterns when necessary. Why, in 1994, do we not have easy access to the price and cost data collected by all payers in the state so that we can make informed choices about providers, programs and services? Would not this economic data be useful to health-care providers themselves so that they would chose the most clinically and economically appropriate interventions?

Today, through more and more expensive insurance programs we pay for quality services, some appropriate and some inappropriate, some very expensive and some which could be less expensive. Sometimes our insurance pays for poor and inefficient services. So far a legislatively-sponsored blue-ribbon committee and political rhetoric have not provided the buying public with the price and cost information collected at their expense. By not creating a mechanism to assure that third-party payors must provide this information, our elected officials leave the public in the position of dependent children in the health market place. By not demanding access to information, we, the public, excuse ourselves from mature decision-making.

Through a failure of will, Hawai'i has stopped short of universal coverage and experiences rapid inflation in its health-care costs.

Improvements Needed

Several steps can be taken to reach the goal of universal coverage and to check health care inflation:

• Amend the Prepaid Act to include temporary employees and dependents.

• Amend the "premium supplementation fund" of the Prepaid Act to subsidize businesses with fewer than eight people which have trouble paying their health premiums. The fund was established for such a purpose but current requirements block effective relief to small businesses. Until 1992, the Small Business Association of Hawai'i did not even know of its existence.[13] Not more than $100,000 has been spent out of this fund since the enactment of the Prepaid Act. Consequently, it has a reserve of $2.3 million and has not provided sufficient relief to small businesses.

• Set up an insurance fund to which all self-employed are required to contribute.

• Place Federal categorical funds which cover immigrants into the same fund.

• Require all insurance payments under Prepaid, Medicare, QUEST, the health benefit portion of workers compensation, the new insurance fund and the Federal categorized funds to be pooled and have one standardized benefit package. Providers would benefit from reduced paperwork and foster more predictable payment from a single plan.

• Require all providers to bid for the number of citizens they can adequately serve within a capitated rate or budgeted amount.

• Require each contracting group of providers to submit an easily readable report on the costs, utilization rates, outcomes and quality indicators of their performance prior to each year's marketing effort and renewal of contract. Much of this is already done under the Federal Employees Health Benefit Program which contract with insurers and health maintenance organizations.

Currently, the state has narrowed the scope of a competitive market to many but not to all of the low income population. The state hopes to check the inflationary growth in its sponsored insurance programs through the QUEST Program. This goal is laudable, and hopefully the state will achieve it. But it runs the risk that providers as a group will raise prices or incur costs at higher rates for the privately insured who have not been included in the competitive market designed in the QUEST Program. The 1994 legislative session with its call for more study about whether cost information should be made available to the public suggests that special interests and their legislative supporters may not want competition but continued oligopolistic control.

Conversely, by taking this incremental step called QUEST and making it a successful check on inflation in publicly-sponsored programs, the state may induce the employers to expect such competitive developments in the privately insured market. Such has been the process which evolved in Arizona over the last decade where employers have offered a wide range of managed-care options to their employees after the state demonstrated significant economies in its managed-care strategy for indigents in its ACCESS program. If we would take the steps outlined here or similar steps, we can achieve universal insurance access in Hawai'i within an open competitive system which would rein in current health-care inflation.

References

1. Advertiser/Channel 2 News Hawai'i Poll of 605 Island residents, February 12-17 Margin of error, 4 percentage points. *The Honolulu Advertiser*, April 10, 1994.
2. Tom Leonard, All About Business in Hawai'i, *Pacific Business News*, 1994:49.
3. Andrew W. Dick, "Will Employer Mandates Really Work? Another Look at Hawai'i," *Health Affairs:* Spring (I) 1994: 342-349.
4. J.C. Lewin and P. A. Sybinsky, "Hawai'i's Employer Mandate and Its Contribution to Universal Access," *Journal of the American Medical Association* (May 1993): 2538-2543.
5. Dick, *op. cit.* : 346.
6. Dick, *Ibid.* : 345.
7. *Health Forum*, Healthcare Association of Hawai'i, Vol. XI, 3, April, 1994: 2.
8. *Health Care in Hawai'i*, U.S. General Accounting Office, February 1994: 9. (or 1-56). Referred as GAO/HEHS-94-68 Health Care In Hawai'i.
9. GAO *Ibid.*

10. *Health Trends In Hawai'i,* The Hawai'ian Medical Service Association Foundation, 1994: 46. This average masks the reality that the level of uninsured on the Neighbor Islands, e.g., Kaua'i, Hawai'i, Moloka'i, Maui. Those uninsured can obtain services from the state hospitals which are required to accept all patients regardless of their level of insurance coverage.

11. Correspondence dated 5-3-94 between Robert Grossmann, Executive Director of the Hawai'i Primary Care Association and author.

12. *Health Trends op. cit.,* p. 47.

13. Interview with Sam Sloan, May 3, 1994. Also Christine Rodrigo, "Health Costs Threaten Fund," *Pacific Business News,* November 9, 1992.

CHAPTER SIX

Myths and Lessons Learned from Hawai'i

BOB GROSSMANN

Looking at Hawai'i's experiences over the past eight years as context for its claim to lead the national health-care reform effort, we find important myths and lessons about our system.

Both the myths and lessons help to highlight the fluidity of the issues surrounding the health-care industry. The financial, legal, and policy pressures are staggering. President-Elect Clinton summed them up at his 1992 economic summit in Little Rock, when he stated that without reform the nation would be bankrupted by health-care costs. The State of Hawai'i is facing similar pressures, because of the high inflationary costs of obtaining such care.

Without significant changes in how health care is given and reimbursements for that method, Hawai'i's system could be in serious jeopardy in less than five years, unless health-care inflation and cost-shifting are abated. The General Accounting Office (GAO, 1992) found that Hawai'i has not been immune to rising costs, and that Hawai'i's per-capita health care expenditures from 1974 to 1982 kept pace with the national average of premium inflation. To arrive at an honest dialogue on the key issues, the myths must be better understood.

Hawai'i, even as a model for health-care reform, has not escaped the power of the myth. One of them, voiced in recent years, is that no new funding is needed or that it can be captured largely through Federal matching, e.g., enhanced Medicaid funds to expand health-care access. The argument that "no new funds are needed" is based on the theory that enough savings can be captured through improving administrative efficiencies, reducing fraud, and restructuring reimbursements, while expanding access toward the goal of universal insurance coverage. The theory becomes myth at the point of reality, because of the length of time and the political will needed to capture the "savings" from the system without limiting current benefits. Increasing access for those currently uninsured—especially in the confines of the traditional medical model—will necessitate the infusion of new capital into the health-care system. Cost containment could reduce expenditures below 1993 levels, but even heroically-successful measures are only likely to bring health-care cost inflation in line with the general inflation rates of other commodities. Furthermore, dependence on an ever-increasing pot of Federal Medicaid funds is also unrealistic, even with a Democratic president. Health-care costs are so out-of-control that President Clinton is likely to cap Federal spending, but the government will most likely allow states greater flexibility on how they can spend Federal health-related dollars.

The theory of "no new funding is needed" became counter-productive in Hawai'i's 1993 legislative session, when efforts to pass further reform measures clashed with toughening economic times when the state budget approached "zero growth," after years of hefty surpluses. The Waihee administration proposed raising cigarette taxes, a health-care provider tax, users' fees, and increased billing for mental and personal health services. Health-care reform is clearly linked to the overall "health" status of the state's economy.

A second myth is that an employer-based system for access to health insurance will eliminate the gap group. This myth becomes exposed during high levels of unemployment seen, for example, after the closing the Hamakua Sugar Company on the Island of Hawai'i, after natural disasters such as Hurricane Iniki, or a downturn of tourists from North America. A gap group continues to exist, although more generous Medicaid[1] and the State Health Insurance Program (SHIP) have reduced the figures since the passage of the Prepaid Health Care Act (PHCA) in 1974 (Lewin, Palmer & Grossmann, 1992). In reality, health care is still a privilege for those enjoying economic security. Hawai'i has been successful in keeping the gap group low in comparison to other states.

However, on November 6, 1992, the Department of Health issued a background paper, "Measuring the Uninsured Population in Hawai'i," which claimed: "The State of Hawai'i offers the nation's only universal guarantee of financial access to health care for all of its people." Such a claim goes further than mere access to health insurance and adds to the myth that all persons without the resources to pay for health care services have either a public or private program that *guarantees* (emphasis added) their health-insurance needs. On a positive note, the Department of Health has claimed survey results indicating that 3.75 percent of residents lacked health insurance in 1991. The state's approach has limits and contradictions.

For instance, SHIP was not an entitlement program, but was capped initially at $10 million per annum. Hence, when enrollment reaches a specific number, either the access gates must close or the program goes into deficit spending. Medicaid has its own "barriers" to enrollment. In 1992, Governor Waihee vetoed H.B. 3672, which would have allowed government emergency hires to have access to the Public Health Fund, thereby giving these employees equal standing with other "full-time" state workers. Additional cost was the main argument offered for the veto, even though the law would have set the same standard for government that is set for the private sector by the PHCA (i.e., requiring all employers to give coverage to employees who work at least 20 hours per week for four consecutive weeks.)

A third myth could be defined by the statement that "access to health insurance equals access to health care." Although access to health insurance may mean protection from catastrophic bills, just having medical insurance does not guarantee, for instance, either appropriate or timely care. The problem of achieving full immunization rates is an example.

Although the cost for immunizations may be covered by insurance plans, state-supported clinics or HMO's, the rate of those children fully immunized by the age of two is still not 100 percent. Preventive measures, even when covered by insurance plans, are generally not well used. The statewide proportion of children born in 1986 and adequately immunized by age two was found to be only 61 percent; from a 1992 Department of Health phone survey, the lack of awareness of the need for immunizations was found to be the leading barrier (32 percent) to higher immunization levels (Baumgartner, Grossmann & Fuddy, 1993). At the other end of the medical spectrum, access to the medical system can result in overly invasive procedures, negative outcomes, or over-medication. Copayments and deductibles can also result in significant yearly medical bills for individuals. To reiterate, having health insurance does not always equal getting appropriate medical care.

In addition, states have groups that are disenfranchised

from the medical delivery system. The poor health statistics for Native Hawai'ians, sadly, exemplifies this point.

Native Hawai'ians represent about 20 percent of Hawai'i's resident population, but this group accounts for about 40 percent of the morbidity and mortality rates. A few statistics[2] for Native Hawai'ians are needed:

- Overall death rate is 34 percent higher than the national average.
- 50 percent higher infant mortality rate and a 61 percent higher chronic liver disease rate in comparison to the rest of the state.
- Diabetes is 222 percent and heart disease is 44 percent higher than the national average.

The need for culturally-meaningful medical approaches for disenfranchised groups, such as the Native Hawai'ians, may be more important than access issues. National reform efforts need to assure that reimbursements are flexible to allow, in some cases, more indigenous healers in conjunction with the traditional medical model. Hawai'i, through Federal funding, is starting to establish a Native Hawai'ian Health Center on each island with a significant native population. For these groups, disease prevention and health promotion must be part of both state and Federal approaches. To affect poor health statistics of the Native Hawai'ians, 10-15 years of sustained effort are needed.

A final myth deals with a state's overall approach to health-care reform. Experience from the key states with health initiatives—Oregon, Washington, Minnesota, Vermont, Florida, or Hawai'i—shows that reform has been most effective when achieved through increments, instead of trying to get an entire health-care package through in one legislative session (Milbank Memorial Fund, 1993).[3] Hawai'i's 1993 legislative session lends credence to this position.

In 1992, Deputy Director of Health for Health Resources Administration, Pete Sybinsky, made the important policy decision to delay any health-care reform bills sponsored by the Executive Branch until the following legislative session, in part, to benefit from the 1992 recommendations of the Governor's Blue Ribbon Panel.

Unfortunately, the decision to wait did not coincide well with the state elections that year for Senate and House of Representatives. With the "retirement," earlier in the year, of both the

President of the Senate and the Speaker of the House and with many new faces in the Legislature, the opening of the session brought an entire new slate of committee membership (including both the Senate and Health Chairs dealing with health and finance). The two key Administration bills for health-care reform measures, 1) to create a Health Commission and 2) to mandate some community rating for health insurance, did not even make it past the first hurdle (first lateral) in the House.

This blow to "Hawai'i—The Health State" clearly demonstrates the need to educate and keep issues discussed every year in the Legislature, in order to avoid a loss of momentum. The belief that an entire health-care reform package could be finessed through the Legislature in one year resulted in the loss of the state's cutting edge in such reform.

Inherent in the overall debate in Hawai'i is an underlying assumption that the health industry will respond to free market pressures to self-regulate the runaway health-care spiral experienced at both the state and Federal levels. Effective cost containment may be the single greatest challenge. Few would debate the reality that when one is sick the demand for health care becomes very inelastic. Nonetheless, better outcome data and information about respective health plans could result in educated consumers who would select among plans sufficiently to assert some level of market pressure. Unfortunately, many of the reimbursement mechanisms are more related to rate charges and other factors not covered by insurance.

For instance, in May, 1993, the Department of Health's Community Hospitals raised rates an overall average of 63 percent. Shortly thereafter, HMSA raised insurance premiums by 9.9 percent for groups of fewer than 100 employees.

An estimated 40 cents of every dollar spent on health care in Hawai'i is for private health insurance. Another 25 cents is for "out-of-pocket" medical expenses. These latter expenses will rise, too, if benefits are decreased by self-insured companies, unions, or insurance plans.

Behind the myths of the health-care reform movement are very acknowledgeable accomplishments and meaningful social goals. The goal to assure that health care is a right and not a privilege for everyone in society is a worthy one. Governor Waihee signed House Bill 1906, creating the SHIP initiative as Act 378-1989, which clearly stated that: "The Legislature finds that it is a matter of compelling public interest to provide for the health and well-being of all the people of Hawai'i." In a market-driven economy, the issue of access is largely driven by financing and the tough "coming-to-terms" with what will be offered to everyone as a standard benefit package. The lessons learned from Hawai'i's health-care reform efforts over the past seven years have helped shaped the broad public interest goals and the specifics of what minimum standards should be maintained. What are these lessons?

Lessons Learned

1. Planning for universal coverage is easier with a smaller "Gap Group."

In 1969, the Legislative Auditor's Office estimated our "gap group" at 17 percent. After the enactment of Hawai'i's 1974 PHCA, the size dropped. Hence, once it is reduced to a manageable level, innovative state programs are more affordable and politically achievable to further close the gap. However, under the PHCA, coverage for dependents is voluntary, and dependents are likely to be dropped as cost pressures increase. Health coverage for dependents needs attention in both state and Federal plans.

2. Data about medical expenditures and hospital discharge data are difficult to obtain due to proprietary pressures.

For example, the Department of Labor does not even collect data on the number of people with employment-based health insurance. Hawai'i and other states are strongly considering legislation that will require such reporting. Mandatory reporting would need to be translated into Federal plans to assure effectiveness in cost containment, consumer education, and measurement of quality outcomes at regional levels.

3. Care will still be needed for those who are medically-indigent or are unable to get health care through insurance.

Even with excellent access to insurance in Hawai'i, community health centers will continue to bear the brunt of non-emergency room walk-in visits by individuals who have no health insurance. A review during the 1992 legislative session found approximately 40 percent of all such clients to be uninsured. Reimbursement structures must be flexible to support these vital services—often to the homeless and immigrants—frequently delivered by nurse practitioners and social workers practicing as a medical team with other health care providers. This is especially true as state health departments continue to get out of the business of providing direct services.

4. Health reform must stress prevention and primary care.

A good example is the need for universal immunizations. Because Hawai'i's hepatitis B rate approaches up to ten times that of the mainland U.S., a universal three-dose infant immunization program was started in September, 1991. Still, an affordable and adequate supply of vaccine is essential and needs to be guaranteed at the Federal level.

5. Leadership and a strong relationship are needed between the executive and legislative branches of government.

Evidence from the various states involved with health-care reform suggest that a good leader or leaders are needed to spearhead the direction of reform measures.

6. Insurance must be portable.

Although the PHCA has made a major contribution to reducing the number of uninsured, health-care insurance linked to employment does not allow for immediate transportability of one's health insurance within or among states. However, through insurance reform, the elimination of waiting periods and exclusions, and transferability among state programs can reduce some of the real concerns about not being able to leave a job without the worry of also losing one's health insurance.

7. States do have an important role to play in the national health-care reform efforts.

Examples abound where a state has shown tremendous leadership in launching a new program that may serve as a model to other states or even for the entire nation. For example, in Hawai'i, our SHIP plan, with some good innovations, followed Washington state's Basic Health Plan. Hawai'i has also introduced exemplary programs for statewide needle-exchange programs and prenatal care for pregnant women at high risk for substance abuse (BabySafe).

The State of Minnesota's Health Care Commission sets targets of reducing the growth rate of health-care costs by

10 percent per year for five years beginning in 1993. Vermont extends community rating, guaranteed access to health insurance and portability requirements to the nongroup markets.

Conclusion

The juxtaposition of myths and lessons helps to separate rhetoric, accomplishments, and challenges. Myth, as it becomes public policy over time, must be viewed separately from the broad public interest goals, such as Hawai'i's objective to achieve universal access. Myths tend to separate politics from economic reality, so that health-care issues then become separate from the nuts and bolts of the health-care industry. The latter is affected by factors like those of the automotive industry: competition-driven risks and profits, monopoly control, market share, fair practice and insurance issues. Because life itself and its quality are so dependent on our health status, the health care industry may be less elastic than other markets.

The summation of lessons learned raises key questions: what should be the role of state and Federal governments, and what level of health care should be guaranteed regardless of one's economic status? Currently, with about 40 million Americans lacking health insurance, the issue of access must be first defined as an issue of social inequity and injustice. The nation as a whole must reach toward the conclusion that to have a basic fabric of social well-being, the wellness of the individual must be at the heart of the reform effort. Universal access to health care will not be achieved without restructuring our health-care delivery system.

The Seventeenth Legislature and the Governor's Package of Bills for Health-Care Reform

The year 1993 was earmarked for the introduction of several bills that would shape the legislative framework for renewed health-care reform efforts since the passage of the State Health Insurance Program (SHIP) in 1989. In fact, the Department of

Health (DOH) made a conscious decision not to introduce any substantial health-care reform bills in 1992, but to wait until a package of bills had been pulled together for the 1993 legislative session.

DOH, in 1993, introduced two key health-care measures to establish a health commission and to mandate community rating for businesses with up to 100 employees. The 1994 session saw DOH trying to test the waters on a measure to establish a health alliance for Hawai'i, the Department of Commerce and Consumer Protection introduced companion measures (H.B. 3315; S.B. 2997), Relating to the Regulation of Nursing, to allow prescriptive authority to nurses in advanced practice. The Department of Human Services introduced a measure to repeal SHIP and transfer funds and staff to the Health QUEST program.

Unfortunately, the 1993 bills were introduced into the legislature without sufficient community-wide review. Without such review, major policy issues must then be worked out within the limits of the legislative process, or fail. The underlying health-care and insurance issues are complex and define the strengths and weaknesses of Hawai'i's health-care system.

Issues Surrounding Community Rating

A basic definition of community rating is that "all groups would be charged the same rate for the same health coverage, with the rate being based upon projections of combined health experience across the various groups." The main benefit is the pooling of risk over the largest possible group, thereby reducing the negative economics of risk selection, risk pricing, and cost-shifting. Total community rating for a state would also include, for example, options for individuals and dependents. Hawai'i, since the Prepaid Health Care Act (PHCA), has benefited from a voluntary community-type rating system but unfortunately, inflationary pressures has diminished the extent of community rating in Hawai'i.

One way that deviation from standard community rating is achieved is through a "tier" structure or price bands within a given group. For instance, Plan IV offered by the Hawai'i Medical Services Association (HMSA) has nine tiers that vary in price by 5 percent per band. Plan IV applies to groups over 10 and up to 100 employees; as of August, 1992, HSMA had an estimated

550,000 members in Plan IV spread across the 45 percent price differential. True community rating would establish just one price for the entire group; passage of the legislation would have resulted in some prices increasing and some decreasing, but the overall impact would depend on the relative numbers in each band. The legislation had not anticipated possible increases in premiums, especially for younger, healthier families who might respond by dropping dependent coverage.

For instance, after the State of Vermont passed a community-rating mandate, companies began dividing employer groups into individual sub-sets so that risk selection could proceed unabated. Such a law should also effectively regulate the differences between health-related indemnity insurance and personal health-care insurance. Community-rating bills are not cost-containment measures and are not effective price regulatory measures, unless ceilings are placed on loss/profit ratios (comparisons between earned premiums with losses and adjustments for fair administration costs). Hawai'i's proposed bills had many limitations and could well have driven non-Hawai'i based insurance companies out of the market.

Issues in Creating a Health Commission or Alliance

The 1993 "Hawai'i Health Commission" bill also had an interesting twist of fate. Instead of creating an entirely new section in the Hawai'i Revised Statutes (HRS), the Department of Health decided to co-mingle the powers and duties of the commission within the existing Chapter 323D of the law that defines the State Health Planning and Development Agency known in the community as SHPDA.

This unfortunately was a "coup de grace," as the bill was interpreted—especially by physicians testifying on behalf of the Hawai'i Medical Association and the Hawai'i Federation of Physicians and Dentists—as being regulatory. At issue were concerns about creating a commission that had the power to set medical-practice guidelines or ways to develop indicators of health outcomes or treatment effectiveness. Creating such a body within a newly-defined SHPDA was interpreted by conservatives as being too risky; liberals did not see the commission as having enough "teeth" to get a real handle on cost containment or to define quality.

The effort to delete the original language and replace it with commission-forming language was seen as being very narrow and too much as a "Blue Ribbon Reconstruction—Phase II," even though the department attempted to structure the language to emphasis cost containment through competition and not through regulation. Hence, although the Hawai'i Health Commission bill was heard in both chambers, the proposed draft by the department did not move forward, and Senate draft missed, by one vote, the crossover deadline. The Director of Health had argued strongly that not passing the bill would leave Hawai'i to the mercy of the Federal plan being proposed by the Clinton Administration, and the lack of passage would result in Hawai'i losing its health-care reform reputation.

In 1994, the Administration introduced companion bills to establish a quasi-public agency to be known as the Hawai'i Health Alliance (H.B. 3460; S.B. 3036). The Hawai'i Health Alliance measure built on the suggested 1993 Health Commission and the notion of President Clinton's health alliance concept, where a state-wide agency would be established with the power to negotiate premium rates and choice of health plans through market forces, facilitate cost-containment measures largely through consumer education, handle funds and complaints, and undertake studies of the health-care delivery system. The Hawai'i Health Alliance notion was reduced in the House to the notion of a commission with only the power to *assess* the creation of a mandated alliance. The bill did not emerge from conference committee.

Only the Administration's bill allowing prescriptive privileges for advanced-practice nurses (amended as S.B. 1249, C.D.1) passed its final reading in both chambers and authorized the transfer of SHIP funds and staff in the budget bill. This limited success of measures introduced in both 1993 and 1994 was due, in part, to the interplay of a national plan and the inability to build on Hawai'i's policy strengths and weaknesses.

The Clinton bill, known as the National Health Security Act, was too complex and convoluted for mark up by Congressional committees. The President's state-based health-alliance concept was viewed as an additional costly layer of bureaucracy; hence, although key Congressional leaders supported the need for health-care reform, alliances à la Clinton were already dead in Washington, DC, before the end of Hawai'i's 1994 Legislative Session. Ironically, as the year for health-care reform at the national level slipped further into debate, the Hawai'i State Legislature closed, for a second year in a row, without significant health-care reform other than prescriptive authority for nurses in advanced practice. Still, the legislature was educated on the need to protect Hawai'i from possible negative impacts of national health-care reform, through repealing the sunset clause of the PHCA, if a national health plan is enacted.

References

1. The QUEST program allows enrollment to 300 percent of Federal poverty; those below 134 percent will not have to pay monthly premiums. The MOMI levels for pregnant women and their first-year-old children stay at the 185 percent level.
2. Statistics presented by the Office of Hawai'ian Health to the Board of Health in 1992.
3. The Milbank Memorial Fund is an endowed private foundation involved with health and social policy since 1905.

Bibliography

Baumgartner, Eric.T., Grossmann, Bob, & Fuddy, Loretta. (1993). "Hawai'i's Near-Universal Health Insurance—Lessons Learned." *Journal of the Poor and Underserved, 4, 3,* 194-202.

General Accounting Office. (1992). "Access to Health Care—States Respond to Growing Crisis." Washington, DC, 28-29.

Governor's Blue Ribbon Committee. (1992). Report to the 1993 Hawai'i State Legislature titled, "Health Care Cost Containment Recommendations."

Lewin, John C, Palmer, Karen S., & Grossmann, Robert S. (1992)."Health Care in the State of Hawai'i," *Journal of Health Care Benefits*, (May/June), 16-20.

Milbank Memorial Fund. (1993). "The States That Could Not Wait. Lessons for Health Reform from Florida, Hawai'i, Minnesota, Oregon and Vermont." New York, N.Y.

CHAPTER SEVEN

It's Not as Pathetic as It Seems

JIM SHON

In February, 1991, a public-health nurse wrote to the Governor of Hawai'i about a client who had AIDS:

> *Being an emergency hire, he had no medical insurance, no sick leave time nor vacation time accrued during all the months he worked for the State. Even the State Health Insurance Plan would have been inadequate for his medical needs, or for other persons with progressive diseases . . . The only way he could get the medical care he needed would be to quit his job, go on welfare, and have Medicaid pay for his medical expenses. The thought of needing to do this was so repugnant to him, that he continued to work until last week when he became too weak and dizzy to function . . .*

Could this be the "Health State?" I wondered. Ever since John Waihee became Governor and selected Dr. Jack Lewin as his health director, we were on the cutting edge of new ideas. We embraced the goal of universal access. We held the line against the kooks who wanted to send sick people to the isolation of Moloka'i. We expanded budgets; this was easy since we had budget surpluses. Smoking-control laws, de-institutionalization of the developmentally-disabled, peer education programs for teens: year after year the legislative agenda was progressive and aggressive.

Health was hot. Jack Lewin and his creative ideas were all over the media. As Chair of the Health Committee for Hawai'i's House of Representatives, I found that nearly every public hearing attracted the media. I learned how to preside over a raucous auditorium filled with those passionately for and against fluoridation of drinking water. I learned how to produce the quotable sound bites for nightly news.

There was so much to do, and so little time to do it. AIDS was a new challenge. We put together an Omnibus AIDS funding bill in 1988, unique because it was a supplemental budget year, and separate funding bills were frowned upon by the money committees, but especially because it was the first package of support for private non-profit organizations dealing with AIDS in our state (and perhaps the first in the nation). It set a pattern for subsequent omnibus funding bills for mental health, primary care, and substance abuse. We stood firm on confidentiality. We enacted the first statewide needle exchange program to control HIV spread among drug users.

It was a time to challenge conventional wisdom. New mandated benefits were added to everyone's health package—well-baby check-ups, mental health, substance abuse—all in the face of strong opposition from the health-care establishment, especially HMSA (the Hawai'i Medical Services Association, Hawai'i's dominant Blue-Cross Blue Shield health insurance company). We pushed for prescriptive privileges (the right to prescribe drugs independently) for advanced-practice nurses as a way to extend health care.

Some doctors reacted with intemperate denunciations, especially the very conservative Federation of Physicians and Dentists, who felt that despite similar practices in other states, it was a danger to patients, and that doctors should be at the economic and spiritual center of the system (as opposed to the patient). (In 1993, the Federation pushed through a bill to prevent HMSA from offering prevention programs because it might infringe on the revenues of physicians. In 1994, the Federation sought to exempt specialists from participating in managed-care plans. One of their leaders campaigned heavily to elect Pat Saiki Governor).

We initially lost on prescriptive privileges and on fluoridation, but it was still an intoxicating time. Still, you could see that for all our self-praise, coverage for over 90 percent of the working population, and a generous Medicaid program, there were major gaps. People dropped through the cracks.

Back to that letter to the Governor:

> . . .He had told his family, his physician, his work supervisors, the Maui AIDS Foundation Case Manager, and myself, that his work was very important to him.

He had worked since he was 15 years old, and took pride in his work. The thought of not being able to support himself, to depend on the welfare system and his family to support him, as well as other stresses, were too much for him. Last week he ended his life.

How could this happen? You see, he was a so-called "emergency-hire." The law requiring state employees to be offered health insurance is fairly clear. It says if you work for 20 hours a week, for three months, you are in. Lots of emergency hires have worked for a lot more than three months. Some, for years. Ah, but now the bureaucracy finds its way to negate eligibility. Our state writes rules to further refine the wisdom of the Legislature. In the rules you will discover that a month is defined as 30 consecutive days. So if you miss one day, you have not worked a month.

To take advantage of this curious refinement, each state agency then proceeds to terminate each emergency-hire employee before every 30th day, thus rendering them ineligible for benefits. Great system, eh?

Being do-gooders, we passed a bill to correct this injustice. Being without consistency, the Governor, champion of the Health State, vetoed the bill!

In the newspaper report on the veto, Dr. Jack Lewin, clearly embarrassed by his leader's anti-health action, was quoted as saying, "It's not as pathetic as it seems." In fact, it was pretty pathetic.

The fate of the emergency-hire bill, and the tragedy of the Maui employee who took his life, are keys to understanding Hawai'i's system. From afar, we look great. We cover more than any other state. We are less expensive by far.

And we are sometimes hypocrites.

We are great on paper. HMSA had 623,074 enrollees in 1992, while Kaiser, our major competing HMO (Health Maintenance Organization) had 189,414. More than 100,000 were enrolled in Medicaid, and about 20,000 in the State Health Insurance Program (SHIP). This adds up to over 900,000 people "covered" in a population of just over a million. Well over 90 percent!

We are progressive and affordable. A comparison of 1991 monthly insurance rates shows Hawai'i with $94 a month for a single policy, $263 a month for a family. Compare this with California at $141 and $503, or Massachusetts with $217 and $508. If it weren't for the high cost of living, and especially the high cost of housing, people might flock to Hawai'i just to get health care. Since 1991 our rates have begun to escalate faster than before, yet we were and still are cheaper partly because we collect premiums from a broader base. Everyone who works 20 or more hours a week in the private sector is in the system. (The state, as we have seen, has ways of exempting itself, as with "emergency-hires.")

Under these rosy circumstances, you might think being Health Chair was an easy job. Just sit back and enjoy the most successful system in America! Not so fast. Look more deeply.

The first thing we might notice when we go beyond the self-congratulations is that there are still lots of folks who are hurting; many of them don't have much clout. There are the mentally ill, whose treatment in Hawai'i won us the distinction of having the worst mental-health system in the nation. There are the Native Hawai'ians, whose health status is unbelievably poor. There are the homeless, those with HIV, teens, the elderly, and those alienated from the system by language and culture.

Ninety percent of our efforts during Governor Waihee's years (1986-1994) was spent on this 10 percent of the population. Our system is great for the "average American," but, like so many systems, falls short of the promise of universal care.

My heart still aches for the Mom with the severely-disturbed teenager, who is prone to violence, often out of control, can't be left in school. She must care for him at home, because there just aren't any specialized services. Home Alone and unable to cope. She loves her son, but she can't live with him.

And what of the homeless young mother who can get food stamps and shelter, but no child care while in school to help get a job? We have programs for this or that part of a person's life, but no programs for the *whole* person!

Where is all this leading? Is there a common affliction or bureaucratic virus responsible for the problems of the mentally ill, the emergency-hires, teens, persons with AIDS, you name it?

Yes. That common disease is fragmentation. "Divide and Founder" could be our motto. We are so isolated and intimate a society that we often fail to recognize the implications of a very uncoordinated, fragmented system.

Like Hawai'i's distinct and sometimes self-absorbed islands, the agencies and programs which make up our health-care archipelago are barely visible to each other. Each has its own turf, home rule issues, budgets, and politics. Each is proud to stand alone and resist absorption into a coherent whole.

The Health-Care Archipelago

Join me briefly in the metaphor of the *archipelago*.

There are several major "islands" in Hawai'i's Health Care Archipelago. The "Capital" is located on Prepaid Island, home of our historic and famous Prepaid Health-Care Act of 1974. With the help of a Federal exemption, we were the only state that could require all employers to contribute to employee health insurance. It's the centerpiece of our system. An overwhelming percentage of our population (80 percent) "lives" on Prepaid Island. The Department of Labor and Industrial Relations administers Prepaid Isle, because it was originally a labor-union idea.

Prepaid Isle is dominated by two huge landholders: The Hawai'i Medical Services Association Estate on which live 56 percent of its health insured population; and the Kaiser Estate, with 18 percent of this population. Both HMSA and Kaiser control important facilities, contracts and programs through which they influence health care throughout the islands.

The "Big Island" of course is Medicaid. Its population is growing. There were 97,950 Medicaid recipients in December, 1992, up from 86,286 in January, 1992. The state's contribution alone is over $220 million. (The overall cost of the program in 1992 was $345,378,840). Rules, regulations and "waivers" are spewed by the Federal and state Medicaid active volcanoes like rivers of lava, creating new territory, but often disrupting or even destroying those caught in its path. Everything about Medicaid Island is big, including its 40-page application forms and its $55 million deficit in FY 93-94. The population of Medicaid Isle is not nearly as high as Prepaid Island, which has about 850,000, but its raw influence is felt throughout the Islands.

Medicaid people (known sometimes as *"HCFA-ites"* —pronounced HIC-fa-ites—after the Federal Health Care

Finance Administration which runs Medicaid) speak their own obscure dialect. Sometimes translators are required before the *HCFA-ites* can be understood. Their society is also very hierarchical, and they spend a lot of time figuring out who should be eligible to live there. There is a long-standing dispute with the Health Department people who live mostly on Visionary Island, over immigration to Medicaid Isle and reimbursements for department programs.

For citizens unable to reside on either Prepaid or Medicaid Isles, there was a special SHIP (State Health Insurance Program, a lean benefit package for those in the "gap" between Medicaid and regular insurance) which moved up and down our health-care chain. You could stay on SHIP if you had to (nearly 20,000 did), but had to wait at least three months to get a boarding pass. It had its own mini-clinic and sick bay, but couldn't replace the facilities on the larger isles. Like any large vessel, SHIP had a growing cost, up from an original $10 million to over $14 million, and its actual cost to providers was open to dispute.

In 1993 and 1994 Medicaid Isle successfully moved to "take over" the State Health Insurance Program (SHIP). The proposal, called HealthQUEST (an acronymic mouthful for Quality care, Universal access, Efficient utilization, Stabilizing costs, and Transforming the way health care is provided to public clients), seeks to reduce the benefits of Medicaid and create a "seamless" program for SHIP's 20,000 eligibles, Medicaid's general assistance 8,100 eligibles, and Aid To Families with Dependent Children's (AFDC) 61,000 eligibles. No doubt some of Hawai'i's islands see this as little more than piracy on Medicaid's part. With HealthQUEST, Medicaid takes the driver's seat for health reform. (Some policy makers are nervous because the original QUEST proposal had 88,100 participants, which has since grown to 106,000. There is also dissatisfaction with the attitudes of *"HCFA-ites"* who seem to gloss over cost over-run estimates, and downplay the importance of specialized indigent care.)

While SHIP was a comparatively large craft, it was joined by a large number of sampans and rowboats known as the Non-Profit Fleet. They operate outside of the traditional land-based medical care islands, providing a wide range of services from education, to case management, abuse prevention and counseling, advocacy, drown-proofing, and emergency rescues. They are more flexible and efficient than facilities on the major islands, but are extremely dependent on fuel and funds from the land-based population. Their financial needs have grown to over $100 million as more people are identified treading water for services outside the usual medical system.

Many boats in the Non-Profit Fleet spend a lot of time on the smaller islands. These are the Community Health Center Atolls. Operating on $9.7 million in 1992, seven clinics served over 55,000 different clients. Stranded or foundering citizens are picked up by the Non-Profits and delivered to the Community Health Centers, who see lots of folks who can't afford the main islands. Occasionally the big SHIP stopped there too (3.7 percent of health center clients came from SHIP in 1992). Today the nine community health centers also take care of nearly 20,000 people with no health insurance, representing nearly 40 percent of their clients.

The Community Health Atolls don't get much respect. In 1993 the SHIP program was given more than $7 million in additional funds, while the Atolls were kept at their 1992 levels. In the QUEST program, Community Health Centers struggle to maintain adequate reimbursement rates.

Just off Big Medicaid Isle you can see a new island forming. It's Family Hope Isle, future home of the long-term care financing administration. It is not yet completely above water. Nobody knows when it will be inhabited. The plan is to transport residents from the archipelago to the main islands for their long-term care needs. The Long-Term Care Shoals—nursing homes—are already overcrowded, with long waiting lists from seniors who want to immigrate. These residents are even more anxious as to their fate in recent months, as Medicaid Island successfully pushed through an additional tax on them in 1993. Some who have been paying their way fear they will be driven into accepting permanent citizenship on Medicaid Isle. Anxiety further increased as the 1994 Legislative Session failed to make a commitment to fund the Family Hope Program. Some fear this island will *never* be inhabited.

The Department of Health is known as the Isle of

Vision, or sometimes Hallucination Isle. With 6,000 inden-
tured servants camped on its shores, it is not sure if it wants
to provide services, create programs, prevent disease, or
merely be the home of the Health-Care Wizard of Oz. It has
its own hospitals, mental health, developmental disabilities, and environmental health duties. Attached is the State
Health Planning and Development Agency (SHPDA),
which grants permits called "certificates of need" for those
who want to build facilities or purchase expensive equipment. It interacts with the rest of the islands in many ways.

The Isle of Vision built the SHIP, funds the Non-Profit
Fleet, and its Director has been the primary spokesperson
for Hawai'i's system, but its reputation is diminished by a
continuing inability to adequately fund and improve mental health. It is an effective advocate for prevention programs—smoking regulations and helmet laws—but these
have yet to be embraced by those who run the show on
Prepaid Isle. Its ambivalent mission stems from the challenge of keeping up with the disparate, isolated islands.

There is no single police force for the archipelago. Consumer Protection Isle regulates auto and life insurance rates,
but they do not yet visit any of the Health Estates on Prepaid Isle. The workplace is "protected" by another group
from OSHA Island, but their vessels are old and they appear less and less frequently. SHPDA tries to keep track
of the number of beds and machines, but has no control
over what goes on in most of the private doctors' offices.
No coalition of these police forces attempts to coordinate
efforts or share data. Perhaps the only unifying force is Big
HCFA, far away in Washington, issuing regulations which
are followed for fear of losing Federal dollars.

As if things were not complicated enough, two independent commonwealths have special contracts with businesses and individuals in the archipelago. They are Workers Compensation Kingdom, and No-Fault Auto Reef. Each
has a completely separate system for financing health
payments. While there have been discussions as to
whether they should be unified with the Health-Care
Isles, these have been fruitless.

It would be wonderful to report that the Legislature is able to overcome this fragmented world and create a unified vision. But this is not the case. We have divided reality into parallel boxes, each committee more or less corresponding to a set of programs or a department. A health-insurance bill must pass through several committees with completely different territories, with completely different orientations and missions. In recent years, the House and the Senate seem to be living on different planets, each with its own peculiar power struggles which affect all important policy matters.

At the very least you might safely say that no single force could single-handedly dismantle or destroy this fragmented system. Even this apparent insulation from wholesale destruction was proved not to be true, as some radical proposals to do that did surface in the 1994 Legislative Session.

One bill sought to declare that all medical specialties, including such exotics as forensic pathologists, were to be considered "primary-care providers." (I suppose there is a crude logic here: if you need a forensic pathologist, you sure don't need to see any other specialists!) Not understanding the importance of administrative leadership in health, the Legislature did pass bills which eliminated the Deputy Directors of Health who oversee the areas of environmental health, mental health, substance abuse, homeless health, AIDS, smoking, and childhood abuse and immunizations. This was done not by the Health Committees but by the Finance Committees, who saw only salary savings and the future given that the next governor would have to return and beg for the positions all over again.

The impact of this policy on the ability to recruit high-quality administrators, as well as the one-year delay in administrative leadership, seems never to have occurred to the Legislature. Of even greater concern: the positions cut from the budget are the administrative advocates for our disenfranchised and uninsured.

It is understandable that legislative politics sometimes lapses into petty personal feuds and rivalry between the Executive and Legislative branches. When the system is fragmented, it is unable to protect itself from the impacts of those conflicts.

From the broader political perspective in Hawai'i, where legislative leaders apparently do not know or appreciate the health-care system, perhaps it really *is* as pathetic as it seems.

The Future

There is a temptation to regard Hawai'i as typical among state systems. But among those interested in health reform there is a clear trend in another direction. From Vermont to Florida to Minnesota to Washington state, there is an attempt to consolidate new and old powers under one administrative roof. They recognize it is nearly impossible to understand, let alone regulate, health care when it is scattered to the four administrative winds. Strong support seems to be evident in bi-partisan circles to get a consolidated handle on the runaway health costs. This translates into insurance reform (Hawai'i doesn't even regulate health insurance, although a bill to begin that passed the 1994 Session), control of hospital costs, a certificate-of-need process (we still have one), and other measures *in one commission.* Vermont has vested geat power in a three-member authority.

What is extremely interesting is that the private sector of powerful stakeholders is taking all of this seriously. All over the land health providers are joining HMOs and other managed-care networks. Large employers in Minneapolis and other cities are insisting on negotiations with these networks as a preliminary dry run for the Clinton Health Alliances to come.

Hawai'i has enjoyed the recognition of being ahead, but in a few years we may be behind, and some would have us discard features which have brought us relative success. We may be unable to respond in advance to the Clinton managed-care world in a timely way, certainly not fast enough to anticipate congressional action or even to influence the final national plan.

There is reason for hope, as the costs of health insurance in Hawai'i may actually spur the business community to push for some cost-containment measures. There is even the beginning of a dialogue on how to combine regular health insurance with the health component of workers' compensation, and even no-fault auto.

If that happens, a thorough discussion of the structure of health regulation by the state would be in order. Perhaps our own failings will drive us to a more unified and coordinated system, more rationally constructed. In this sense, perhaps *it's not as pathetic as it seems.*

PART THREE
Who Dares to Care?

CHAPTER EIGHT

The Health-Insurance 'Gap Group'
Hawai'i's Uninsured and the Use of Non-Physicians

BY GREGORY P. LOOS, M. JAN PRYOR, AND DANIEL DOMIZIO

As various health-care reform proposals are considered, issues related to the composition of the health work force increasingly become a focus of attention. Concern for the looming cost implications of the generalist-specialist imbalance, and for the uneven provider distribution that limits health care access, has renewed interest in the future supply of primary-care providers.

Like many Americans, people in Hawai'i need improved access to affordable health care; this is particularly true for the medically uninsured. This chapter identifies populations of uninsured in Hawai'i and the use of non-physician primary-care practitioners (NPPCPs) such as, physician assistants (PA's), nurse practitioners (NP's), and certified nurse midwives (CNM's). While retrospective data is considered, the focus of this analysis is on the years 1994-2000.

First, we estimate the state's uninsured population under the newly-proposed capitated managed-care system; they are identified by type and location. Second, we consider the plausible influence of NPPCPs on improved access to health-care services for populations in need in Hawai'i, and their potential to curb escalating medical costs among these same populations. Finally, the current professional environment in Hawai'i for NPPCPs, which influences their recruitment and retention, is discussed. Our position is that capitated managed care will not reach targeted populations, nor succeed financially, unless the present environment in the state improves to encourage greater recruitment and retention of NPPCPs. Implications drawn here for Hawai'i apply equally to the nation. Sadly, professional, financial, geographic, cultural, and attitudinal barriers to the increased use of NPPCPs exist, and the medically-underserved communities suffer the most due to this restrictive environment. The National Health Service Corps defines a medically-underserved population as those people who have to travel 30 or more miles for health care, and a medically-underserved area as a community where the ratio of population to physicians is greater than 3000:1. Currently, Hawai'i has an acceptable ratio of physicians. However most are disproportionately located in Honolulu, leaving a vast geographic majority of the State medically under-served. Some of the currently most under-served communities are listed in Table 1.

Table 1: Adjusted Physician-to-Population Ratio, by Area, 1992	
Area	**Ratio**
Puna, Big Island	1:23,203
Ka'u, Big Island	1: 2,219
Hamakua, Big Island	0: 1,864
North Hilo, Big Island	0: 1,541
Hana/Haiku, Maui	1: 6,631
Moloka'i	1: 4,911
Lana'i	1: 3,352
Subtotal: Selected Neighbor Island Districts	1: 8,744
Kahuku, O'ahu	1: 2,121
Laie, O'ahu	1: 5,847
Ka'a'awa/Hauula, O'ahu	1: 7,780
Kahalu'u, O'ahu	1:15,736
Hale'iwa, O'ahu	1: 703
East of Hale'iwa, O'ahu	0: 1,520
Wai'alua, O'ahu	0: 4,890
Subtotal: North Shore O'ahu West of Kahalu'u	1: 3,162

To redress these circumstances, Hawai'i has explored a variety of innovative programs during the last two decades. Each has met with limited success. Despite such programs as Hawai'i's pre-paid mandatory health insurance, a "gap-group" state health insurance plan (SHIP), and a recently-enacted statewide system for Native Hawai'ian health services, many communities are still without needed health care. Some sub-populations are significantly less served than others. These include: 1) rural poor; 2) urban indigent; 3) migrant workers;[1] 4) immigrants and minority cultures; 5) single women and their children; 6) the uninsured; 7) the isolated elderly;[2] 8) the mentally ill;[3] 9) the homeless; 10) teens; and 11) the substance-abusing community.

Impact of Reform on the Uninsured

The Health Care Financing Administration (HCFA) awarded Hawai'i a Section 1115 Demonstration Waiver to provide a health-insurance approach consisting of the creation of a significant purchasing pool, coupled with the development of a basic capitated benefit plan focused on preventive and managed care, to provide affordable quality health and medical care to the under-served[4]. The health-care reform plan is entitled Hawai'i Health QUEST (an acronym for Quality care, Universal access, Efficient utilization, Stabilizing costs, and Transforming health-care provision to public clients; hf. QUEST). It advertises increased quality of, and access to, care at reduced cost. As a capitated system, it includes several strategic options to curb medical costs. Unfortunately, these same strategies may increase the number of uninsured. Factors which may contribute to increased rates of the uninsured include: discontinuance of cost-based reimbursement; individual enrollment premiums; and disenrollment for non-compliance.

The first, discontinuance of cost-based reimbursement, decreases provider incentives to conduct outreach services to distantly-located communities, to dislocated and/or disenfranchised individuals, and to minority clients who may use English as a second language. These services are likely to be discontinued as unnecessary cost centers. Though the State Department of Human Services (DHS) may withhold monies from providers to undertake these services themselves, it is not yet clear that DHS has sufficient resources to manage the oversight of QUEST, let alone assume additional functions.

DHS has determined that outreach and cultural/language services will be optional for QUEST bidders. Capitation lends itself to cost reduction by, among other strategies, discontinuing ancillary services. Federally-qualified health centers, which typically provide these services in minority/underserved communities, will have to shift their thinking to serve only those who come in to the clinic for care. These inconsistencies abound under managed-care programs; truly successful programs cannot cut the cost of care by restricting access to care. Later care or curative interventions do accrue costs that are far greater.

Second, with individual enrollment premiums, it is conceivable that many large families may forego paying for any health insurance for part of the family. Though all families with incomes below 134 percent of poverty will be provided free coverage under QUEST, those families with incomes in excess of this level must pay a premium on a sliding scale.

However, in a state with a high cost of living like Hawai'i, it is equally conceivable that they might not insure at all. For example, as much as 25 percent of the population has made the economic decision to do without automobile insurance because they face pressing fiscal demands.

The final concern is that providers may disenroll QUEST members for non-compliance with medical-care procedures, unruly behavior, and/or for lapsed premiums. Presently, "non-compliance" is not defined, nor are grievance procedures for discontinued members. However, it is easy to envision that many of the public clients and high-risk populations noted earlier may find compliance difficult, especially if outreach and translation services are not available, or if their financial resources are intermittent.

DHS will decide to disenroll based on recommendations by plans. DHS will be responsible for the assurance of adequate outreach and cultural/language aspects for the program. Presently, four outreach teams, each comprising a nurse-practitioner and three health aides, are planned. However, this may be inadequate for the numbers of QUEST enrollees.

Other uninsured and under-served populations include individuals who are geographically and/or socially isolated, and those with health conditions not included in the QUEST benefit package. Presently, oral health, mental health and long-term care represent continuing gaps in service.

Many high-risk populations such as the homeless, the severely disabled, single-parent families, teens, the isolated elderly and rural poor will remain uninsured and unserved. In Hawai'i, the estimated number of homeless may reach 10,000. Eighty-five percent of Hawai'i's homeless are unemployed, and 60 percent of all homeless are uninsured. QUEST will only be provided to those who are eligible and who request services. Without adequate outreach services many homeless people likely will remain uninsured.

For example, homeless services provided by one primary health-care center have been curtailed by 30 percent. The DHS states that the Department of Health will provide indigent care. However, this may be impossible due to the state's continued economic downturn. Moreover, without needed outreach services, homeless populations are unlikely to seek early care. Sadly, the DHS doesn't seem to appreciate this point:

> . . . While the Project hopes to improve health-care access to all residents. . . only those who request services can be assisted. There will be those who for reasons only known to themselves will not seek health-care coverage. Unfortunately, some of the homeless are currently, and probably will continue to be, among those who do not seek health-care coverage.
>
> *DHS: Responses to legislators'*
> *questions on QUEST, October 1993*

Individuals who are severely disabled, including the mentally ill and children with special health-care needs (CSHCN), should be eligible for benefits under Social Security Income (SSI) programs. QUEST recipients diagnosed as seriously mentally ill will be eligible to participate in separate behavioral health managed-care plans requiring additional monthly capitated charges if they seek enrollment.

Currently, 45 percent of the state's 1,000 designated CSHCN receive Medicaid benefits. This population will be transferred to QUEST under the experimental waiver. For some families, the individual membership premiums may be prohibitive. In such circumstances, non-CSHCN family members may be voluntarily disenrolled to accommodate the needs of the disabled child.

Six percent of the state's 18,000 family planning clinic users are presently covered by Medicaid, and another 48 percent

are uninsured. These same individuals will be eligible to enroll
in QUEST if they can afford the premiums and remain
compliant. However, many clinic participants are teens and
single-parent mothers who may not be able to make continued
premium payments, and/or may be inconsistent users of the
clinic and judged non-compliant.

Hawai'i has many similar populations who may not
choose or be eligible to enroll in QUEST. Some of these include
retirees under 65 years; migrant laborers; Pacific Islanders from
the Basin nations; emancipated minors; undocumented
residents; recent immigrants, and refugees. Many of these
groups remain socially and culturally isolated, on the economic
fringe, and may fail to be enrolled for circumstantial reasons.
Others may be ineligible.

In 1992, Filipinos who fought in World War II were
granted citizenship, and many have chosen to come to Hawai'i
to reside with family. For this and other reasons, the state
anticipates an influx of 10,000 in-migrants annually for the next
several years. Many will not be eligible for medical coverage
through the family's medical plan, nor able to afford Health
QUEST[5]. Other in-migrants may be ineligible for QUEST since
only legal residents and individuals having a Social Security
number may enroll.

Considering these many populations that may remain
uninsured with the advent of QUEST, the state policy-makers
and health-care providers must consider alternate strategies to
reach, enroll, and serve these consumers, improving health-care
access for all residents, while controlling care costs.

Ironically, the state may decide to cut back on its purchase-of-service contracts and other services on the grounds
that the QUEST bidders should be caring for all the clients'
medical needs. There is concern that any purchase-of-service
agency that does not become a plan subcontractor will likely
lose its cost-based reimbursement for services it provides to
many of the state's underserved populations.

State policy-makers must consider alternative strategies
to reach out, enroll, and serve the uninsured and under-served.
This must be accomplished by improving access to health care
for all residents while controlling cost, not by sacrificing access
to control costs. Historically, the prime factors limiting achieve-

ment of these objectives have been the geographic availability of qualified health personnel and the availability of medical payment programs to cover the under-served. QUEST will address the latter issue partially, only if members are not disenrolled.

As to geographic distribution, the outer islands have a particularly difficult time in recruitment and retention of trained health personnel. The result is an increase in morbidity and mortality due to critical shortages of health-care services appropriate for and acceptable to the needs of rural populations.

If the success of QUEST is measured by improved access to health care among its targeted populations, the program will need to reach out to these communities and to provide needed services more efficiently. QUEST's success will be strongly tied to the willingness of service agencies to use non-physician providers, and the availability of NPPCPs capable of providing community-based, family-centered, culturally-competent care.

It has been proven that NPPCPs provide increased access to health services in many practice settings, both in rural and inner city areas; in health programs for the poor and minorities; for people without health insurance;[6] and for people with AIDS,[7] at a level of care equal to or better than MDs. Further, minority NPPCPs have been reported more likely than their non-minority peers to work in public institutions and clinics and in primary-care specialties; they are also more likely to work with minority and low-income patients.[8]

Need and Support for NPPCPs

There is an abundant need for a broad range of services supplied by a greater number of NPPCPs than are presently available. This need derives from significant factors including:

- the relative excess of non-primary-care specialist physicians;
- demographic changes in the population;
- the existence of populations particularly in need of primary-care services;
- the rising cost of health care;
- the need to improve the quality of provided health care services.

The disproportionately large number of specialist physicians trained over the last 20-30 years has left many parts of our society without access to primary-care physicians. Although large amounts of time, energy and resources have been committed to remediating this problem over the last two decades, the imbalance persists.

Demographic changes, such as the urban drift of the rural unemployed, the large influx of immigrant populations from Asia, Pacific and the Americas, and the move away from the urban center of the upper and middle classes, have all encouraged the shift of health-care resources toward those areas where people can pay for them, i.e., suburban areas of the City and County of Honolulu. What is left is a patchwork of under-served populations in rural settings and the central city.

Special populations are invariably in short supply of primary-care providers. The already large and growing population of the old and aging in Hawai'i is generating an increasing demand for long-term care. Although few NPPCPs have gone into geriatric medicine, their utilization in this area has worked well, extending primary-care services to a much larger number of clients than would otherwise be possible with the limited number of physicians willing to practice in this area.

For instance, it is difficult to extend consistent care to migrants and their dependents. Health-status indicators for these groups are as bad as for any other under-served population. Immigrants often arrive in relatively poor health and, once here, encounter cultural, linguistic and economic barriers to accessing our health care system. NPPCPs working with these populations have served as clinicians, translators, health educators, and advocates in ways for which physicians rarely have time. Many ethnic minorities have some of the lowest health-status indicators. Hawai'i's indigenous peoples frequently show the epidemiologic pictures of Third World countries.

The AIDS epidemic has burdened the health-care systems of communities. NPPCPs have played significant roles as care providers, educators, and in the nation-wide research efforts to develop treatment protocols. Additionally, the homeless population and the substance-abusing community are groups which have tended to be disenfranchised by the health care delivery system. NPPCPs could be appropriately utilized to provide better services to all of these special populations.

The high cost of health care in the U.S. has stimulated

growth of the mid-level health-care professions because utilization of NPPCPs has been a proven method of delivering high-quality, cost-effective services in virtually every type of practice setting. For example, newly-graduated NPPCPs earn $35,000-$40,000 annually. The average salary for all NPPCPs is $45-$50,000; those with 10-20 years of experience earn $55-$60,000 a year. PA's in rural and primary-care settings earn less. NPPCPs in Rural Health Clinics are reimbursed by Medicaid at 100 percent of the physician rate while costing much less to employ. NPPCPs who work as surgical assistants earn much less than a surgeon and usually free up another physician who can use his/her time more effectively.

In the 1970's and 80's, many small hospitals were forced to eliminate their residency programs in an effort to save costs. In those institutions where NPPCPs were hired to replace house staff, the facilities were able to maintain their levels of services.

NPPCPs can perform a variety of primary health-care roles. They can serve as a substitute for the physician where no physicians are available; they can supplement the work of physicians, improve the efficiency of care by performing delegated services; and they can perform a complementary role, to enhance the effectiveness of care by undertaking roles for which they are uniquely qualified.

Quality of health care is enhanced by the use of NPPCPs. The U.S. is near the bottom of industrialized nations in standard measures of quality of life (e.g. maternal and child mortality, longevity). Most of this is due to lack of access to basic preventive health and primary-care services. Studies have clearly shown that NPPCPs improve access, improve delivery of primary-care services, and enhance patient education strategies.

Primary care is that level of services which bears the responsibility for the vast majority, perhaps 99 percent, of the health problems of the population in any given area. In order to fulfill that responsibility, primary care has four unique functions: it is the first contact, and thus aids access to care; it is longitudinal, affording the personalization of medical care; it is comprehensive, helping to make care available for 99 percent of health problems in the population; and it is coordinator of care, encouraging its continuity.

Among all health professionals, NPPCPs are the most

cost-effective and ideally prepared health personnel to perform primary-care services. These NPPCPs all share several attributes: the quality of their services is consistently high, they perform tasks which might otherwise be performed by physicians, they lessen the demand for physicians in any given setting, they lighten the load on the physicians already present, they cost less to train and sustain in practice (thus reducing the overall cost of delivering health care), and they improve access to care simply by being present. Whenever they are utilized fully and allowed to perform the tasks and services for which they are trained, NP's, PA's and CNM's have been effective at improving the health-care system for clients and physicians alike.

Similarities and Differences in NPPCP Types

Although PAs, CNMs and NPs are often collectively referred to as "mid-level" practitioners, or simply "mid-levels," they are also called "non-physician providers." Important similarities and differences exist among them.

There are several similarities. Most of these practitioners are trained in programs which require baccalaureate degrees for admission and which grant a certificate and either a second baccalaureate or a master's degree to their graduates. National Board exams and continuing education are required. While studies demonstrate that non-master's prepared NPPCPs are more likely to be employed in primary-care and to practice in rural areas and small towns, there have been no differences in clinical and board examination performances between graduates of certificate and master's programs,[9] and each level of graduate is thus equally competent clinically.

"Mid-levels" are trained to assess patients independently and to develop and implement treatment plans for them, placing greater emphasis on psycho-social dynamics than physicians typically do. Such plans might include the immediate referral onward to a back-up physician, or the ordering and interpreting of lab test and X-rays and the prescribing of medications. They are trained to work within, and to utilize, the health-care system which surrounds them and backs them up. In their respective ways, each of these practitioners is trained to initiate encounters with patients and manage their care while relying upon close working relationships with physicians in their practice settings.

In day-to-day terms, although there might be considerable differences in backgrounds and/or professional interest, there is little difference between the practice of a PA generalist working in a family medicine setting and that of a Family Nurse Practitioner. Indeed, they often work side by side as effective colleagues in a variety of clinical settings, and are regarded as interchangeable by Health Care Financing Administration in rural clinics. CNMs, of course, have a primary clinical focus on women's health obstetric management. And they, too, have close working relationships with back-up obstetricians in the management of high-risk, complicated cases.

The differences between these practitioners are broadly divided here into three areas: background, role, and relationship to physicians. NPs and CNMs invariably come from a nursing background; licensed Registered Nurses, most with Bachelor's of Science in Nursing (BSN) degrees, elect to go into training for "advanced practice" in a variety of areas such as women's health, pediatrics, family health. They never relinquish their nursing identity and regard their practice as advanced nursing practice, quite independent of physicians as such. Their relationship to physicians is collaborative and collegial, with clinical consultation taking place on an as-needed basis. In some venues around the country, nurses in advanced practice can bill independently for services performed. All nursing practice is regulated through specific laws and a state Board of Nursing[10].

PAs, on the other hand, come from a variety of health-care backgrounds (including nursing) and are trained specifically to work in partnership with, and dependent upon, supervising physicians who bear ultimate legal responsibility for the PA's practice. PAs are trained to work in a broad variety of settings and perform tasks at levels of responsibility which are practice-dependent. Thus, you find PAs not only in isolated rural health centers and inner city clinics (as you would NPs or CNMs), but also in Emergency Rooms and orthopedic or cardio-thoracic surgical theaters, for example. Regardless of setting, there is always a supervising physician, and PAs never bill independently. Autonomy has not been a strong theme within the PA profession.

The character and capacity of the PA practice is not mandated by specific licensure. Instead, the PA is permitted by a state to practice in a specified setting with a specified supervising physician. Their practice is regulated through the same state medical practice laws and Boards of Medical Examiners that regulate physicians.

NPPCPs In Hawai'i: Professional Realities

The development of NPPCPs disciplines more than 25 years ago was spurred by the need to increase health-care access for underserved populations;[11] this same need is equally pressing today. Professional status, rewards and support are essential determinants of recruitment and retention of NPPCPs in underserved areas. Unfortunately, Hawai'i's present environment is not conducive to the training, recruitment, and use of NPPCPs. Restrictive scope-of-practice laws for NPPCPs in Hawai'i deter their willingness to practice in this state. For Hawai'i to remain the "Health State" under managed care, it is imperative that this environment improve.

Mid-level primary-care practitioners, PAs, CNMs, and NPs, have been providing basic health service in a variety of settings in Hawai'i for more than 20 years. Though their contributions have been significant, the medical establishment has resisted their presence, and their utilization has been limited. Consequently, their numbers remain small in relation to what they might be in a less professionally hostile environment. This brief looks at some factors which contribute to the professional practice realities of these clinicians and points to those areas where change would make the most difference.

After 25 years of successful practice in Hawai'i and nationwide, there are just over 100 NPs, around 50 PAs (non-military), and only 16 CNMs practicing in the state at present. Despite the clear-cut need for more primary-care service providers, and the existence of many under-served populations and communities, non-physician practitioner utilization in Hawai'i has been, and continues to be, sparse. Foremost among the reasons for this is the resistance of a conservative medical establishment which is unrelenting in its opposition to non-physician practice of any kind.

Hawai'i's health-care system can be characterized as primarily private practice/specialist-based and for-profit in nature. The laws and regulations which apply to the health-care system and its various practitioners were written to sustain those characteristics. They were written in Honolulu where 85 percent of the state's physicians practice. The competition among them is intense. It is no wonder that "mid-levels" are viewed as unnecessary and dangerous competitors. Numerous efforts to change the laws to encourage a move toward a more community-oriented, not-for-profit, primary-care basis for the health-care system, and to increase the use of non-physician providers, have almost all died in the state Legislature. Simply put, the Legislature continues, with the encouragement of the Hawai'i Medical Association, to accept and sustain the idea that you must be a physician to be able to provide quality care.

In Hawai'i, it is as though the national and international experience of the last quarter-century with NPPCPs has not occurred. Many thousands of these clinicians manage hundreds of thousands of patients and write millions of prescriptions every year. Although careful studies indicate that service-delivery costs are cut, quality of care is uncompromised, and medical liability is reduced when they are included in the health-care team, an exact opposite image is portrayed by the medical establishment and accepted by the Legislature here. Many involved in these dynamics say that this pattern will not change without sustained pressure from within and considerable pressure from outside the local system. Perhaps recent national initiatives for health-care reform and "managed competition" will make that pressure.

Federal and state policies need to be shaped to make more efficient and effective use of NPPCPs, and to encourage them to practice where they are most needed[12]. For example, current criteria for designating primary-care health professional shortage areas (HPSA) do not include NPPCPs. Policies can be developed to standardize scope-of-practice laws and credentialing procedures. Reimbursement policies for NPPCPs could be standardized. Incentives can be offered to institutions to expand NPPCP training, in particular, to focus on primary-care, emphasizing practice in under-served communities. Training institutions must include more than Schools of Medicine.[13]

Meanwhile, PAs, NPs and CNMs in Hawai'i will continue, in limited numbers, to work as they have with one clinical hand behind their backs restricted to routing clinical tasks, unable to write prescriptions for treating basic problems which they identify, and limited to settings where physicians are present. And under-served communities will continue to be neglected. It is ironic that the only population in Hawai'i fully taking advantage of non-physician providers is the basically healthy military, where Federal, not state, guidelines prevail.

It will probably be the drive toward cost containment and the cost-effectiveness of non-physicians in the health-care system which forces the issues, but whatever the factors that produce the pressures needed for change in Hawai'i, non-physician practice will take off only when a number of specific circumstances evolve:

1) The general public must be better informed about PAs, Nurse Practitioners, and CNMs. Otherwise, utilization will remain limited;

2) The physician community is not a monolith. Many MDs understand what PAs have to offer in their practice settings and fully support their increased use. When these physicians speak out, it invariably helps to turn the political tide;

3) The public health community and the State Department of Health must recommend and adopt policies supportive of primary-care and NPPCPs;

4) Legislators must learn, from unbiased sources, more about non-physician providers, and they must be encouraged to take the political risks needed to support new legislation;

5) The Board of Medical Examiners must promulgate new rules to allow PA's to write prescriptions in concert with their supervising physicians. And all non-physician providers should be able to practice in settings where they are physically separated from their back-up physicians.

Conclusions

Hawai'i's reputation as the "Health State" is on the line; without change it will not survive the brighter light of national scrutiny. Because managed care is likely to play a featured role in a reformed health-care system, policy-makers need to examine the impact of such care on medical practice, physician supply, and access to primary-care providers.

Health-system reform in general and managed competition in particular are likely to generate contrary pressures on physician supply. At the heart of these reforms is the commitment to provide the state's un- and under-insured populations with access to basic coverage, increasing demand on the system, and, hence, the draw on physician services. Workforce deficiencies include too few generalist and too many specialist physicians, too few minority physicians, poor geographic distribution, and poor incentives to reach out and serve those populations in greatest need.

The state's existing and emerging "gap" group populations will not be served well under capitated managed care because needed outreach and decentralized provider services are not mandated and cannot be cost-effectively provided unless the state and professional working environment evolves sufficiently to recruit and retain NPPCPs. To personalize the delivery of health care, to extend health services to those who lack adequate care, and to improve access to and utilization of available services, physicians in Hawai'i must be willing to transfer more responsibility to non-physician practitioners.

Considerable research has been generated on the acceptability, cost effectiveness, and exchangibility of these providers for physicians in the provision of primary-care. Within their areas of competence, PAs, NPs, and CNMs provide care of a quality equivalent to that of physicians' care. Moreover, NPPCPs are more adept than physicians at providing services that depend on communication with patients and preventive actions. These are precisely the complementary services that the public-health clients targeted under QUEST require. The State Medical Practice Act must be revised, and the supply structures must be improved, to enable NPPCPs to provide a valuable source of primary and preventive care in Hawai'i.

References
1. The islands of Maui and Hawai'i have a significant number of Mexican/ Latino migrant farm laborers and imported hotel workers.
2. Currently Hawai'i is the oldest-lived state in the Union, and the elderly are the fastest-growing age segment.
3. Hawai'i has been rated 51st out of 51 states for the past five years due to inadequate provider-to-consumer service ratios for the mentally ill.
4 "Part-time" employees are those who work less than 20 hours a week, or less

than four weeks of consecutive employment. Sadly, the 3,000 "emergency hires" working for the state of Hawai'i and city of Honolulu, are not provided with health-insurance benefits. Many of these individuals will need to rely on QUEST.

5. A recent case at one state primary health-care clinic: A visitor to O'ahu, daughter of a World War II Filipino veteran, needed an immediate rabies vaccination. (A dog bit her just before her visit.) Sadly, she had no health insurance and the state had to absorb the $600 charge.

6. Fowkes, V. (1993). Meeting the needs of the underserved: the roles of physician assistants and nurse practitioners, *in* Clawson, DK, and Osterweis, M. (eds). The role of PAs and nurse practitioners in primary care. Washington: Association of Academic Health Centers. 69-84.

7. Scherer, P. (1990) Comparing NP with MD care for people with AIDS. *Am J of Nursing.* **90,** *43.*

8. Schafft, GE, Cawley, JF (1990). The physician assistant in a changing health care environment. Rockville, MD: Aspen, 1987; and Fowles, VK, McKay, D. (1990). A profile of California's physician assistant. *Western J of Medicine,* **153,** 328-9.

9. Starfield, B. (1992). Primary Care: Concept, Evaluation and Policy. New York: Oxford Press.

10. Cruikshank, BM, Lakin, JA. (1986). Professional and employment characteristics of NPs with master's and non-master's preparation. *Nurse Practitioner.* **11,** 45-52.

11. Schnare, S. (1991). Entry into practice dilemmas: a review of research and health care environment impacts. Unpublished manuscript, Harbor-UCLA Medical Center, Torrance, CA.

12. Hansen. C. (1992). *Access to Rural Health Care: Barriers to Practice for Nonphysician Providers.* Bureau of Health Professions, Health Resources and Services Administration (HRSA-240-89-0037). Rockville, MD: DHHS.

13. State of Hawai'i Legislative Reference Bureau (1970). *New Patterns of Health Care; The Physician's Assistant.* Report #2. Honolulu: LRB.

CHAPTER NINE
Specialist vs. Primary Care
(À La Carte vs. Plate Lunch)

What type of provider is best qualified to manage the primary health care of Hawai'i's people? The highly trained sub-specialist who is the recognized expert in their area of expertise? Or is it the well-trained generalist who may not be an expert in a given area, yet knows the broad base of medicine, the "jack of all trades, yet master of none?" This could be labeled à-la-carte versus platelunch health care. This chapter provides insight into the definitions of primary care as well as how primary care and specialists are trained and oriented. With the changes sweeping our country in the areas of health-care reform, the information provided will help the reader to understand our current health-care environment, the role of primary care, and potentially some of the solutions for our health-care crisis.

The term, "health-care reform," has been bantered around as the solution to solving the current health-care crisis facing America. Health-care reform will fix the problem. Health-care reform will put the health-care triangle of cost, access, and quality back into proper alignment (Figure 1). Health-care reform will hopefully take us into the twenty-first century with a medical-industrial complex that is a "lean-mean fighting machine." The primary driving force behind this initiative, no matter what your political alliances, has become cost. With health care representing 14 percent of our Gross National Product (GNP), it's no wonder. This load to the overhead of small and large businesses alike directly affects their profitability, their abilities to compete and create capital for expansion, and, in the long term, their viability. As a nation, we also face the prospect of being opted out of world markets, again affecting the economic viability of this country and ultimately our standard of living.

Besides cost, access to health care has re-emerged as an important issue in health-care reform. Access has always been a problem for the underserved and needy of this country (e.g.,

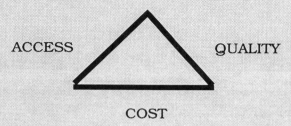

HEALTH CARE TRIANGLE:
ACCESS, COST, QUALITY

ACCESS   QUALITY

COST

HEALTH CARE MUST:

Δ BE ACCESSIBLE TO ALL SEG-
MENTS OF HAWAI'I'S PEOPLE
Δ BE AFFORDABLE AND COST-EF-
FECTIVE TO ALL
Δ MAINTAIN ITS *QUALITY* IN AN
ENVIRONMENT OF LIMITED AND
EVEN SHRINKING RESOURCES

THIS TRIANGLE MUST BE MAIN-
TAINED IN STRATEGIC BALANCE
AND ALIGNMENT IF WE ARE TO DO
THE BEST WE CAN IN THE DELIVERY
OF HEALTH CARE.

FIGURE 1

rural, inner city, and indigent populations). It has more recently become an increasing problem with the proliferation of sub-specialists who do not practice in rural areas. This is coupled with the substantial drop in graduating medical students entering primary care specialties. In 1992 only 14 percent of graduating medical students entered primary specialties.

Finally, both health and non-health care professionals have come to look skeptically at the issue of quality. Many feel a two-tiered system of care has evolved. For those who can pay for it, the sky is the limit: all the technology, procedures, medication, or physicians you could possibly want. The poor and underserved lack access to basic acute-care and preventive health-care services. Although they may have coverage (i.e., Medicaid), many providers cannot provide care because of substantially low reimbursements. When practices approach 30 to 40 percent indigent or Medicaid, many offices are unable to accept more such patients because it threatens financial viability. The overheads to run primary-care practices vary from 60 to 75 percent; hence providers cannot practice economically when reimbursements are at low levels. In large institutions such as hospitals, this low reimbursement rate is ultimately shifted to other payors resulting in increasing health-care premiums. Thus, increasing disparity evolves between the costs for private insurance and care for the indigent.

In addition, even basic health-care services such as immunizations, prenatal and well child care are not given to a substantial number of our citizens. When measured by standard health-care outcomes with other industrialized nations (e.g., longevity, maternal-child morbidity and mortality), the U.S. is very near the bottom of the list. Additionally, the U.S. has the highest per capital spending on health care, yet over 39 million Americans lack access to needed medical services.

The primary care physician (PCP) has re-emerged in the health-care reform debate. The PCP has been labeled as the best health-care provider to manage the medical needs of an individual or family unit. In many of the managed-care or health-maintenance organization (HMO) programs, these PCPs have become medical managers, the "quarterbacks," who become responsible for managing the total health care and the accompanying financial and medical resources available for the care of the patient. In many of these settings, payors have found that PCPs more cost-effectively manage resources, provide the largest access available (because of their breadth of training) and become responsible for maintaining the overall efficiency of care (e.g., they manage costs, quality and patient satisfaction). The issue of who best delivers primary-care services will certainly emerge in the health-care reform debate. For in the fee-for-service arena, specialists historically have and continue to provide a significant amount of primary health care.

Toward A Definition of Primary Care

Primary care has been defined as first-contact health care delivered by practitioners who take responsibility for the coordination and management of a patient in health maintenance and therapy. Figure 2 presents definitions of primary care by the American Academy of Family Physicians, Hawai'i State Primary Care Association, American Society of Internal Medicine, and American College of Obstetricians and Gynecologists.

Characteristics of a primary-care practitioner, as defined by the Institute of Medicine (1977), are: 1) takes responsibility; 2) broadly-based knowledge/skills; 3) cares for common problems; 4) manages health care for an individual/family; 5) preventive (physicals, immunizations); and 6) health care advice.

Also defined by the Institute are the three principal functions of primary-care providers--first contact care, longitudinal responsibility, and coordinating use of the health-care system-- and five attributes of primary care. These are: accessibility, comprehensiveness, coordination, continuity, and accountability. Trained primary-care practitioners who function by covering the largest number of these characteristics, functions, and attributes best serve their patients. Many specialists and sub-specialists deliver some of these specific determinants; however, primary-care practitioners fulfill many more.

Figures vary greatly, but from 9 to 34 percent of primary health care in this country is delivered by specialists. This variability is highly dependent on the definitions of primary care which are used in different studies. However, when people identified a "personal" physician or "regular" doctor by name, 79 to 88 percent of patients thought these physicians were general or family practitioners, general internists or pediatricians.

Training of Primary Health-Care Providers

There are distinct differences in the training and orientation of the major primary-care specialties in medicine. Family physicians, pediatricians, internists, and in some settings obstetricians-gynecologists (OB-GYNs), have been identified as pri-

DEFINITIONS OF PRIMARY CARE

American Academy of Family Physicians

Primary care . . . emphasizes first contact care and assumes ongoing responsibility for the patient in both health maintenance and therapy. It is personal care involving unique interaction and communication between patient and physician. It is comprehensive in scope and includes the overall coordination of the patient's health problems . . . biological, behavioral or social. Appropriate use of consultants and community resources.

Hawai`i State Primary Care Association

Primary health care includes those services provided to individuals, families and communities, at a first level of care, which preserve and improve health. Primary health care encompasses services which promote health, prevent disease, treat and cure illness.

American Society of Internal Medicine

Primary medical care is characterized by . . . first contact care for persons with undifferentiated health concerns; person-centered, comprehensive care that is not organ- or problem-specific; an orientation toward the longitudinal care of the patient; and responsibility for coordination of other health services as they relate to the patient's care. Physician-providers are trained, practice and receive continuing education in . . . health promotion and disease prevention, assessment and evaluation of common symptoms and physical signs, management of common acute and chronic medical conditions, [and] identification and appropriate referral for other needed medical services.

American College of Obstetricians and Gynecologists

Primary and preventive care is the entry point to the health-care system involving direct patient involvement; continuity in relationship between physician and patient . . . awareness of the significance of disease to the family structure. . . [early detection and] long-term prevention of serious illness; general health care, i.e., diseases other than those of the reproductive tract; application of skill and judgment regarding consultation and referral, when required . . . availability on a 24-hour basis.

FIGURE 2.

mary-care practitioners. They approach patient care with varied knowledge, skills and attitudes.

Pediatricians and internists train over three years and
generally spend 24 months of these three years in the in-patient
setting and 12 months in the out-patient setting. There may be,
occasionally, out-patient clinics of a half a day a week for each of
these specialties. However, within these out-patient clinics, there
is no cohesive orientation towards primary care that includes
minor surgery, behavioral science, and practice management.
Nor are there other ambulatory primary-care programs that
would enhance the training of these specialists in areas outside
of pediatrics and internal medicine.

The training of OB-GYNs is four years long. More than
three years of this training experience is in-patient and less than
a year is in ambulatory and out-patient clinics. Obstetricians
become highly trained sub-specialists. Their orientation is on
high-risk obstetrics and sub-specialties within obstetrics, including infertility, endocrinology, and surgical disease. Little time is
spent in exposing them to diseases outside the female realm such
as internal medicine, its sub-specialties, behavioral science, or
practice management.

Family practice residency, over three years, is equally split
between in-patient and out-patient training. It is characterized
by increasing ambulatory experience coupled with continuity
of care of family groups from the first year to third year of training. All ranges of skills are learned and practiced in continuity
on the resident's own patient panel throughout the three-year
training program. Incorporated within the family practice module are behavioral science, practice management, and other skills
necessary for a successful primary care physician. Family practice faculty role models actively practice and teach residents and
students within the family practice module. This module has its
own curriculum as mandated by the Residency Review Committee.

As can be seen from the above descriptions, these different primary-care practitioners have different orientations in the
care of their patients. There is no doubt that pediatricians are
primary-care practitioners for children, that internists are primary-care practitioners for adult diseases, and that obstetricians
can certainly deliver primary care in the areas of obstetrics and

gynecology. However, these same practitioners are highly trained to deliver many sub-specialty skills within their areas. It is this orientation that has led many of the pediatricians and internists into sub-specialties of cardiology, pulmonary, gastroenterology, hematology, oncology, etc. Nationally, approximately 70 percent of general internists and 40 percent of pediatricians enter sub-specialty training. This has contributed further to the present shortage and infrastructure problem of primary-care providers.

Over the past 25 years has arisen another group of primary health-care providers. These "mid-level" non-physician providers (NPPs) or physician extenders consist of nurse practitioners (NPs), advance practice nurses (APNs), physician assistants (PAs), and certified nurse midwives (CNMs). APNs, CNMs, and NPs generally require R.N. degrees before an additional two years of training leads to certification. PA training can be at a bachelor-degree level or two years additional training after the bachelor degree which leads to certification.

The majority of these NPPs are used in primary-care settings, closely linked with the clinical practitioner with whom they work. Some go on to specialty training working as physician extenders of sub-specialists in surgery, intensive care, and medicine. The different primary-care practitioners, physician or non-physician, bring differing strengths and weaknesses to the patient populations they serve.

Specialty Health-Care Providers

After the Flexner report in 1910, the education of physicians shifted toward scientific and research-based medical education. The results were medical specialties defined by age (adult internal medicine, childhood pediatrics) and sex (obstetrics and gynecology). The pace of this specialization quickened after World War II, enhanced by graduate medical education and National Institutes of Health (NIH) funds to develop research and fellowship programs in areas of sub-specialization. Thus were developed organ-specific sub-specialties such as cardiology, gastroenterology, hematology-oncology, pulmonary.

The proliferation of sub-specialists has not abated. Much of this has been attributed to the persistent lack of incentives, academic stature, role modeling, professional respect and economic rewards in primary care. Specialists and sub-specialists command, in many instances, salaries two to ten times higher than their primary care colleagues. In many instances, their overheads are lower (maintained by hospitals with operating rooms, expensive technology and equipment); they have shorter working hours, and the high professional respect garnered by being the recognized expert in a particular field. In academic centers and teaching hospitals, this power and respect overflows into the teaching agendas of residents and medical students. A lack of primary-care role models exists in these settings, resulting in a low percentage of medical students entering primary-care training programs.

The training differentiation of specialists generally occurs early in their medical education. By the third year of medical school, barely having been exposed to the different clinical disciplines, students are forced to make career choices. Many students headed toward medical or surgical specialties structure their fourth year toward "electives" in their chosen field, thus further promoting this early differentiation. By graduation, many of these students are already pointed toward specialized medical careers without ever having become comfortable with the broad areas of primary care. In many instances, the rudiments of primary care as it interfaces along all specialties (i.e., dermatology, cardiology, gynecology, psychiatry) are not learned, nor is clinical comfort and competence obtained.

Because of this, specialists generally are not trained nor oriented toward encompassing the total individual. They also are not aware of the integrating aspects of health care within the context of an individual within their family and the family within their community. They thus have a greater tendency to refer more quickly to a sub-specialist for medical problems which may only need a primary health-care practitioner.

The Present Health-Care Environment

Hawai'i has a shortage of primary-care practitioners. Although the John A. Burns School of Medicine residency programs have trained adequate numbers of internists and pediatricians, as well as OB-GYNs, the Hawai'i Medical School has historically graduated less than 6 percent of its graduates into family practice. This compares with 13 percent nationally and the projected 25 percent needed to correct the family-physician shortage. Much of this low percentage in Hawai'i has been attributed to students having to go away to the U.S. mainland in order to complete family medicine residencies. The result has been a "triumvirate" of primary health-care practitioners. This "triumvirate" has consisted of internists, pediatricians, and OB-GYN physicians.

There is a need for more family physicians available to the underserved and rural areas of Hawai'i. Additionally, managed-care plans and medical groups are actively seeking them to be the "gatekeepers" to manage health-care services. Some Hawai'i graduates have attempted to go into general internal medicine to practice in remote neighbor-island areas. Many have left disappointed because they did not learn enough of the primary-care skills necessary to deliver the broad spectrum of health care to patients in rural areas (i.e., pediatrics, GYN, and minor surgery). They have also been frustrated, in small rural hospitals, by the lack of technology needed to maintain their internal medicine skills. The "triumvirate" of primary-care model has created a significant problem of access for many underserved areas in the neighbor islands (Molokai, Hilo, Lanai, etc.). An analysis of physicians graduating from American medical schools (1976-85), has revealed that family physicians are more likely to practice and stay in rural areas than are other primary-care specialties. For this reason, the obvious need for a Hawai'i-based family-practice residency has become apparent.

Between 1976 and 1981, a family-practice residency in Honolulu was started at Kaiser Permanente. Half of the funding for this residency was from Federal monies, 45 percent was contributed by Kaiser Permanente, and another 5 percent by the state. A handful of Hawai'i graduates entered and completed these residencies. When Federal funding ended in 1981, the residency was closed because the Medical School and state were not prepared for funding. This created a rift between the family-practice community and academic institution, which only recently has been repaired. In February, 1992, after five years of active work by the Hawai'i Academy of Family Physicians, a clinical Department of Family Medicine was again started. This department moved from one full-time equivalent to three over the following year and a family-practice residency of six per year was anticipated to start in July, 1994. In September, 1993, this residency was approved by the AMA's Residency Review Committee. It will be in central O'ahu (Mililani) under the John A. Burns School of Medicine and Wahi'awa General Hospital.

The overall costs for health-care GNP (8.1 percent) in Hawai'i are below the U.S. national average. This has been attributed primarily to a significantly low hospitalization rate, one of the more expensive segments of health-care costs. However, recent premiums for health care (borne almost entirely by employers) have been increasing at rates approaching 20 percent per annum. Employers are concerned that their very viability will be influenced by health-care costs. One of the largest Hawai'i hotel chains recently had a premium increase of $1 million per year for its 3,000 employees, equal to over 50 new jobs. This has resulted in many employers seeking health premiums in the form of HMOs and managed-care products which require primary-care case managers.

The Primary-Care Case Manager or primary-care gatekeeping concept emerged in the late 1970s. The former term, is preferable because "gatekeeping" implies the inhibition of health care, whereas primary-care case manager implies access to the management of health care. The goal of primary-care case manager programs is two-fold: (1) cost effectiveness, and (2) ensured access. The two features are: (1) the gatekeeper's assumption of utilization management responsibilities. Here the case manager agrees to exercise discretion in decisions which affect health resource consumption and to be monitored for performance. (2) The restriction on physician choice by patients, which affects their health-care seeking patterns. This results in patients being "channeled" to their gatekeepers, thereby enabling them to provide care and to perform utilization management functions.

The public's awareness of accelerating health-care costs is coupled with paradigm shifts occurring in the environment in regards to values that have to change if we are to get control of health care successfully. Steve Shortell has pointed out several of these paradigm shifts: (1) A change in focus from acute care toward a continuum of care, (2) from treating illness toward maintaining wellness, (3) from caring for individuals toward health-care systems becoming responsible for health status (out comes) of defined populations, (4) from market share toward covered lives (capitation), (5) from filling (hospital) beds toward care provided at appropriate levels (managed health care), (6) from managing department and organizations toward managing markets and networks, and (7) from coordinating services toward actively managing quality. Many of these shifts should result in enhancement of reimbursement for primary care, enhancement of services that are knowledge and judgment based rather than procedurally driven, an emphasis on preventative health-care services, and increasing Federal and private supports to develop primary-care training programs of all types.

Many state legislatures (e.g., Texas) are mandating line-item budgets that promote primary-care training in medical schools. Additionally, in order to get control of government health-care costs, they are encouraging the development of managed-care Medicaid programs. Already more than 39 states covering 3.6 million Medicaid recipients offer managed-care programs; Hawai'i's Health QUEST (Quality care, Universal access, Efficient utilization, Stabilizing costs, and Transforming provision of health care) being one of the newest initiatives. Employers and consumers are also starting to demand information about their health-care costs and outcomes. Outcomes research, market-driven health care with competition, as well as informed consumers will all be a part of the health-care equation as we approach the next century. Providers who can provide value, defined as cost-effective, quality outcomes for defined patient populations, will be the survivors in the next century.

Managed health-care plans have the data showing how value in access, quality and cost are enhanced when well-trained primary-care practitioners are delivering health care. The Federal government has mandated Medicare reimbursements under the Resource Based Relative Value System that is enhancing support of primary-care providers. President Clinton's health-care task force will accelerate health-care reform toward managed care. Discussions of managed competition, global budgeting, a national health-care board, and elimination of health-care benefits as a nontaxable item, will cause large flows of patients into managed-care plans and into HMO's. Figure 3 outlines some of President Clinton's proposed health-care reform agenda.

Community Health Centers and Ke Ola O Hawai'i

At the national level, there has been a movement toward the development of community health centers. Federal funds have been earmarked for the development of community health centers as well as Area Health Education Centers. This has been done to move health-care practitioners of all types into communities to train as well as subsequently live and practice. The community health center movement has been spearheaded by the Hawai'i State Primary Care Association. In addition, the Kellogg Foundation granted the Medical School $6 million in 1991. Ke Ola O Hawai'i was formed specifically to develop community multidisciplinary academic training programs for medical students, nurses, social workers, and public health students. Three Ke Ola sites have been developed: the Queen Emma Clinic, Waianae Comprehensive Care and Kalihi-Palama Clinic. This is being coupled with plans for Area Health Education Centers.

These could parallel the Kellogg project but are oriented toward continuing medical education and training programs for communities. To further stimulate the development of primary care in 1992, the Hawai'i Academy of Family Physicians assisted in the passage of House Bill 2835–Act 41: the primary-care incentive bill. Its intent was to create incentives for recruitment and retention of health-care practitioners in under-served areas. It emphasized creating training programs and clerkships for students in family medicine as well as training programs for nurse practitioners, physician assistants and other health-care professionals. In April, 1992, the State Legislature also passed Act 70, which established a system of community-based primary-care health centers located in under-served areas. The Hawai'i State Primary Care Association sponsored this legislation. These initiatives are being carried out under the direction of the Department of Health and organized via the Primary Care Roundtable. During the 1993 legislative session, House Bill 1363 established a family-practice residency training program with a rural health clinic rotation site in Hilo.

The Health-Care Infrastructure

The present U.S. and Hawai'i health-care system is an inverted pyramid with an imbalance of primary care to sub-specialty physicians. In Canada where health-care costs are 10 per-

CLINTON'S HEALTH-CARE REFORM AGENDA

Health care will be an important piece of Clinton's economic reform package. Throughout his presidential campaign, Governor Clinton stressed health-care reform as a top priority. The Jackson Hole Group (JHG) initiated the concept of "managed competition" which appears to be the centerpiece of his reform package. Elements include:

✔ A National Health Board (NHB) which would set standards and collect health outcomes data,

✔ National Spending Targets, set by the NHB,

✔ A core benefits package to all Americans,

✔ Employer responsibility for provision of health benefits with employer tax benefits only for the lowest priced plan,

✔ a government plan to replace Medicaid,

✔ increased use of managed care networks,

✔ insurance reform with return to community-based rating without exclusions for pre-existing conditions,

✔ medical malpractice reform,

✔ tax credits for Research and Development (R&D),

✔ focus on community-based care and primary and preventive care.

As you can see from the Clinton Health Care Plan, managed care, primary care and community-based care will be important elements in the proposed plan.

"Clinton's Health-care reform Agenda," Hogan & Hartson's Medical Technology Coverage & Reimbursement Update, December, 1992, No. 7, pg. 7.

FIGURE 3

cent of GNP, 51 percent of practicing physicians are family doctors. Steven A. Schroeder, President of Robert Wood Johnson Foundation, says the most aggressive attempts to address our health-care problems will be jeopardized by the lack of primary-care physicians. Clearly the infrastructure of our health-care system will need to be fixed if reform is to be successful.

Approximately 45 percent of Hawai'i physicians belong to the Hawai'i Medical Association (HMA). Of the total 1,189 HMA physicians, 756 (64 percent) are sub-specialists and 433 (36 percent) are primary care. The goal in correcting the present sub-specialty/primary-care imbalance would be to create a system with a strong primary-care provider base. These would be linked with sub-specialists who would provide consultation and medical care. It is estimated that the primary-care base should approach 50 percent of our provider work force. In a recent *New England Journal of Medicine*, Richard Kronick, *et al.* outlined the estimated number of full-time equivalent (FTE) physicians and hospital beds needed under managed competition (Figure 4). Primary-care FTEs closely approach 50 percent.

Correcting the present imbalance in the health-care pyramid will require the creation of a U.S. health-care work force policy that gives direction into the next century. Fitzhugh Mullan addresses these issues of physician work force policy. He states that even if all residency programs began graduating 50 percent generalists in 1993, it would take until 2040 for the physician work force to reach 50 percent primary-care strength. If all graduating medical students entered generalist training in 1993, it would take until 2004 to reach the same 50 percent goal.

For work-force policy development, he recommends focusing in five areas: (1) training physicians in family medicine, general internal medicine, and general pediatrics; (2) reflection of the nation's ethnic diversity in the work force; (3) distribution of physicians in geographically-equitable ways; (4) maintenance, rather than increase, of the current physician-to-population ratios; and (5) establishing the supply needs for nurse practitioners, primary-care physician assistants and certified midwives.

Accomplishing these goals will challenge the present health-care provider infrastructure. Improvement of the present work-force balance will require short- and long-term orienta-

FIGURE 4: Estimated Number of Full-Time-Equivalent Physicians and Hospital Beds Needed, According to Size of the Health Plan.

SPECIALTY OR TYPE OF SERVICE	NUMBER OF ENROLLEES				
	20,000	60,000	120,000	300,000	450,000
Primary care (family medicine)*	10.0	30.0	60.0	150.0	225.0
Gen'l. Hosp. Services:					
OB-GYN	2.2	6.5	13.0	32.6	48.9
General Surgery	1.1	3.2	6.3	15.8	23.7
Orthopedics	0.9	3.0	5.9	14.9	22.3
Emergency medicine	0.9	2.9	5.9	14.7	22.1
Anesthesia	1.0	3.0	6.0	15.0	22.5
Radiology	1.2	3.6	7.3	18.2	27.3
Psychiatry	0.8	2.3	4.6	11.4	17.1
Cardiology	0.6	1.7	3.4	8.5	12.8
Urology	0.5	1.5	3.1	7.7	11.5
Subtotal	**9.2**	**27.7**	**55.5**	**138.8**	**208.2**
Tertiary hospital Services:					
Thoracic surgery	0.2	0.5	1.0	2.5	3.8
Neurosurgery	0.1	0.4	0.8	2.0	3.0
Subtotal	**0.3**	**0.9**	**1.8**	**4.5**	**6.8**
Other specialties**	4.1	12.2	24.3	60.8	91.2
Total	**23.6**	**70.8**	**141.6**	**354.1**	**531.2**
Hospital beds	**40**	**120**	**240**	**600**	**900**

*Staffing will vary depending on the mix of family practitioners, internists, and pediatricians.
** The other specialties: opthalmology, otolaryngology, dermatology, pathology, hematology and oncology, neurology, gastroenterology, allergy and immunology, pulmonary medicine, nephrology, and rheumatology.

tions. In the short term, retraining programs to improve the primary-care skills of both primary- and specialty-care providers will be needed. In the long term, graduate medical education funds will need to be increased and reallocated toward generalist training programs in primary-care specialties. NIH funds will also need to emphasize more research in primary and community-oriented agendas. Something is also to be said about training more physician extenders. The costs to train these primary-care providers is an order of magnitude less than to train resident physicians. Estimated average costs are $7,000 per year to train a physician assistant, $10,000 per year for a nurse practitioner and $100,000 per year for a family practice resident. The total cost then to train a physician extender after college or nursing school would range between $14,000 and $20,000 as opposed to a primary-care physician costing $300,000 after medical school.

Access, Cost, Quality

Primary-care providers deliver care to the broadest segments of our populations and provide first contact, comprehensive and continuous care. Consequently, they are generally more accessible for undifferentiated patient problems and settle in rural areas more than do specialists. Just as the specialist becomes the "expert" in a particular area of medicine, the primary-care provider must become comfortable with how "the masses" may present with acute or chronic, medical, surgical, or psychiatric problems. This makes them the "expert" along the horizontal breadth of illness and wellness and requires them to be comfortable with "knowing what they don't know."

There is much discussion and controversy about whether generalists or specialists are better able to deliver cost-effective care. In one HMO setting involving 344,474 patient months and 640 physician contract years, Dr. Walter Lane demonstrated that primary-care physicians with more than six years of practice experience generated less medical costs per member per month than those with no primary-care training and especially those with sub-specialty training. His figures parallel an HMO in Hawai'i where pediatricians and family physicians generated far fewer costs per member per month than did general internists or sub-specialty internists who acted as gatekeepers.

The issue of quality has often been the public's reason for seeing specialists for all maladies. This is fine if an individual only needs to see a physician on occasion for one recurring problem. What happens to someone who has several simultaneous or recurring medical problems? Is the patient to see multiple specialists in order to get the best care? Does this not lead to confusion for the patient and high costs for care? Would a medical coordinator or manager of health care be a better solution to this problem?

Thus, we see that à la carte care may not be the answer. Additionally, the lack of continuity, medical coordination and communication can itself become a quality issue for patient care, especially for complex cases, the elderly or those on multiple medications. What is needed is a primary-care case manager, broadly trained, who can care for 90 to 95 percent of an individual's health needs and coordinate the care which requires specialty referral and expertise. When a medical problem needs specialty case management (i.e., chronic kidney dialysis, organ transplantation, acute cancer chemotherapy, etc.), then a sub-specialist will be needed to maintain expertise and quality. The close linkage between the primry care provider and sub-specialist will assure health-care coordination, responsibility and accountability for a PCCM. This will give the patient maximum accessibility to health care, coupled with cost-effective care and accountability for quality.

Conclusion and Recommendation

The future of health-care delivery in the United States and Hawai'i will be significantly influenced by the infrastructure of health-care providers. Much discussion and debate will occur regarding who are the best primary-care providers to form the base of the provider pyramid. Such discussion should clearly distinguish *functionality* in primary-care determinants rather than definitions based on specialty turfs.

The driving forces of health-care reform will be led by cost, followed by access and quality. The balance necessary to keep the health-care triangle in strategic alignment will directly affect the side of the triangle most dear to physicians, that of quality. Much of our ability to maintain this balance will be based on developing a strong, solid base of primary-care practitioners. These medical-manager "quarterbacks" must be closely linked to our sub-specialists if we are to maintain quality in health care and provide the broad access and cost-effective care that Hawai'i's citizens deserve.

Bibliography

Clinton's Health-Care Reform Agenda (1992). *Hogan and Hartson's Medical Technology Coverage and Reimbursement Update,* (December) **7**, p. 7.

Richard Kronick, PhD; David C. Goodman, MD; John Wennberg, MD; and Edward Wagner, MD, MPh(1993), "The Marketplace in Health-Care Reform—The Demographic Limitations of Managed Competition," *The New England Journal of Medicine,* **328**, 2, (January 14) 148-152.

Walter Lane, MD and Terry Sincich, PhD (1992). "Selection of Cost-Effective Primary-Care Physician Case Managers," *Medical Interface* (October).

Fitzhugh Mullan, *Health Affairs Supplement* (1993). 138-151.

Roger A. Rosenblatt, MD, MPH; Michael E. Whitcomb, MD; Thomas J. Cullen, PhD; Denise M. Lishner, MSW; and L. Gary Hart, PhD (1992). "Which Medical Schools Produce Rural Physicians?" *Journal of the American Medical Association,* **268**, 12, (September 23/30) 1559-1565.

Stephen M. Shortell (1992). "Transformation of a Hospital System to a Health Care System of the 1990s," *Hospital Strategy Report,* **4**, 7, (May) p. 4.

CHAPTER TEN

Overcoming Giants

NANCY MCGUCKIN-SMITH

Let us go up at once, and possess it; for we are
well able to overcome it.   *Numbers 13:30*

It was close to the midnight deadline for bill introduction into the 1990 legislative session. The lights shone in the
office of Representative Jim Shon, as did the work of a handful
of nurses who were committed to crafting a bill to grant prescriptive authority to advanced-practice nurses. Just days before, the decision had been made. These nurses determined it
was time: Hawai'i should become the thirty-sixth state to enact
legislation to increase access to primary health-care services.

Nurse practitioners and other advanced-practice nurses
across the country had been prescribing medications to their
patients for over 20 years. The nurses in Hawai'i believed that
if they were granted the authority to prescribe medications
within their area of expertise, they would bring efficiencies to
the health-care system and would increase consumer access to
much-needed primary health-care services. Advanced-practice
nurses in Hawai'i were already making patient assessment, diagnosis, and determining the medications the patient needed.
However, the problem was that the nurse had to either call or
physically track down the physician who would then sign the
prescription, more often than not without seeing the patient.

From the nurses' point of view the public-policy issue
was straightforward. Numerous studies showed this was a safe
practice, increasing people's access to primary health-care services. All the nurses wanted was to help people receive safe,
excellent, timely care, and to make the system more efficient.

So began a journey of heartbreak and joy, a five-year journey of tales that when told can only bring a greater appreciation
of Hawai'i's political process, of individual courage, and the
fruits of the faithful diligence shown by Hawai'i's nurses and
their supporters.

The 1990 Legislative Session, in terms of prescriptive
authority, began quietly enough, but ended with all the fanfare

of a three-ring circus. A bill which would grant nurse practitioners and other advanced-practice nurses the ability to prescribe drugs was introduced on time by Rep. Jim Shon, Chairman, House Health Committee. The bill was heard and passed by that committee with supporting testimony by nurses, John Lewin, M.D., Director, Department of Health, and Kaiser Permanente, but with surprisingly scant testimony in opposition by the physician community.

By the time the bill was scheduled for hearing by Rep. Mazie Hirono, Chairwoman, House Committee on Consumer Protection and Commerce, the Hawai'i Medical Association, whose leadership had been away at a conference, and the Hawai'i Federation of Physicians and Dentists were a bit more aware of the bill and its potential implications for the delivery of health-care services. Physicians in specialty practice, who had never worked with advanced-practice nurses, testified in strident opposition, arguing in colorful terms that the passage of such a bill would be extremely harmful to the people of Hawai'i. Notwithstanding, Rep. Hirono indicated she would pass out the bill but only if a listing of the drugs from which the nurses could prescribe was attached. Within 24 hours the nurses provided a formulary of drugs used by advanced-practice nurses in Mississippi. The bill, in its amended form with drug listing attached, was passed out of committee.

As the bill passed first crossover, the opposition by physicians heated up. One of their major political rallying cries, used effectively for the remainder of the 1990 session and into the 1992 session became: "They (the nurses) didn't tell us. . .they should have told us they were going to do this."

Senator Daniel K. Inouye, a long-time supporter of the nursing profession and of prescriptive authority for advanced-practice nurses, submitted a letter to Senator Andrew Levin in support of passage of the bill. In response, a letter in March, 1990, to Senator Inouye from the president of the Hawai'i Medical Association (HMA), indicated the temperament of the physician community:

> . . .The issue of nurses prescribing (certified nurse practitioner) without the supervision or approval of a physician (licensed medical doctor or M.D.) must assume

that a *medical diagnosis* has been made by the nurse (or why is he or she prescribing medication without approval of a physician)...

...The manner in which this bill was introduced, heard, and passed through the State House of Representatives is an insult to common, decent people... The Hawai'i Medical Association has been in existence for 134 years. Its offices are known and our telephone number is in the telephone book. There was no attempt to make contact with us...

Senator Inouye's response to Hawai'i Medical Association was just as reflective of the temperament of the nursing community:

...As my letter to Chairman Andy Levin indicated, this is, in fact, a movement I support. Based upon two studies that have been developed by the Office of Technology Assessment, which is the scientific policy arm of the Congress, I have absolutely no reason to expect that if our State Legislature makes a determination to expand the scope of nursing practice along the lines proposed in this legislation, that those who receive care from those practitioners will receive anything but the highest quality of care...

...Your comments regarding the manner in which this particular legislation was introduced, heard, and passed through the State House of Representatives, as 'an insult to common, decent people,' is really a matter upon which I cannot comment...

...I would further point out, however, that in all candor, it does not surprise me that the nurse practitioners' leadership in Hawai'i would not feel an obligation to discuss its legislative objectives and strategies with your profession's leadership. It is true that for a long time professional nurses viewed themselves as 'handmaidens of physicians.' However, times do change. I am confident that the leadership of the Hawai'i Nurses Association no longer considers themselves to be subordinate to any other profession.

Senator Andrew Levin, Chairman, Senate Health Committee, attempted to mediate the issue between the nurses and the physicians. The nurses were willing to compromise to a degree but the physicians' position was firmly "Just Say No." Nevertheless, Senator Levin passed the bill out of his committee and on to Senator Russell Blair, then committee chairman of the Senate Committee on the Judiciary.

It was at this juncture that nurses learned a valuable lesson. Physicians are a political force to be dealt with, particularly in the Senate. The Committee hearing room was full of people spilling out into the corridor. The hearing started out with a slide show, by Dr. Phillip Hellrich, Hawai'i Federation of Physicians and Dentists. The slide show, which went on for about one-half hour, graphically depicted drug reactions that could happen to patients. Perhaps the nurses should not have been amused, but they were. For all nurses, let alone advanced-practice nurses, are educated to diagnose drug reactions.

But the humor stopped there. Nurse after nurse was questioned about their education, their ability to make a diagnosis, and their ability to provide even basic health care without a supervising physician in attendance. Nurses such as Tiffany Coleman, CNM, RN, a certified nurse midwife who had been delivering babies for 15 years, was questioned about her knowledge of drugs and pain-killers such as Demerol. Alexandra Hunt, MSN, RN, a family nurse practitioner, who graduated from Yale with a Masters in nursing, and was practicing at Kokua Kalihi Valley Health Center, was questioned as to whether or not she knew what she was doing. It was suggested that the care she was providing patients was second-class and harmful. Jane Starn, Ph.D., R.N., pediatric nurse practitioner, and Professor, School of Nursing at the University of Hawai'i, was questioned as to how she could determine the accurate diagnosis of a sore throat or an ear infection. Valisa Saunders, MSN, RN, geriatric nurse practitioner and clinical nurse specialist with Kaiser Permanente who cares for elderly patients in long-term care facilities and in their homes, was seriously questioned as to how she could possibly determine what was wrong with a patient and make a decision as to when to call upon a physician for assistance.

The bill died that night, and so did the naiveté of the nurses. It was a complete victory for the physicians. The nurses had been humiliated. But in the days, months, and years to come Dr. John Lewin would endure scathing remarks and treatment from his physician colleagues for his support of prescriptive authority. Geri Marullo, MSN, RN, Deputy Director, Department of Health, would endure much the same as her boss. Rep. Jim Shon was specifically targeted by the physicians as the "#1 elected official to be defeated in the 1990 elections."

In the 1990 elections the physicians forwarded Dr. Lei Siri Hundall to run against Rep. Jim Shon in the primary. When Rep. Shon won the primary the physicians then supported the Republican candidate Mark Au. The nurses spent countless hours on Rep. Shon's campaign, and the physicians contributed time and thousands of dollars to his opponents' campaigns. Rep. Shon won the 1990 election; the margin of victory was 64 votes.

Lessons learned in 1990: 1. In Hawai'i, if you are a nurse, you must first tell the physician what you are going to do and get their permission before you do it. 2. Physicians have a great deal of political power in the Senate. 3. It doesn't particularly matter what you know but who you know. 4. Incorporate Golf 101 into Nursing School curriculum. 5. Help your friends and give lots of money to political campaigns.

In the summer of 1990, the advanced-practice nurses once again discussed the prescriptive-authority issue among themselves. There was a great deal of internal professional debate about the issue. It was abundantly clear to the nurses that the legislators had very little knowledge about the profession of nursing and in particular about what advanced-practice nurses were doing in the community and across the nation. It was recognized that time was needed to gather information on the issue from other states and from other nursing organizations. The nursing community decided to defer approaching the law-makers on the prescriptive authority issue in the 1991 Legislature and instead concentrated on trying to educate legislators, physicians who would listen, and the broader community.

With unwavering commitment, Rep. Shon again introduced legislation granting prescriptive authority to advanced-practice nurses in the 1992 Legislative Session. Again, the bill was passed by the House Health Committee, House Committee on Consumer Protection and Commerce/House Committee on the Judiciary, and the first crossover by the House of Representatives. The arguments of the physicians could be predicted. Undocumented and unfounded assertions that second class health care would be delivered to poor people. Nurses would "hang out their shingles" and practice "medicine." And, they summarily recalled and again proclaimed in 1992 that in the 1990 Legislation Session "they (the nurses) did not tell us they were going to do this."

During the 1992 session, many in the health-care community were supportive. Many physicians who worked with the nurses in community clinics came forward and personally testified on behalf of the bill. Kaiser Permanente became a strong ally, and hence became a target of the non-Kaiser physicians. Old sentiments about Kaiser surfaced from the physicians in private practice who were testifying in opposition.

Hawai'i Medical Association and the Hawai'i Federation of Physicians and Dentists continued their strident opposition to the bill. In addition to using a tactic of fear, women physicians, one of whom was once a nurse, were brought forward to testify in opposition to the bill. But other physicians such as John Lewin, Kim Thorburn, M.D., Medical Director, Department of Public Safety, and Robert Hollison, M.D., President, Hawai'i Academy of Family Physicians, testified in support of limited prescriptive authority, if advanced-practice nurses worked with or were in some way supervised by physicians.

Clearly, there was growing dissension among physicians. It was also clear there was a growing consensus in support of the bill among the nursing community and others in the health-care industry. Help came from The Hawai'i Public Health Association, the Hawai'i State Primary Care Association, Kokua Kalihi Valley Health Center, Kalihi-Palama Health Clinic, Waianae Coast Comprehensive Health Center, Bay Clinic in Hilo, the Healthcare Association of Hawai'i, and the Hawai'i Long-Term Care Association.

During the legislative hearing more than 75 advanced-practice nurses gave remarkably clear descriptions of how they practice on a day-to-day basis: providing undisputed testimony that they are already seeing patients, making a diagnosis, determining the drugs which are needed and then having to find the physician to sign the prescription. Representatives and Senators were educated, lobbied, and provided with volumes of documentation from the now-40 states which had granted prescriptive authority to their advanced-practice nurses.

The House of Representatives was becoming quite familiar with the nurses and physicians arguments, but what about the Senate? As the bill passed from the House to the Senate the lobbying of Senator Donna Ikeda, Chairwoman, Senate Committee on Consumer Protection, to hold a hearing on the bill intensified. A hearing was finally scheduled, with the stipulation from the Senator that testimony could be given from only five people on each side. The hearing lasted three hours and after a five-minute recess the Committee reconvened and announced, "There are not enough committee members who agree on this bill. It is held in committee."

Once again, it was obvious that the physicians who so stridently opposed prescriptive authority for advanced-practice nurses could ultimately rely on the Senate to prevent passage of a bill which could only help meet the primary health care needs of Hawaii's people.

Lessons learned in 1992: 1. Same as in 1990.   2. Help elect friends of nursing to the Senate.

The change of leadership in the 1993 House of Representatives had a major effect on the ability of the nurses to garner backing for prescriptive authority. Speaker of the House Joseph Souki was familiar with the issue but had signalled his serious questions about the ability of nurses to make a diagnosis and therefore prescribe drugs. Rep. Julie Duldulao was the new chairwoman of the House Health Committee, replacing Rep. Shon. Previously Vice-Chairwoman of the Committee, she had appeared to hold but lukewarm support for the issue. Rep. Robert Bunda was the new chairman of the House Committee on Consumer Protection and Commerce, replacing Rep. Mazie Hirono. His sentiments were even less certain. The Senate leadership also changed; however, Senator Donna Ikeda continued to chair the Committee on Consumer Protection.

By now 43 states had granted some form of prescriptive authority for these highly-qualified nurses, and support for the bill was growing in Hawai'i as well. Not knowing the response to the query, the nurses approached Rep. Duldulao to ask for her support. She not only spoke strongly for the bill but also agreed to introduce legislation. Rep. Hirono also introduced a bill into the House of Representatives. In the Senate a bill was introduced by request by President James Aki, and a bill was introduced by newly-elected Senator Brian Kanno.

With four bills alive in the Legislature, the nurses thought that perhaps a bill would pass in 1993. However, early-on, the rumor was heard "Not this year. The prescriptive authority bill will not pass this year." "Why not?" And yet, the physician leaders of Hawai'i Medical Association were most certain the bill would not pass. What did they know that the nurses didn't? The nurses would soon find out.

Hearing day, February, 1993. The hearing started late and no one truly knew why until after the hearing when it came to light that Rep. Bunda and Rep. Duldulao had what can be politely called a "disagreement" about the bill before the hearing. It proceeded with more than 50 nurses, about ten physicians, and more than ten health-care agencies in support of the bill in attendance. The nurses calmly gave eloquent and explicit testimony as to why they believed the granting of prescriptive authority would help in the provision of primary-care services, as did the health-care agencies who had been supporting passage for years. The physicians again stated their opposition to the bill and their unwillingness to compromise on any aspects. "Just Say No," fear, and money had worked for three years; why change tactics now?

Rep. Duldulao moved to pass the prescriptive-authority bill. Her Committee on Health voted to support the motion. Rep. Bunda made a motion in opposition to Rep. Duldulao's motion. His Committee on Consumer Protection and Commerce voted to support his motion, but not without dissenting votes from those who had year after year supported nursing's initiative. With the bill lost in the House of Representatives for 1993, Rep. Duldulao, in remarks which will forever be remembered, asserted in strong and unequivocal terms that those members who had voted to defeat prescriptive authority had bowed to special interests, and furthermore as far as she was concerned the uncompromising strident opposition of the physicians was absolutely uncalled-for and had gone too far. There was no substantiation for such opposition; the nurses had compromised and compromised and the physicians still "Just Said No."

And so on an extremely emotional note the bill calling for prescriptive authority died an early death in the 1993 session. But Rep. Duldulao was not finished. A resolution surfaced which called for the interested parties to enter into dispute resolution on the subject with the "The Judiciary Center for Alternative Dispute Resolution." Nursing testified in support of the resolution with technical amendments, the physicians testified in strong opposition to the resolution and couched their arguments by indicating their refusal "to mediate on the issue of quality of patient care." The hearing on this resolution lasted for three hours and was finally passed but died for lack of a hearing in the House Finance Committee.

In summer, 1993, nurses, physicians, the Department of Health, and the Department of Commerce and Consumer Affairs received communication from The Judiciary Center for Alternative Dispute Resolution indicating that Rep. Duldulao had made a request, with the concurrence of Speaker of the House Joseph Souki, to enter into discussion on the issue of prescriptive authority. Three meetings were held. Nurse representatives attended the meetings with the authority to negotiate with the physicians. The physician representatives attended the meetings with no such authority and proceeded to derail the discussion by indicating they could not address the issue of prescriptive authority until national health-care reform became a reality and until the role of nurse practitioners as primary-care providers under the new Hawai'i Health QUEST program was clarified. Nursing submitted documentation as to the safety of care provided by advanced-practice nurses. The physicians provided no documentation as to the adverse effects on consumers.

The 1993 demise of the bill unified nurses. The public sector nurses, represented by the Hawai'i Government Employees Association , joined the Nurses Prescriptive Authority Coalition. By the end of 1993 the Board of Nursing, almost every nursing organization in Hawai'i, and almost every health-care organization and agency in Hawai'i, except organized medicine, supported the endeavor to obtain prescriptive authority.

In fall, 1994, the change in Senate leadership had a powerful impact on the issue of prescriptive authority. Sen. Norman Mizuguchi became President of the Senate; Sen. Milton Holt became the chairman of the Senate Committee on Consumer Protection. In addition, the national health-care reform being forwarded by President Clinton called for the increased utilization of advanced-practice nurses as primary-care providers. By now 46 states had granted prescriptive authority to advanced-practice nurses, and Hawai'i "The Health State," and model for a reformed health-care system could hardly withstand the contradiction of being a progressive health state and still not allowing their highly-qualified nurses to prescribe.

In winter, 1994, Sen. Milton Holt held an informational briefing on the role of the advanced-practice nurse in the delivery of health-care services. And while the briefing was intended to speak in broad terms about the role these nurses would play in delivering primary health care services, the conversation devolved to the issue of prescribing by nurses. At the conclusion of the briefing Sen. Holt indicated that "something needed to be done." And with this brevity, the powerful chairman of the Senate Consumer Protection Committee signalled that in 1994, the Senate would deal with the issue.

Governor Waihee introduced the prescriptive-authority bill into the 1994 Legislative Session as part of his administrative package. Speaker of the House Joseph Souki, Rep. Tom Okamura, and others in the House Leadership fully supported Rep. Duldulao and her Health Committee in passage of the bill. Sen. Holt became the standard-bearer for nurses and the issue in the Senate. The Governor, the Speaker of the House and the House Leadership, Sen. Holt, Sen. Kanno, and the Senate Leadership, took ownership of what was to become known in 1994 as "The Nurses' Bill." The physicians, in true form, continued to oppose the idea of nurses prescribing.

On May 2, 1994, as the nursing community looked on, the Legislature passed a one-sentence bill calling for the granting of prescriptive authority to advanced-practice nurses. Hawai'i became the 47th state to recognize the important role of nurses in health care.

The public-policy implications of allowing advanced-practice nurses to prescribe medications are profound. True health-care reform will be allowed to flourish in Hawai'i. The Hawai'i State Legislature, in a single piece of legislation, has increased and enhanced consumer access to advanced nursing care in community settings. Access to primary health-care is improved for individuals and families; health education, the treatment of minor illnesses, and continuity of care in the monitoring and treatment of chronic diseases will be achieved.

In the beginning the nurses wanted to help people and help the health-care system be more efficient; in the end, giants were overcome and the vision was obtained.

PART FOUR

Harm Reduction
and Other Heresies

CHAPTER ELEVEN

Drug Policy in Hawai'i
Is the Cure Worse than the Problem?

DONALD TOPPING

Despite the considerable efforts of the thousands of people in Hawai'i who are engaged in our War on Drugs, the unfortunate fact is that the battle is not being won.[1]

In spite of the conclusion drawn by Attorney General Warren Price in 1989, Hawai'i continues to follow the policies of the Federal War on Drugs, described by a growing number of critics as self-destructive and unwinnable. While other communities in Europe, Australia, Canada, and even the U.S. are beginning to look at all substance abuse as a public health issue, Hawai'i's policy-makers, as well as those who carry out those policies, seem committed to the criminal/punitive approach of the War on Drugs which seeks to achieve a drug-free society through interdiction, eradication, arrest, trial, and mandatory sentencing of offenders. Prevention education and treatment programs are also included in the effort, but clearly are second-string players as far as financing is concerned.[2]

After more than two decades of steady escalation of the War on Drugs, and no apparent success in eliminating, or even reducing the amount of drugs (except for *paka lolo*[3], surely the time has come to raise some questions. What is the demon that we are fighting? How much is it costing us, in dollars as well as social disruption? How successful have we been in eliminating drugs and creating a better community? Is there perhaps a better, health-oriented approach to the problem? Why are we not considering alternative approaches? Finally, why have we let ourselves come this far without seriously asking these questions?

History

The evolution of drug policy in Hawai'i began with the first anti-drug law, enacted in 1856 and aimed at the opium-smoking minority of the newly recruited Chinese labor force. This first law, and its 13 amendments (added between 1856 and 1900), were ostensibly motivated by concern for the health of the Chinese laborers, as well as that of the Hawai'ians, who had a "sociable nature and readiness to acquire any new thing."[4]

Unlike today, licensed physicians in nineteenth-century Hawai'i could import and sell opium on demand. The price for one of the limited licenses was $30,000, a tidy sum in those days but obviously a sound investment from which both government and physicians profited, while the addicts were assured of good-quality dope at a reasonable price. As an indicator of the potential profit, the Moreno Bill (1880) included the proposal "to have the Kingdom of Hawai'i replace Hong Kong as the opium manufacturing and exporting center of the Pacific."[5]

Drug-related legislation in the Territory of Hawai'i followed that of the Federal government, which progressively stressed prohibition and punishment, particularly after 1930 when the Federal Bureau of Narcotics was established under the directorship of the tireless anti-drug crusader Henry J. Anslinger. As their fight against alcohol began to lose ground following the repeal of the 18th Amendment in 1933, the prohibitionists and the enforcers turned their sights from alcohol to "drugs" as the menace. According to Theodore Vallance, between 1961 and 1992, "at least eighty-two federal laws have been enacted. . . that relate at least in some significant part to the drug problem."[6]

Although President Richard Nixon "declared victory in the war on drugs in 1973,"[7] the problems persisted. Anti-drug legislation escalated during the 1980s under the influence of presidents Reagan and Bush, culminating in PL 100-690, the Anti-Drug Abuse Act of 1988.

> This omnibus drug control bill contains provisions relating to virtually every aspect of the federal effort to curb abuse of narcotics and other dangerous drugs.[8]

This, as well as the numerous other Federal laws, had direct application to all 50 states, including Hawai'i.

The lawmakers of the State of Hawai'i fell in step with the U/S. Mainland in waging the "War." With the passage of each new anti-drug law came tougher penalties. Throughout the 1980s, chapters 329 and 712 of the *Hawai'i Revised Statutes* were amended and expanded to mirror the ever-changing Federal laws (e.g. mandatory sentencing, assets forfeiture, definitions of proscribed paraphernalia, addition of new drugs). The 1985 Index to the Hawai'i Revised Statutes has ten pages of references to drug laws (but less than one page for divorce).

Although Hawai'i's anti-drug laws are listed under the broad heading of "Health," their content and language indicate that our policy-makers view drug use primarily as a criminal offense, and not a public-health issue. Chapter 329 (Uniform Controlled Substances Act) not only lists all of the illicit drugs; it also includes enforcement procedures and penalties. Ironically, any Department of Health (DOH) employee can be empowered with police authority to make arrests for drug-law violations.

At the same time, the DOH bears the burden of providing support for most of the State's prevention and treatment services through its Alcohol and Drug Abuse Division. In addition to its own programs, ADAD provides significant amounts of funding for other state groups, as well as a number of private organizations which offer treatment services (e.g. Salvation Army, YMCA, Aloha House). In all, there are more than 30 such agencies. However, even with its multi-million dollar annual budget,[9] ADAD's mission exceeds its limited resources, which were to be reduced in 1994. One casualty of the reduction is that the number of publicly funded methadone maintenance slots was to be reduced by one-third in 1994, from 160 down to 104.[10]

Substance Abuse A 'Health Issue'

An increasing number of countries in the world are coming to see substance abuse as a health issue. Why doesn't the United States, Hawai'i included? Could it be that we have been persuaded by the intemperate metaphor and rhetoric of war, as in the wars on cancer, poverty, hunger and illiteracy, as well as those against communism and Saddam Hussein? In view of all the effort, expense and anguish connected with the War on Drugs, and the admitted lack of success, one might well ask, "Who are the combatants, and why are they fighting?"

On the attack are, according to Alexander Cockburn in *The Nation* (Nov. 15, 1993), the combined forces of 54 Federal agencies, plus at least ten from the state. Their goal: to eliminate from society illegal drugs and the people connected with them. While it is difficult to pin down the exact number of drug warriors, their multi-billion dollar annual payroll suggests there are plenty. (The budget for the federal Office of Drug Policy alone is over $13 billion for FY '93.)

And who—or rather *what*—is the enemy? Although the rhetoric has declared it a War on Drugs, in reality it is a war on ourselves, for which we all bear the costs and consequences.

But let's assume, for the moment, that the War really is against drugs, even though drugs can't fight back. What are these evil drugs, and why are we fighting only some of them, while ignoring the ones that pose the greatest threat to our health and safety: alcohol, tobacco and prescription drugs?

The target of the war is a whole "passel" of drugs (89 separate ones) listed under Schedule I in Chapter 329 of the *Hawai'i Revised Statutes*, plus any precursor or paraphernalia that might be used to manufacture, process or consume them. The

list includes heroin, cocaine, marijuana, amphetamines, and all
their derivatives. And the list keeps growing as more and more
synthetic drugs, such as crystal methamphetamine and MDMA
("Ecstasy") are invented.[11]

Why these particular drugs? Because they have been
defined by the U.S. Drug Enforcement Agency as mind-altering,
of no proven medical use, and harmful to the consumer. There
is also the popular belief that some of the Schedule I drugs lead
to uncontrolled and violent behavior. The claim that the inges-
tion of these drugs causes mood changes is not even debated.
That is precisely why people take drugs, including such stimu-
lants as coffee and tea. The other claims are open to question.

For example, in an educational pamphlet produced and
distributed by the Australian Centre for Education and Information on Drugs and Alcohol, the following information is given
about marijuana:

Cannabis has been used medicinally for many centuries. Research-
ers now believe that cannabis is valuable in the treatment of glau-
coma, nausea, anorexia nervosa, epilepsy and asthma. Research
is continuing to support these effects.

The Drug Enforcement Administration's administrative
law judge, Francis Young, after extensive hearings on the medicinal value of marijuana concluded that the drug "is one of
the safest therapeutically active substances known to man."[12]

The conclusion that drugs are in themselves truly harmful is also open to debate. It appears to be a matter of degree
and opinion, which is diverse. For example, in the bi-monthly
newsletter, Drug-Free Hawai'i, the following statements appear:

People using psychoactive drugs are not in control of their behavior . . . Often they become dangerous to themselves and others.
Psychoactive (mind-altering) drugs create an insatiable, uncontrollable desire for more.[13]

On the other hand, Stanton Peele, for example, reports
from his studies that "very few young people who try drugs
ever become regular users, and fewer still get 'hooked.'"[14]
Nadelmann, among others, claims that "the dangers associated
with cocaine, heroin, the hallucinogens and other illicit substances are . . . not nearly so great as many people seem to
think."[15] With such contradictory claims by experts, one can't
help wondering who is right. Most drug analysts would agree,
however, that drugs in general are not good for people, and addiction of any kind can be debilitating, if not devastating.

Conspicuously absent from this or any other list of illegal drugs are the two most harmful and addictive substances

gal drugs are the two most harmful and addictive substances ingested by humans: alcohol and tobacco. While the figures may vary, they consistently show that these two popular substances are directly responsible for widespread addiction,[16] hundreds of thousands of deaths each year, and indirectly responsible for thousands more when second-hand smoke, drunk driving, and the violent behavior that alcohol frequently induces are factored in.[17] And yet, both substances are available every day at your nearest supermarket, just a few feet away from the milk and candy bars. This hypocrisy has come to be accepted as normal.

In short, some critics of the War on Drugs are saying that the Schedule I drugs are not nearly as addictive or evil as the War propaganda would have us believe. Marijuana has been used for at least 12,000 years[18] by millions of people in nearly all parts of the world. Yet, there are no reports of widespread addiction, death from overdose, or violence associated with its use. Even the *Merck Manual of Diagnosis and Therapy* states, in reference to marijuana users, ". . .the term dependence with its obvious connotations probably is misapplied."

Cocaine may well be another unfairly maligned substance. It is well known that the coca leaves have been used as a stimulant by people of the Andean regions of South America for centuries. As Benjamin and Miller point out, "Prior to World War I, cocaine and opiates were generally legal in this country, readily available over the counter or even by mail order." Cocaine was a central ingredient in Coca Cola until 1903.[19] And yet, one hears very little about the horrors of addiction or behavioral problems during those days.

And it is argued by Stanton Peele and others that only a very small percentage of those who experiment with illicit drugs ever become addicted to them (Cf. Peele 1989; Alexander 1990; Siegel 1989).[20] According to Siegel, a pharmacologist at UCLA, "The occasional user of narcotics and other drugs is more common than people realize."[21] Lee N. Robins of Washington University in St. Louis studied Vietnam War vets who became addicted to heroin during duty in Vietnam, and found that only 12 percent had become readdicted after their return to civilian life. It would appear, then, that with the possible exception of tobacco and heroin, the two substances defined as most addictive,[22] the "deadly" drugs of Schedule I are not as pernicious as claimed by the drug warriors.

Why, then, if the prohibited drugs are not as deadly as they have been popularly portrayed, are we engaged in this seemingly endless, futile and costly war against them? And if they are deadly, or even dangerous to health, why do we not approach them in the same way that we deal with other health problems, such as alcoholism, influenza, and the deadly HIV? The answers appear to be money, fear, and the willingness to believe without questioning the incessant War propaganda generated by the numerous agencies, such as the DEA, FBI, CIA, NIDA, Partnership for a Drug-Free America, whose employees depend on the continuation of the War on Drugs for their livelihood.

The total amount of money connected with the War on Drugs is nearly impossible to calculate, as is the number of beneficiaries, which include thousands of employees of the scores of agencies and organizations that serve to enforce, incarcerate, educate and provide treatment. Others profiting from the effort include drug traffickers, as well as the manufacturers of guns and security devices and the merchants who sell them to the combatants. Drug-testing laboratories also thrive.[23]

The economist Roger Miller claims that drug trafficking is the second largest business in the world, following weapons sales, but ahead of petroleum. The $13 billion appropriated this year for the federal "drug czar's" budget is only the tip of the economic iceberg, whose submerged portion includes the budgets of hundreds of state, city, and county agencies throughout the country, not to mention the costs of housing of the many thousands of prisoners now doing time for crimes of possession and sales.

Even trying to determine the dollar cost of the War on Drugs in Hawai'i has thus far proved impossible. There are too many players supported by interlocking sources of funds to permit an easy cost analysis. In a typical "Green Harvest"[24] operation, for example, we may find the combined resources of the U.S. Army, the National Guard, the Drug Enforcement Agency, the State Department of Land and Natural Resources, the city and county police, the State Department of Public Safety, and probably others. In 1987, when "Green Harvest" sweeps were conducted only twice a year, the reported cost was $1,218,687. This figure has undoubtedly escalated considerably since 1992, when "Green Harvest" was made an ongoing program, with sweeps conducted throughout the year.

The cost of marijuana eradication programs is small when compared with the total costs of patrolling harbors, airports, post offices, and the many streets and neighborhoods where drugs are sold. Not to be overlooked are the enormous costs of the arrests, court trials and incarceration of offenders who are guilty of commiting victimless crimes. Indeed, the cost of incarceration of drug law offenders quite possibly exceeds all of the other costs combined. For the fiscal year 1992-93, Hawai'i had 2,851 sentenced felons behind bars, nearly 15 percent of them doing time for drug offenses.[25] With an annual per capita cost of $26,737 for housing inmates, this adds up to nearly $11.5 million a year just for keeping Hawai'i's non-violent drug offenders locked up!

Obviously the War on Drugs is big business. It keeps a lot of people employed in both legal and illegal enterprises. The money alone gives the War on Drugs a momentum that would be hard to slow down, much less stop.

The social costs of the War on Drugs are enormous. It impacts all of us in one way or another, especially those who inadvertantly get caught in a War zone. We see more and more families broken up by mandatory sentencing laws. Young mothers are separated from their babies. Private property can be invaded without warrant, confiscated and turned over to the state. The growth of violence, such as turf wars and armed robberies, is yet another cost of a war against ourselves that has been generated by anti-drug laws. The violence leads to the growing paranoia and fear that grips much of our society.

Ironically, it is this growing fear that helps to propel the War on Drugs. We are taught to fear illegal drugs and the people who use them. Many drug education programs teach that drugs lead to violence, a lesson which is reinforced nightly by violence-laden television shows which seem to thrive in our society. The message from government and media sources is that illicit drugs are the menace to be feared, and that the only solution is to eliminate them. So deeply embedded is this fear that we are afraid to consider alternatives to the War on Drugs, such as decriminalization or controlled availability.

Perhaps the strongest factor underlying our willingness to continue the futile War on Drugs is our mass acceptance of the anti-drug propaganda. All wars are sustained through propaganda. The War on Drugs is no exception. It underscores the validity of the old maxim, 'truth is the first casualty of war.'

While some of the widely distributed information about drugs is based on reliable studies, much of it gets distorted in the transmission. The "Reefer Madness"[26] image of the 1930s persists today among much of our population, in spite of the fact that millions of Americans have used illegal drugs without the dreaded effects of addiction, impotence, loss of memory and motivation, and violence, as portrayed in much of the educational materials and through commercial television programs. And yet, the majority apparently are still willing to accept the standard myth that drugs are the villain in this War, a villain that must be eliminated irrespective of the amount of harm that is generated in the process.

And, perhaps nostalgia plays a role in the unrelenting pursuit of the War on Drugs. We are a country desperately searching for something we feel we have lost. A purity of soul. A noble cause. We know intuitively that something is wrong. If only we could roll back the clock to a "kinder and gentler" era. But, as our recent involvements in Panama, Grenada, Somalia, and Haiti suggest, we have not yet learned that war is not the way to get there. And neither is President Clinton's $22-billion "Crime Bill," which aims to put 100,000 additional police on the streets and build more prisons.

As the War on Drugs has intensified, what are some of its consequences? Perhaps the most obvious one is the dramatic increase in state prison populations, which, according to Benjamin and Miller, is "up over 100 percent since 1980, and more than 250,000 above capacity." Some critics (cf. Nadelmann, 1989) see this explosion in the prison population as a direct result of "government-subsidized crime," in which the only plaintiff is the government itself.

But, what about the benefits from the War on Drugs? There must be some. Nationally and locally, some authorities are making guarded claims about the reduction of cocaine use among occasional users. And there is clear evidence that marijuana eradication efforts in Hawai'i have been successful: the price has soared to make it the most expensive marijuana in the entire country ($600-$800 per ounce, according to recent police reports). Although there are no hard data to prove a correlation between the escalating costs of marijuana and the increase in the use of more available, affordable, and dangerous substances, it seems too obvious to ignore.[27] Recent police reports (October, 1993) show a marked increase in the use of crystal methamphetamine ("Ice") and "Rock" cocaine,[28] and the recent appearance of a new synthetic called methcathinone ("Cat"), all available at street prices that make them cheaper "per high" than marijuana. Sadly, school surveys indicate that alcohol consumption among intermediate and high school students is on the rise.

Is it possible, then, to claim any substantial benefits from the efforts of the War on Drugs? Even the hardliners are unable to make any defensible claims, aside from the occasional newsbreaking drug busts, or the eliminations of drug lords, which have little impact on the international narco-business.

The criticism of the War on Drugs is mounting. The U.S. Attorney General Janet Reno, as well as President Clinton's appointed Director of the Office of Drug Policy Lee Brown, have expressed their dissatisfaction. The Surgeon General, Joycelyn Elders, stated publicly that legalizing illicit drugs "would markedly reduce our crime rate." Yet, there are those who point to the War's isolated successes, and argue for more time and support to achieve the ultimate goal of a society free of drugs. One cannot escape the analogy with the argument during the 1970s for continued escalation as the solution to the Vietnam War.

Is there a viable alternative to the current policies? Isn't there the possibility of another approach which would squarely address the problems associated with substance abuse, and yet not generate the social ills that are a direct consequence of the War on Drugs: violence in the city streets, proliferating black markets, invasion of privacy, erosion of civil liberties, the spread of contagious diseases, burgeoning prisons, and, not least, the enormous economic drain of tax dollars?

One alternative that has been proposed is the Libertarian argument for legalization of all drugs. While that may appeal to some, it does not appear as a viable alternative. In the first place, the very notion offends the great majority of people. Secondly, it ignores the very real problem of addictive people, who, if not addicted already would very likely become so, particularly if the currently illegal drugs were promoted and advertised the way alcohol and tobacco are now. In addition, there is the formidable problem of how to regulate production, distribution, sales and taxation. At the present time, legalization does not seem to be a likely or desirable alternative.

Another approach, now followed in the Netherlands and Australia, is to separate the "soft" drugs (*paka lolo* and hashish) from the "hard" drugs (opioids, amphetamines and hallucinogens) and concentrate the interdiction efforts on the latter group. This approach alone would result in a savings of time, effort and money now spent on marijuana eradication programs, arrests, and incarcerations. However, it is still a prohibitionist approach, which has never worked, and it would continue to ignore the social and health problems generated by the War on Drugs.

Harm Reduction

Another alternative now is advanced by leading experts from the fields of health, law enforcement, and politics in other parts of the world. They are calling this alternative approach "Harm Reduction." As its name implies, its goal is to reduce the harm associated with substance use and abuse, whether it be the social harm of crime and violence, or the physical harm resulting from shared needles, overdoses, and adulterated drugs. Hawaii's Needle Exchange Program is an example of the Harm Reduction approach in practice, albeit on a limited scale.

The idea of Harm Reduction is to reduce, even to a small degree, the harm caused by the use of drugs. It accepts that there will always be, as there have always been, drug users and abusers. A drug-free society is simply not realistic, even if all the currently illegal drugs were to vanish. It further takes the point of view that drug users, even addicts, are first and foremost human beings who may need help, not criminals to be punished. In general, the proponents of Harm Reduction see the victims of substance abuse from a perspective of compassion for fellow human beings and public health.

Given these premises, what does Harm Reduction purport to do, and how does it go about it? On the individual level, the Harm Reduction approach aims to prevent harm to the user, and to provide assistance to individuals in helping them change self-destructive behavior. Specifics of this approach would include providing clean needles to confirmed addicts, and even prescribed doses of heroin or methadone as needed to prevent sickness or anti-social behavior. The approach also stresses health care and counseling services to those who want to reduce or completely stop their use of drugs. Total abstinence is not required.

The Harm Reduction approach also stresses prevention of substance abuse through education that is based on objectively researched data, not on popularized myths and distortion of fact. This approach has proved to be highly effective in the reduction of tobacco consumption in the U.S. during the past decade. Even the majority of those who continue to smoke have turned to filtered cigarettes that are lower in tar and nicotine.

On the social level there is the likelihood of several positive outcomes, especially reduced crime and improved health. If drugs, or their substitutes, are made available to addicts, the current black market and its attendant crime and violence would be severely weakened, if not eliminated. With this reduction in crime and violence, citizens would feel proud and free to walk their city streets again at any time of day or night, without fear, as they do now in such places as Amsterdam and Sydney, where methadone is made readily available to heroin addicts.

Even if only half of the purported claims of the positive effects of the Harm Reduction approach were true, it would still seem to have advantages over the War on Drugs. What, then, is standing in the way of trying it?

As I see it, there are three major obstacles to change. The first is the vested interests: the many agencies and organizations, and their thousands of employees, whose primary mission is to carry out the War on Drugs. Fewer in numbers, but just as entrenched, are those involved in the government-funded mandatory treatment programs to which the clients are very often "sentenced" by the court. Not to be overlooked are the pharmaceutical companies, which want to maintain their lock on the sales of the increasingly popular and highly profitable drugs—such as Prozac, Xanax, and Valium–all of which qualify as mind-altering substances. And, of course, legions of criminals profit by continuing to sell illegal drugs. In all, these add up to an impressive number who would be hit by any change in policy.

The second obstacle to change is the widespread acceptance of the many unsubstantiated myths about drugs and their effects, which are given credence by politicians, bureaucrats, educators, preachers, and law-enforcers. Volumes of objective, scientific studies on illegal drugs, available in libraries,[29] are ignored in favor of the simplistic, distorted claims found in education, popular literature, and legislative records. The media play on the sensational and violent aspects of the drug trade.

The third obstacle is the pervasive war-like mentality that has gripped our nation–Hawai'i included–the notion that violence can be eliminated through more violence. Admitting defeat is never easy. Vietnam taught us that. We have, as a society, seized upon a truth, that war is the only answer. Despite the mounting evidence that the War on Drugs is not working, we can't seem to let go. It is self-perpetuating, even though it is a war against ourselves.

Is there hope for change? Let us remember that Hawai'i is known for its leadership in public health and civil liberties. It was one of the first states to recognize a woman's right of reproductive choice. It led the nation with its needle-exchange law. It is among the few states with a prepaid health care act. On all these issues, Hawai'i has taken an enlightened stance.

Hawai'i now has another opportunity to provide leadership to the rest of the nation on an urgent public health question. Do our policy-makers have the will, the wisdom and the political courage to reconsider the unproductive and self-destructive policies of the War on Drugs, and seek an alternative approach? I can only hope so.

What alternative measures might Hawai'i adopt in the War on Drugs without waiting for changes in national policy? Each of several possibilities depend on a shift in attitude from making war to making peace through healthful measures.

A starting point would be to create a better balance in the way Federal and state funds are used. The present ratio–70 percent for interdiction, 30 percent for prevention and treatment–could be reversed. This could provide funding for more drug-treatment slots to help those who are ready to help themselves.

The judiciary could implement an alternative court system, modeled after the Dade County Court.   First-time, nonviolent offenders would be referred to treatment and/or maintenance programs rather than jail, provided they have not committed crimes against others. This would require a substantial increase in the number of treatment programs, but not necessarily an increase in tax dollars. It could be accomplished through redistribution of the appropriated funds, as suggested above, supplemented by monies forfeited by convicted drug dealers.

Hawai'i could also repeal the mandatory minimum laws relating to drug offenses to give judges the discretion to take individual circumstances into account when sentencing. This could result in reducing unhealthy conditions of our prisons.

The concept of community policing, now gaining favor in several North American cities, should be promoted. This approach stresses the role of the police as social worker as well as a guardian against harm.

Hawai'i could establish additional methadone clinics, including the neighbor islands. Studies show that providing methadone to heroin addicts lowers the crime rate by removing a major incentive to commit crimes, and enables the addicts to be gainfully employed rather than spending their time finding their next fix. It would also help to eliminate the risk of poisoning through the use of contaminated street drugs.

Hawai'i's needle-exchange program could also be expanded. An increasing body of evidence indicates that such programs reduce the spread of AIDS, link addicts with needed health and human services, and encourage many of them to enter treatment programs (when available).

The State's prevention/education programs and materials should be thoroughly reviewed and evaluated for accuracy, credibility and effectiveness. Certainly, alcohol and tobacco should be included in all drug-awareness programs.

These are all features of the Harm Reduction approach, which more and more communities throughout the world are looking to as a preferable alternative to the War on Drugs. What might be some of the results?

Some potential results of changes proposed above: 1) less drug-related crime; 2) an easing of court backlogs and prison overcrowding; 3) more drug-treatment chances; 4) more effective drug-education programs; 5) less HIV and other bloodborne disease among injection drug users and in the general community; 6) a more compassionate approach to individuals with substance-abuse problems who are, after all, human beings needing help, not punishment.

Would a Harm Reduction approach lead to more drug use and abuse? Evidence from The Netherlands, Australia and other communities tells us, "no." Would there be a noticeable reduction in the kinds of harm to individuals and society? Based on the evidence so far, the answer is "yes." In view of these positive experiences elsewhere, what is stopping us from at least seeking alternatives to the tried and failed policies of the past that have only brought harm, in one way or another, to all of us?

References

1. *A Survey of Hawai'i's War on Drugs*, February, 1989. The Department of the Attorney General, Honolulu, p. 48.

2. Exact numbers are not available, but funding for prevention and treatment in Hawai'i is consistent with the Federal level: 70 percent for interdiction and incarceration; 30 percent for prevention and treatment.

3. The Hawai'ian term for marijuana. The literal translation, according to the 1986 *Hawai'ian Dictionary*, is "numbing tobacco."

4. Lim-Chong, Lily and Harry V. Ball. (1988). "Opium and the Law: Hawai`i, 1856-1900. Unpublished ms., p. 4.

5. *Ibid.*, p. 13.

6. Vallance, Theodore R. (1993). *Prohibition's Second Failure: the Quest for a Rational and Humane Drug Policy*. Westport, CN: Praeger, p. 135.

7. Benjamin, Daniel K. and Roger Leroy Miller (1991). *Undoing Drugs: Beyond Legalization*. Basic Books, Harper Collins Publishers, Inc., p. vii.

8. Vallance, p. 140.

9. The budget for the State Department of Health's Alcohol and Drug Abuse Division for Purchase of Services (for treatment) in FY 92-93 was $10,052,701.

10. As reported by the Chief, ADAD, at Sterile Needle Exchange Oversight Committee meeting, October 21, 1993.

11. *Newsweek*, December 8, 1993, lists six popular new synthetic drugs. A pharmacologist at the University of California at Berkeley "has researched 179 potential intoxicants in one psychedelic chemical family alone." (p. 62)

12. Isikoff, Michael. (1988). "Administrative Judge Urges Medicinal Use of Marijuana," *Washington Post*, Sept. 7, p. 42.

13. *Drug-Free Hawai'i: the Newsletter of the Coalition for a Drug-Free Hawai'i*, V, IV, September/October, 1993, p. 2.

14. Peele, Stanton. 1989. *The Diseasing of America*. Lexington, MA: Lexington Books, p. 2.

15. Nadelmann, Ethan A. 1989. "Drug Prohibition in the United States: Costs, Consequences, and Alternatives." *Science*, **245**, 939-947.

16. Douglas Talbot, as reported in Peele, 1989, claims "that 20 or more million Americans are alcoholics." (p. 25)

17. The Fall, 1992 issue of the *Carnegie Quarterly* states: "Each year, more than 400,000 Americans die as a result of smoking-caused diseases and 200,000 from disease and accidents caused by alcohol."

18. Abel, Ernest L. (1980). Marihuana: the First Twelve Thousand Years. New York: Plenum Press.

19. Alexander, Bruce K. (1990). *Peaceful Measures: Canada's Way Out of the War on Drugs.* Toronto: University of Toronto Press, p. 174.

20. Siegal, Ronald K. 1989. *Intoxication: Life in Pursuit of Articial Paradise.* New York: E.P. Dutton

21. Quoted in *Science News,* 1989.

22. Benjamin and Miller claim that tobacco and heroin are used almost exclusively by addicts. Such drugs as marijuana, cocaine and alcohol are often used casually.

23. Raymond E. Sakamoto reports that Hawai'i spends $333,000 per annum for court-ordered urine testing of juveniles alone. "Detection of Juvenile Drug Use: Effects of Age at Testing, Court History, and Counseling." University of Hawai'i Department of Sociology Colloquium Presentation, April 29, 1993.

24. Code name for marijuana eradication program in Hawai'i.

25. Inhouse Department of Public Safety Data Book, June 30, 1993.

26. *Reefer Madness,* a 1936 propaganda film, was widely distributed among schools, churches and prohibitionist groups. Its exaggerated message was that smoking marijuana led to insanity and death.

27. Attorney General Warren Price predicted such a shift in 1989. (*A Survey of Hawai`i's War on Drugs,* p. 64).

28. Commonly known as "Crack" cocaine on the Mainland.

29. See, for example, bibliographies listed in the following: Trebach, Arnold and Kevin Zeese (eds.). 1989. *Drug Policy 1989-1990: a Reformer's Catalogue.* Washington, DC: Drug Policy Foundation; Herer, Jack. 1991. *The Emperor Wears No Clothes.* Van Nuys, CA: Business Alliance for Commerce in Hemp.

CHAPTER TWELVE

Caring for the Invisible
The Policy Environment for Alcohol and Drug Issues in Hawai'i

SCOTT WHITNEY AND JOYCE INGRAM-CHINN

> Should substance abuse be considered a disease, its treatment covered by health insurance? Are public dollars best spent on substance abuse prevention or treatment? Is either cost-effective? Should mandatory sentencing for drug offenses be made more flexible, allowing treatment in lieu of jail in some cases? Should we decriminalize marijuana and other drugs?

How would you answer these questions? Do you vacillate between what you personally believe, what you think might be best for the state, and what you think the public would support? These are only a few of the issues that island policymakers may be asked to address over the next few years. Each question is an emerging policy issue in the substance-abuse treatment and prevention field. None can be answered without an understanding of the complexities of the field and the policy environment in which it exists. No question is easily answered; the answers, once formulated, affect all of us. Substance-abuse problems are more complex than most other health-related issues. The following discussion presents four characteristics that must be understood in order to formulate rational answers to the above questions.

Hidden Communities
Two hidden communities within the state must be cared and planned for by the state's health, enforcement and social services systems: practicing and recovering addicts. The first go

about their daily lives silently, unless thrust into the public spotlight by drug busts, motor vehicle crashes or dramatic crimes. The second may belong to such self-help groups as Alcoholics Anonymous, Narcotics Anonymous and Cocaine Anonymous. Members of these two communities do not really differ from each other, in fact, they are the same people at different points in their life histories. Only a semi-permeable membrane separates the two stages of conversion and relapse, allowing for individual traffic back and forth between the two.

Yet whether addicted or recovering, these individuals remain politically silent and hidden from the ebb and flow of public discourse. Neither community has any particular political nor economic clout. It would be unlikely to see a methamphetamine addict at a legislative hearing lobbying for more treatment resources, or a self-identified recovering alcoholic at a public forum debating the merits of drunk driving legislation. They may care, but they chose to remain invisible. The silence of the recovering community is driven by the desire for anonymity as well as by the inward nature of each individual's struggle.

This invisibility fosters that cornerstone of addiction: denial. It extends to family, friends and community. The addict voices it through such statements as "I can handle," or "I really do get a lot of work done after I've had a little coke," or, "I'm not an alcoholic. I still have a job." Clinicians see denial as a primary obstacle to an individual's recovery. Similarly, therapists recognize that denial within the network of the addict's family and friends, often augmented by ignorance or shame, is exhibited in statements such as, "She wouldn't drink so much if things were better on the job," or "He'll get over it; it's just a passing phase." Local cultural values, which make confrontation difficult and discussion of personal problems at work uncomfortable, also encourage this denial syndrome.

A concrete example may help to show how denial perpetuates the existence of the invisible. A few years ago, a statewide drug and alcohol survey was administered to a sample of secondary students. Upon receiving the results of the survey, one school district refused to release the results to either the public or to other state agencies. Instead of considering the results as useful and important information that could be used for planning and prevention efforts, this district's administrators chose the path of denial, defensiveness, and concealment.

Just as the clinician must confront the addict over denial, the public must confront policy-makers who deny the existence of the invisible. But who is the public that should take on this responsibility? Usually consumer and advocate groups have a strong, effective voice in policy debates that directly concern them but, as noted above, the consumer groups in this instance are primarily invisible and those that could be advocates are often shrouded in denial.

An additional dimension of invisibility is found when looking closely at the needs of special populations in the state: Native Hawai'ians, Filipinos, women. Both the administrative and clinical substance-abuse professions in the state are overwhelmingly representative of the dominant cultures. It is no wonder then, that these same professionals question, from time to time, why ethnic populations and women do not avail themselves of treatment. Instead of questioning our "help-giving" and outreach behaviors, professionals routinely blame the victim by wondering why these populations have such "poor help-seeking behaviors."

Research tells us that both addiction and recovery follow very predictable cultural patterns. Hawai'i offers the opportunity to discover how we can culturally pattern our prevention and treatment efforts to reach non-dominant cultures, an opportunity that, for the most part, goes unheeded. Instead of blaming the victim, the planning of treatment services in the state must begin to hear the voices of those whose values and behaviors differ from the dominant norm, a norm that is all too often presumed to be universal.

If neither the addicts/alcoholics, nor their families, nor their peers, nor employers wish to speak publicly, who are the stakeholders who might come forward as advocates, as teachers, as cultural informants, or as policy consultants?

In Hawai'i, this role has historically been filled by two groups: the community-based organizations that provide alcohol and drug prevention and treatment services and the state office which funds the delivery of these services. Unfortunately, both groups could be seen as motivated by self-interest because increased funding meaning increased staff and status. Recent improvements in accountability have lessened these accusations, but a broader representation of the hidden substance-abuse communities is needed for policy-makers to get an unbiased, comprehensive understanding of the issues.

Invisible, But Not Absent

While substance-abusing and recovering individuals may be absent from the public spotlight, the effects of their condition are visible and pervasive. Our health system treats thousands of addicted individuals per year; our prisons house thousands of convicts who committed their crimes while under the influence; the police blotters and emergency room logs are full of burglaries, injuries and crashes that are alcohol or drug related; worker compensation claims are paid to many who were injured on the job because of an alcohol or drug-related incident; and our churches are full of families suffering from the effects of coping with chemically-dependent loved ones.

- As of November 23, 1993, 50 percent of this year's traffic deaths were alcohol related. On the Big Island, this percentage increases to nearly 60 percent (Clark, H., 1993) and (Kresnak, W., 1993).
- In 1991, 135 juveniles and 2,199 adults were arrested for narcotics offenses (Honolulu Police Department, 1993).
- A 1990 report showed 62 percent of probationers, 66 percent of female inmates and 90 percent of male inmates at Oahu Pre-Release Center report a history of drug use (Alcohol and Drug Addiction Division [ADAD], Department of Health).
- For fiscal year 1991, ADAD funded treatment for 4,362 admissions.
- For fiscal year 1993, the 13 emergency room sites that participate in the HEED Study reported 6,511 emergency episodes related to alcohol or other drugs (ADAD/Birch & Davis, 1993).
- Based on the 1991 Department of Education survey, ADAD estimates nearly 10,000 of Hawai'i's youth, ages 14-15, have high or moderate use of alcohol and over 2,500 have high or moderate use of other drugs. These numbers increase to 13,000+ and 5,000+ for students 16-17 years of age (ADAD, 1993).
- 80 percent of domestic violence cases relate to substance abuse (ADAD, N.D.).

•75 percent of child abuse cases involve alcohol and other drugs (ADAD, N.D.).

The relentless statistics show not only the pervasiveness of the problem but also its intransigence. Keala's case illustrates the complex nature of what lies behind these numbers:

> Keala is a stockbroker in the Honolulu office of a major brokerage firm. Her boss, afraid of confrontation, and co-workers, sympathetic to her role as a single parent with young children, overlook her progressively troublesome behaviors: coming to work late, taking three-day weekends, being irritable at meetings and not returning client calls. Today she was in an auto crash following a business luncheon. She and a victim in the car she hit have been hospitalized. Keala was found to have a blood alcohol level of .25 (the legal limit is under .10).

Who has been affected by her drinking? What systems must now exert energy, time and money to deal with this series of events? Her manager and the company's personnel department will now need to respond to her addicted behavior. The police, the courts, the hospital, Keala's auto and health insurance companies, possibly the Department of Human Services if care is needed for the children, and attorneys, if the victim sues, will all become involved. More attorneys will need to handle the actual DUI charge, and even the restaurant that served Keala's lunch-time drinks may need representation to defend themselves against victim liability. The progress of Keala's DUI case will be monitored closely by Mothers Against Drunk Driving (MADD) and will become part of their yearly statistics. She will be sent to DUI school and, hopefully, will seek help from one of the community substance-abuse agencies.

The effects of the invisible are often painfully obvious. Substance-abuse problems have not gone away and will not go away on their own. Keala's case points out the need to do something before the invisibile becomes visible. The personal and public cost of responding to such cases is enormous, engendering the constant plea for more prevention and treatment programs.

'We Are The Good Guys'

In addition to the resounding silence of the primary clients and the habitual denial at the community level, substance abuse treatment professionals have done little to inspire confidence in their methods. While they have worked steadily to professionalize their field, they have remained reluctant to share their skills with other human service providers. While priding themselves in being separate from other disciplines, this separation has fostered both intellectual and scientific stagnation. The field is caught in what one observer has dubbed the "we are the good guys" syndrome.

Because of the attitude that only substance-abuse professionals truly understand the chemically-dependent client, relations with other disciplines and self-help systems have often been strained. Medical professionals are blamed for routinely misdiagnosing and inappropriately medicating substance-abusing patients. Mental-health workers are accused of having little training or skills to meet their substance abusing clients' needs. Child and sex abuse treatment professionals are accused of denying that alcohol and other drugs play a significant role in their cases. Even self-help methods or examples of spontaneous recovery (unaided by professionals) are looked upon with suspicion.

But the substance abuse field is not totally to blame for this "we are the good guys" syndrome. Historically, the other human service professions and even the medical profession have shied away from becoming involved with the chemically-dependent client. Professional schools provide little or no preparation for working in this field. It is common knowledge that the addict population is tough to treat. Treatment is long-term and complicated; the successes do not match expectations and the failures return again and again. Academics seem convinced that teaching addiction counseling skills is either unnecessary or too complex. It is no wonder that health and human service professionals are reluctant to become involved. As demonstrated in the following case review, the delusion persists that the substance-abuse treatment system is the only system that can, and should, become involved in the care of the client, much to his or her detriment.

Stan is a chronic, middle-aged, homeless alcoholic who repeatedly cycles through hospital emergency rooms where the contusions and abrasions resulting from fights or falls or other "street" injuries are treated very competently. While the medical staff might routinely advise him to stop drinking, they do not address the underlying problems of addiction and homelessness (poverty).

Stan also is a frequent client at the local detox unit where he "dries out" and leaves after a few days with the addiction problem tentatively addressed—and perhaps feeling better physically—yet with the underlying problems of poverty, homelessness, poor health, and lack of social support left unattended.

Stan goes to one of the homeless service facilities for food and temporary respite. Here some of his needs are met but his health and addiction—and even the underlying issue of poverty—are not primary concerns of the dedicated staff.

And so the cycle continues. None of the three major systems with which Stan has interacted (primary-health, substance-abuse, and homeless services) has all the answers, or all the services, he needs.

If we were truly serious about meeting the multidimensional needs of clients like Stan, we would have to rid ourselves of the delusion that only one system can adequately treat the substance abuser. To achieve any meaningful improvement in Stan's prospects, the housing and shelter, medical, social services, law enforcement, mental health and income maintenance (welfare) systems would all have to actively plan and cooperate. To do this successfully, cross-training of human service workers is urgently needed, along with incentives and accountability that would pressure existing agencies into collaborative care.

The Elusive Paradigm

Added to the dilemmas caused by the invisible stakeholders, the pervasiveness of substance abuse problems, and the reluctance of the human-service professionals to collaborate, the ever-shifting paradigms of the substance abuse field create additional challenges. Although research and practice are beginning to identify "what works," there still is no single clear model of treatment that emerges from the substance-abuse field.

Substance-abuse treatment, as a discipline, would make great strides if there were one identifiable, effective, predictable way to help people recover. Unfortunately, there is not. Some addicts need medical management of their withdrawal; others can begin their recovery by simply joining AA. The chronic population may need extended non-medical residential treatment, and special populations such as pregnant women, adolescents, Native Hawai'ians and the dually diagnosed (those with co-occurring mental-health conditions) need treatment that requires the close cooperation of several systems.

Just as the treatment profession lacks a simple, easy-to-explain model for treatment and recovery, the public and local policy-makers suffer from fluctuating national policy. The substance abuse policy pendulum has swung, back and forth, over the American scene for the last century and a half.

For example, cocaine was once an accepted ingredient in Coca Cola; now it is proclaimed the most addicting substance on earth. Nineteenth-century citizens drank copious amounts of opiates in their home remedies, yet fifty years later, heroin and opium were dubbed the scourges of Western Civilization.

In our own times we have witnessed the shift from the "Summer of Love" libertarian ethos of the 1960s to the military analogy of Reagan's "War on Drugs" and "Zero Tolerance." New metaphors may evolve, but history tells us that such shifts can be expected in our ongoing American attempt to find a compromise between public control and individual liberty.

As paradigms shift, so do policies. This is blatantly evident in the policy oscillation between a law enforcement, 'get tough' national drug control strategy and one that emphasizes the disease paradigm of addiction and, consequently, rewards medical or public health strategies. The sixties were typified by the augmentation of educational and prevention efforts. Twenty years later the economic metaphor put forth during the Reagan/ Bush era rewarded the military, intelligence, and law enforcement establishments with money and hardware for their 'supply side' interdiction and enforcement activities.

Yet even when then-Drug Czar, William Bennett, announced his conversion back to "demand side" efforts (treatment and prevention) and initiated the "Treatment Works" campaign, the bulk of funding remained on the 'supply side' (interdiction and enforcement): going into the flack jackets and helicopters of a very costly and, as yet unsuccessful, paramilitary campaign.

The Clinton paradigm preferences—and the resulting policies—are still unclear. Drug Czar Lee Brown states his intent to focus more resources on demand but also says efforts should be concentrated on the hard-core addict. These are not necessarily conflicting goals but, once again, there has been no corresponding shift of funds from supply to demand-side efforts. "Follow the money," one local program director says, "and you will find the paradigm. Right now, the money proves we're still in the law enforcement model."

It is further disconcerting that the Clinton administration took more than a year to name a Director for the Substance Abuse and Mental Health Services Administration. This leads one to believe that the Federal administration has still to embrace a clear paradigm out of which alcohol and other drug treatment and prevention policies can be generated.

As policies shift, so do program implementation strategies. The translation of policies into programs is not always well thought out. We can now see how the last administration's 'get tough' policy strategy against illegal drug use has had unforeseen consequences that now face state and local policy-makers. The United States now has jailed a higher percentage of its population than any other industrialized country. The imposition of mandatory and lengthy sentencing for drug offenses has crowded local, state and Federal penal institutions to the bursting point. While the filling of the prisons might have some temporary supply-side impact, it is a costly strategy for the taxpayers and leaves the underlying demand (addiction) problem unaddressed and untreated.

If we listen to the pro-legalization advocates, the answer is to change the policy. However, this unforeseen consequence of a well-intentioned policy may have been avoided if the implementation strategies had been more carefully thought out. Unlike the enforcement policies for illegal drugs, the "get tough" policy for drunk-driving has had success. The specific program strategies to support the tougher drunk driving policy included strengthening of drunk-driving laws coupled with strict new enforcement measures and greatly increased prevention and intervention programs. Renewed focus on public awareness campaigns also had its effect. Skillful program set-up has helped obtain the policy goal: a national decrease in alcohol-related traffic fatalities.

We can learn from this example. Hawai'i policy-makers should first analyze the implementation strategies used to support policies before changing a policy direction. In terms of our 'get tough' policies on illegal drugs, we need to ask, as a state, do we have an integrated program plan to support our drug policy? Have we set up coordinated education, prevention, public awareness and treatment programs to complement the drug laws? We need to analyze our responses to these questions before we can decide whether it is our execution of programs or the guiding policy paradigm that needs changing.

Paradigms generate policies and policies are carried out through the setting up of programs. Should Hawai'i continue to re-allocate its resources for program implementation following each paradigm shift at the Federal level? Or should Hawai'i be more proactive in defining its own direction? Historically, we have primarily done the former--reacted to Federal shifts.

It is now time for us to set our own state patterns and policies so that responsible, effective program planning and implementation can occur. Formulating consensus among the many stakeholders in the substance abuse field could result in more meaningful policies and generate more effective service delivery strategies. We must also be cautious of changing policy directions when results are not immediate. It may be our working strategies, and not the policy, which need changing.

Toward a Working Consensus

Three consistent themes emerge from the preceding discussion: the need to expand stakeholder involvement in the advocacy for the "invisible" and in discussions about the issues emerging from the substance abuse field; the importance of fostering proactive policy development; and the need to develop strategies and incentives for the coordination of services. Osborne and Gaebler (1993), in their Reinventing Government, have addressed the first two themes. The President's Commission on Model State Drug Laws (The White House, 1993), has implied the importance of all three, with a special focus on the third.

Osborne and Gaebler convincingly argue that policy should originate from stakeholders. But, as we have seen, the stakeholders—the practicing and recovering addicts—are not so easily accessible. Their participation cannot always be guaranteed though it is crucial. This means that the responsibility rests on those stakeholders who can meaningfully represent the needs of the invisible population. Some possible candidates are: Substance Abuse Program Directors; staff from other agencies with direct alcohol and other drug assignments; Law enforcement representatives; advocacy groups such as Mothers Against Drunk Driving and the Coalition of Substance-Abuse Directors; correctional and judicial system representatives; and other state and private human service organizations.

Along with the above, additional stakeholders who might have an impact on the substance abuse field include: beer, wine, and liquor wholesalers, distributors and retailers; restaurant and bar personnel; insurance industry (medical and liability); hospital and medical personnel; professional organizations (Hawai'i State Bar Association, Hawai'i Medical Association, Hawai'i Psychological Association, Hawai'i Psychiatric Society); employee/employer organizations (Chamber of Commerce, Small Business of Hawai'i); the Hawai'i chapter of the American Lung Association; and the Cancer Institute.

These interest groups are important to the development of consensus for Hawai'i, yet they still represent, for the most part, only dominant cultural interests. While every interest group need not be consulted on every policy or program implementation decision, those who remain "in the loop" of a more inclusive decision-making process should be as diverse as possible.

The importance of hearing the opinions of stakeholders before making policy decisions is illustrated by the following scenario in which lawmakers deliberate a policy shift toward decriminalization of marijuana. Which stakeholders might be involved and what would their positions be?

Law enforcement, corrections and judicial representatives would most likely testify with varying opinions. Some might support such legislation believing that it would free up prison space and staff whereas others may wish to protect their hardware and personnel budgets. Still others may vehemently oppose such a measure on philosophical, or other personal beliefs.

Unions representing prison workers might speak against de-criminalization for fear that there would be a reduction in the work force.

Substance abuse program directors would oppose such a policy based on the common belief that marijuana is a gateway drug, its use leading to the use of harder drugs.

The medical community might have two opinions. Some might side with the substance abuse professionals; others might support decriminalization so that they can use THC (the active ingredient in cannabis) in their practice.

The local chapter of the American Lung Association would certainly speak against legalization; based on their research, they have consistently spoken against any changes that would make marijuana's use more prevalent.

Lawyers' professional associations may choose not to voice an opinion since some members may have philosophical biases and other members might experience a loss of income due to a decrease in marijuana-related cases.

Farmers' associations interested in growing hemp might also voice their support for legalization.

And so the debate would go, with most stakeholders sharing opinions based on self-interest, a few basing their recommendations on facts. It would certainly be easier for experts, uninfluenced by the whims of public opinion or the pull of political realities, to make policy decisions in a rational, scientific vacuum. But we do not live in such a technocracy.

Returning to the decriminalization example, if we accepted that we do not have the resources to punish or prevent or treat the use of all drugs, and if we decided instead to concentrate on only those drugs that are the most lethal or the most medically costly, then the rational choice would be to criminalize alcohol and tobacco and leave the use of other drugs unsanctioned.

But policy is not, and should not be, made in such a vacuum. Our history, our culture, and our economic system would not allow us to make such rational, but unrealistic, policy choices. The real world of history and stakeholders' opinions always overrides the narrowly-focused, purely rational. So it is crucial to hear from, and learn from, the stakeholders—they are the ones who should shape our policies and programs.

This focus on collaboration with a broad representation of stakeholders can be considered the grassroots implementation of the publication released by the President's Commission on Model Drug Laws, which focuses on cooperation between policy-makers and program implementors within each state. In fact, this 23-member commission, of which Hawai'i's Prosecuting Attorney Keith Kaneshiro was a member, defined their mission as one in which they were . . . "to develop comprehensive model state laws to significantly reduce, with the goal to eliminate, alcohol and other drug abuse in America through effective use and coordination of prevention, education, treatment, enforcement, and corrections" (The White House, 1993, pg.2).

The 44 model drug statutes, if adopted by a state, are seen as the foundation of a drug policy that would result in the accomplishment of the commission's goals. Hawai'i has been a leader in adopting many of the model laws that are within the jurisdiction of law enforcement. Now it is time to give serious consideration to some of the other laws, specifically the adoption of the *Model Alcohol and Other Drug Abuse Policy and Planning Coordination Act* (The White House, 1993, p. E-141). This model act's goals are: 1) to transcend the boundaries of agencies, recognizing the broad nature and scope of alcohol and drug abuse; 2) to establish a rational, long-term planning system to ensure continual, optimal service delivery; and 3) to develop the expertise and capability to monitor a comprehensive system while achieving rigorous accountability. If adopted, these goals would help address the issues raised by the existence of our invisible communities, by arbitrary policy shifts, as well as the "we are the good guys" syndrome. For instance, the model act recommends:

- the establishment of a cabinet level executive council comprising cabinet officers and state agency heads involved directly or indirectly with alcohol and other drug issues;
- council's responsibilities to include statewide planning, establishing budget priorities, evaluations and accountability reviews, proposing policy changes, and establishing communication with stakeholders.

It may be time for history to repeat itself. It may be time for the state's lead policy organization, the Governor's office, to establish a substance-abuse stakeholders' policy council, as was done in the 1970's. This council could be assigned the task of bringing the stakeholders' voice to the legislators and administration. The council could also recommend policy upon which the departments could base their program planning. While the renewal of such a council would not eliminate the responsibility of policy-makers to remain informed of stakeholders' positions, it would certainly serve to encourage both interdepartmental and private-public collaboration.

Although this structure has been used in other states to increase stakeholder empowerment, it is always in danger of becoming just another layer of bureaucracy. It must be emphasized that to avoid this, the councils must have the full political weight and legitimacy of the governor's office behind them.

Such a council might require a structure in which each of the state offices involved in drug and alcohol issues are mandated to develop a plan of action, with documented participation from community stakeholders and evidence of collaborative efforts with each other. The plan would need to include a system of evaluation that involves recovering addicts and alcoholics. This could be thought of as "feedback from customers." Technical assistance could be provided through the Governor's Office of State Planning.

Many otherwise talented administrators and clinicians in the substance abuse field are like the chef who never learned to bake because she was afraid of yeast. The "yeast," in this case, is program evaluation and outcome research. Most professionals irrationally fear such research, yet this "feedback from customers" could allow them to upgrade the quality of their services. Such evaluations should be required of all state programs.

The addition of qualitative research, focused on ethnic populations who have trouble relating to current, dominant-culture treatment and prevention techniques, would also be an important step. Such research could provide more visibility for the beliefs and behaviors of those groups who have not traditionally been part of the planning and delivery efforts of the substance-abuse service system. What little research has been conducted in the past has remained virtually unknown to front-line treatment planners and clinicians, circulating as it does only among the academic journals and conferences that litter the intellectual landscape with their abstracts.

In an accountable world, there would simply be no funding without such planning and research. Such efforts would encourage public stakeholders to respond to the invisible constituencies. The State Department of Budget and Finance could be accountable to the public for assuring that funding was approved only if stakeholders' participation was evident in the planning of funded projects. Other state agencies would also be made accountable both to private stakeholders and to each other.

By undertaking such efforts, policy-makers can learn from the beliefs and values of everyone involved in the substance abuse arena. Administrators and policy-makers need no longer be part of the denial; they can create the opportunity to see the invisible and to hear the voices of Hawai'i's long-too-silent substance abuse constituencies.

Such a giant U-turn toward sanity and responsiveness would not come without some bureaucratic pain, but it would be worth the effort. Abba Eban once noted that individuals and governments seem to act wisely only when they have exhausted all other alternatives. In Hawai'i, we have reached the point where wise action may be our only remaining choice.

Bibliography
Alcohol and Drug Abuse Division (1992-1993). HEED Reports. Honolulu: Department of Health (DOH).
Alcohol and Drug Abuse Division (1993). State Plan 1994-1997. Honolulu: DOH.
Alcohol and Drug Abuse Division Fact sheet. Honolulu: DOH. N. D.
Baker, F. (1991). Coordination of Alcohol, Dru*g Abuse, and Mental Health Services.* Technical Assistance Publication Services Number 4 (Pub. # ADM 91-1742) Washington, DC: Department of Health and Human Services.
Clark, H. (1993, November 24). Crackdown on Crocked Fails. *The Honolulu Advertiser.* p. A6.
Department of Justice. (1992). *Drugs, Crime, and the Justice System.* (NJC Report No. 133652). Washington, DC: U.S. Department of Justice.
Honolulu Police Department. Presentation to the Community Epidemiological Work Group. Honolulu: Research and Development Div.
Kresnak, W. (1993, November 24). Hawai'i Scores C+ on Drunk Driving Curbs. The Honolul*u Advertiser.* p. A3.
Osborne, D. & Gaebler, T. (1993). *Reinventing Government.* New York: Plume.
Staff. (1993). NASADAD Alcohol and Drug Abuse Report (Special Report: Issue No.1). Washington, DC: National Association of State Alcohol and Drug Abuse Directors.
Statewide Drug Prevention and Control Committee. (1991, January). A report to the governor on the Hawai'i statewide drug prevention and control strategy. Honolulu, HI: Office of the Attorney General.

Tomko, A.T. (1993, October 18). ONDCP will be Renewed, Despite Fireworks by Conyers. *Alcoholism & Drug Abuse Weekly*.

The White House (1990, 1991 and 1992). National Drug Control Strategy. Washington, DC: U.S. Government Printing Office.

The White House (1993). President's Commission on Model State Drug Laws. Washington, DC.

CHAPTER THIRTEEN

Community and Compassion
What We Learned from the AIDS Epidemic in Hawai'i

PAMELA LICHTY

The AIDS epidemic of the 1980's caught the United States and the rest of the world unaware. At a time when infectious diseases were thought to be virtually under control in the developed world, the sudden onset of this new epidemic surprised epidemiologists and other health professionals. As the epidemic grew, with its alarmingly-high case fatality rate, they struggled to understand its origins, its nature, and above all how to arrest its spread.

Now, more than a decade into the HIV/AIDS epidemic,[1] our understanding of the disease has deepened; the nature of HIV disease itself has changed; and above all it has caused us to reexamine the way the health-care system itself functions. Dealing with the HIV epidemic has led to major re-thinking in the health care arena, and the management of HIV disease has become an valuable model for effective, humane management of other chronic conditions. The self-empowerment of people with AIDS (PWAs) and their impact on institutions such as the Food and Drug Administration has inspired activists struggling with other conditions such as breast cancer. Hawai'i, with its system of community-based care and its early enactment of a body of progressive legislation, has developed a useful model for the nation as it deals in a compassionate and cost-effective manner with the most devastating epidemic of the late twentieth century.

The rubric of "access" encapsulates many of the issues surrounding AIDS. The epidemic has underscored the vital importance of access: to medical care, to psycho-social services, and particularly—without discrimination—to jobs, housing, and insurance coverage.

AIDS is a unique condition because it affects so many aspects of a person's health; because it can and does affect whole families; and, above all, because of the extraordinary stigma which has accompanied it since its first appearance. Despite its unique properties, however, the HIV epidemic holds many lessons for health-care professionals. Both civil rights and treatment issues surrounding AIDS have raised concerns which had not been linked in the past. As the extraordinary nature of AIDS revealed itself to us in the 1980's, it became clear that in addition to medical care, an effective strategy must include a full array of prevention and education services and psycho-social support services.

Foremost among the useful developments in dealing with the HIV/AIDS medical/social phenomenon has been the rise of multi-disciplinary, community-based care based on case management. In the community, AIDS activists have forced drug companies and the FDA to expedite clinical trials and hence the approval of promising drugs. Waivers have been approved to increase the flexibility of Medicaid.

Thanks to increasingly effective prophylactic treatments, the nature of HIV disease is changing. Whereas in the mid-1980's HIV disease meant two years before the onset of AIDS and then perhaps another two years of life, the average time from HIV diagnosis to AIDS is now ten to twelve years. After a person is diagnosed with AIDS, she now lives an average of two or three years, often longer. AIDS is now considered a chronic condition like heart disease or diabetes.

The HIV Epidemic in Hawai'i

Many observers have noted a certain lag time before mainland fads and fashions surface in Hawai'i. Luckily this pattern appears to hold true for epidemics as well.

The first AIDS case was diagnosed in Hawai'i in 1982, some two years after the first cases were identified on the U.S. mainland. For public-health planners, this lag time was invaluable in designing a strategy to fight the epidemic.

The natural history of HIV/AIDS in Hawai'i has closely parallelled the pattern in mainland cities, although —through luck, preparedness or demographics—Hawai'i has been spared the high numbers of AIDS cases seen elsewhere.

As in many major U.S. cities, Hawai'i's first cases appeared among male homosexuals or bisexuals in the early 1980's. The second wave of the epidemic occurred among injection drug users (IDUs) and their sexual partners, while the third wave, beginning in the early 90's, is appearing in the offspring of IDUs and in heterosexuals, with young adults at especially high risk. As of April, 1994, there were 1,393 official AIDS cases diagnosed in Hawai'i and reported to the Federal Centers for Disease Control and Prevention (CDC).[2] There were 811 AIDS-related deaths reported at this same time. (DOH, AIDS Surveillance Program, March 31, 1994).

Since the mid to late 80's, Hawai'i has had a relatively high per capita rate of HIV infection according to the CDC rank ordering of the states in terms of AIDS cases per 100,000 population.[3] Hawai'i's ranking has varied from 11th highest to 15th highest (at the end of 1993) with a downward trend. This has been variously interpreted as showing the efficacy of prevention and education efforts or, pessimistically, as showing how fast the epidemic is growing on the mainland.

In any case, throughout the 1980's and into the 1990's, Hawai'i has consistently placed in the second tier of states in terms of HIV/AIDS incidence, just below the states which have been the leaders in the epidemic since the early days: New York, New Jersey, Florida, Texas, and California.

Hawai'i's relatively high incidence, which surprises many people, is due to a combination of factors including a relatively large gay population, a large military population, and, above all, Hawai'i's role as a major transit point between East and West, and a place with huge numbers of visitors (approximately 6 million) per year. Tourists on vacation are in a relaxed mood which may translate into risky behaviors putting them at high risk for acquiring HIV. In addition, Hawai'i is a "state of travellers with many of its residents making frequent business and pleasure trips to foreign destinations." (Governor's Committee on AIDS, p. 27) Many of these overseas trips are to destinations where there is an active sex industry and a high prevalence of HIV infection.

A Proactive Response

> The fear [of AIDS] seems to override logic. In a
> recent study, researchers at Arizona State Univer-

sity asked several hundred business and science majors how they would feel about dining with silverware used by AIDS patients on the previous day (and then washed), the previous week and as much as a year ago. Although they were well informed factually about HIV disease, the majority admitted they would feel some lingering unease even after a year. (*Gelman, p. 79*)

Physicians, public health workers, the gay community and civil libertarians in Hawai'i made good use of their time advantage by analyzing the politics of the AIDS epidemic on the mainland. They acted quickly to propose a body of enlightened legislation to offset the social and political side effects of the epidemic. The early days of the HIV/AIDS epidemic were marked with real panic and hysteria. Houses were torched because family members had AIDS; HIV positive children were kicked out of school; and people with AIDS routinely lost their housing, jobs, and often family support. Few extreme incidents occurred in Hawai'i although dozens of people have lost jobs and housing due to discrimination.

All this was before Ryan White, the Indiana teenager with hemophilia, became a tragic folk figure; his virtual canonization via the media bespeaks a sea change in public awareness. In addition, the many celebrities dying of AIDS throughout the 1980's—like it or not—put the spotlight on the illness in a way that a thousand red ribbons never could.[4]

AIDS and The State Legislature

We were denied mortgage insurance, and adequate police services (despite documented and witnessed harassment by the neighbors), lost our home, car, pets, etc. and suffered severe mental, physical, and emotional stress, simply because we were a gay, bi-racial couple ill with AIDS. . . (*William Healy, testimony before Hawai'i State Legislature, 1991*)

In the face of such discrimination, safeguards must be in place to insure access to services. Thus, a series of proactive bills was introduced and enacted into law in Hawai'i. These included informed consent statutes with strong confidentiality provisions specifying the conditions under which a person could be tested for HIV, what could be done with the test results, and under what circumstances exceptions to the informed consent provisions were permitted.[5] Other measures enacted during the late 80's prohibited discrimination against persons with HIV disease in employment, housing, insurance, state-funded services and public accommodations. Among the key players in the passage of this body of progressive legislation were the Life Foundation, the Governor's Committee on AIDS[6], and the American Civil Liberties Union of Hawai'i and its then-staff attorney, Kirk Cashmere. These organizations looked to the epicenters on the East and West Coasts and adapted the most compassionate, public health-oriented legislation that had yet been developed.

Politicians, citizens and some worried health care organizations were looking to the mainland as well. In the climate of fear and sensationalism surrounding AIDS in the mid 80's, they looked to conservative states like Texas for inspiration. Countless bills were submitted which had been adopted verbatim from these other venues.

Each year since 1985, 25-30 bills have been introduced in the Hawai'i State Legislature which specifically mention HIV or AIDS. The vast majority of these bills are what AIDS activists label "punitive." They fall into the broad categories of confidentiality and testing, discrimination, and funding bills. The conservative forces accused the HIV activist groups of "making" AIDS political. Hindsight demonstrates that the politicization of AIDS has more to do with the circumstances in which it first appeared in the U.S. The fact that the first identification of HIV/AIDS in this country was in the gay community and then among injection drug users (largely African-American and Latino) set the tone for the public's reaction. The reality is that this disease first emerged within already marginalized groups. The growing politicization and in-your-face militancy of segments of the gay community (most notably ACT UP) grew in direct response to both the burgeoning numbers of deaths and the deafening silence and indifference of mainstream citizens and government.[7]

In Hawai'i many of the punitive bills called for HIV testing of specific segments of the population, sometimes without informed consent. The testing proposals variously targeted hospital patients (reflecting the fears of hospital workers about transmission despite estimates that an extremely small percentage of Hawai'i's in-patients are HIV positive) and health care workers (after the widespread publicity about six Florida patients acquiring HIV disease from their dentist, Dr. David Acer). But the most common targets were such unpopular groups such as prisoners and sex offenders. Other bills introduced year after year called for creation of a new crime of "intentional transmission" of HIV infection via unsafe sex or shared injection equipment. These latter bills were routinely defeated because of the other routes of prosecution available, the technical difficulties with proving intent, and because legislators saw the inhumanity and counterproductiveness of criminalizing a disease. Such proposals, however, forced HIV advocates to spend countless hours researching legal remedies, organizing opposition, and developing and presenting testimony.

HIV Organizations in Hawai'i

The Life Foundation (the AIDS Foundation of Hawai'i on Oahu) was founded in 1983, shortly after the first cases appeared here. For the first few years of the epidemic it was virtually alone in providing HIV/AIDS education and services.

Most of the early AIDS cases were on Oahu and HIV services were oriented toward Honolulu in the early years, engendering a certain amount of resentment from the neighbor islands. Gradually though, more AIDS cases were reported on the neighbor islands, and soon each island's percentage of AIDS cases corresponded roughly to its percentage of the population. In 1986, AIDS Foundations were established on all major islands: Malama Pono (the Kauai AIDS Project), the Maui AIDS Foundation, and the Big Island AIDS Project. All of these organizations benefited greatly from analyzing the growing pains of the non-governmental organizations (NGO's) on the mainland, and particularly from observing the evolution of the fast-growing Life Foundation.

In 1987 the AIDS Community Care Team (ACCT) was formed. A community-based consortium of more than 20 groups and individuals affected by HIV, ACCT now testifies as one entity at hearings. This coalition approach has been effective in lobbying for both policy and funding bills.

Hawai'i's Needle Exchange Program

In 1990, the Hawai'i State Legislature authorized the State Department of Health to establish a controversial two-year needle-exchange pilot project in Honolulu. Hawai'i thus became the first state to permit legal needle exchange, designed to prevent the spread of HIV, state-wide. (A few legal city-based programs existed in the U.S., and many abroad). In 1992, the law-makers voted to make it permanent.

The story behind this victory for public health and for AIDS prevention is one of hard work, commitment, and above all, a unified approach. In 1989, HIV infection rates were soaring among injection drug users (IDU's) on the mainland and tales of "AIDS babies" were rampant in the media. HIV advocates in Hawai'i decided to use the lead time, which an accident of geography had given Hawai'i, to try to prevent this rapid transmission among IDUs, their sexual partners, and offspring. Led by the Life Foundation, and with the all-important cooperation of the Hawai'i Medical Association (HMA), the Sterile Needle Exchange Coalition was formed in late 1989. Assisted by the Governor's Committee on AIDS and HMA, the Coalition soon grew to more than 20 groups, including the Hawai'i Chapter of the National Academy of Pediatrics, the Hawai'i Nurses' Association, the Hawai'i Public Health Association, the Department of Health, mainstream churches, and every HIV group in the state.

The Coalition organized a media blitz and briefed legislators and law-enforcement officials. They developed a solid lobbying strategy. They did their homework and offered compromise wording to meet every possible concern.

The final bill bore scant resemblance to the original; it was stuffed with oversight provisions, required evaluations and reports. But it did the trick. The needle-exchange program was up and running by July, 1990. Despite inevitable growing pains, it has become a model for progressive legislation and received consistently favorable evaluation from the Department of Health, Federal observers, and the participants themselves. It has proven to be a bridge to treatment, and has become a vital point of contact for providers who regard injection drug users as people first: people in need.

The Hawai'i AIDS Task Group, founded in 1985, has played an important role in forging consensus on problematic policy issues. This university-based group meets monthly, and provides a neutral setting in which to thrash out the implications of current policy debates. Non-HIV specific groups (including some adversarial groups such as the Hawai'i Federation of Physicians and Dentists) are invited to present their perspective, as are visitors from the mainland and overseas.

The Governor's Committee on HIV/AIDS (GCHA), founded in 1987, has played an even more critical role in the public sector. The Governor appoints its 21 members, who represent a cross-section of the community: physicians, social workers, nurses, people with AIDS, academics, and representatives from the major state departments (e.g., Health, Human Services, Education, Labor) affected by HIV disease. GCHA's small staff has a high profile in the State Legislature, as they promote the largely progressive policies painstakingly developed by the members. The Committee has played a key role in explicating the immensely complex social, medical, and political dilemmas raised by the HIV epidemic.

The STD/AIDS Prevention Branch of the State Department of Health is responsible for the programatic side of HIV services. It works closely with the GCHA and, in cooperation with community-based services, has developed a number of innovative programs. Among these are the Hawai'i AIDS Research Consortium (HARC), which conducts clinical trials; the Hawai'i Seroprevalence and Medical Management Program (HSPAMM) which provides biannual medical check-ups and follow-up; the Hawai'i Drug Assistance Program (HDAP) which subsidizes therapeutic or prophylactic drugs; and HCOBRA, which continues (Federal) medical insurance for persons with HIV disease who have lost their jobs. There is also the Community Health Outreach Worker Project (CHOW), which works with injection drug users. Formerly a Federally funded research-oriented project, the CHOW Project is now state-funded and administers part of the statewide needle-exchange program. DOH also has an HIV Coordinator in each county who assists in education, problem-solving and referrals to available services.

The Politics of Funding

Throughout the late 80's and early 90's, the HIV activist groups and their government and non-government allies became more sophisticated in dealing with the State Legislature. In 1988, for the first time, the AIDS Omnibus Bill, spearheaded by Representative Jim Shon, provided state funding to the burgeoning HIV service organizations. (Federal funding, primarily for counseling, testing and prevention education had been flowing to the state since 1985).[8]

Hawai'i in 1988 became one of the first states to obtain a Medicaid Waiver. This permitted a cost-effective and humane funding/treatment approach whereby PWAs can receive the gamut of necessary medical and psycho-social services at home as an alternative to extended hospitalization. A network of organizations such as PacifiCare grew up to provide direct services and volunteer training to in-home assistants.

In the first years of state funding, the growing numbers of HIV service agencies were scrambling for the same piece of the pie, trying to differentiate themselves in the legislators' eyes and trying to out-finesse one another. It became apparent that a unified approach would work better.

The AIDS Community Care Team (ACCT) was founded in 1987, partly in response to this situation. When the Ryan White CARE Act Federal funding became available in 1991, calling for a statewide consortium to distribute funds and coordinate services, ACCT was ready. At that time, it acquired non-profit status, formalized its procedures, hired part-time staff, and focused on presenting a unified front for both funding and policy efforts. This coalition approach was welcomed by state legislators since it simplified their task and eased the painful prioritization of funding that had historically been part of the appropriations game. ACCT developed written agreements asking each member group to commit to lobbying solely for the overall funding. They tried to achieve the same unanimity in terms of policy recommendations. This was more problematic since each organization's board set policy, but there was generally agreement on the major recurring issues surrounding testing, confidentiality, discrimination, and other issues.

The Future

Trends in HIV incidence in Hawai'i in the early 90's continue to parallel those of the mainland. The third wave of the epidemic is manifest in increasing numbers of HIV-infected women and children; the neighbor islands have increasing numbers while Oahu's have never slackened. The groups with the greatest percentage increase in cases from 1991-1993:

By age: 40-49 year olds
By behavior: Heterosexual contact
By gender: Females
By race: Hispanic

(AIDS Surveillance Quarterly Report, DOH, Cases to March 31, 1994)

In some of these groups, such as females, the numbers are small and thus percentage increases are very misleading (e.g., if the number of cases jumps from two to six), but the trends are clear. As indicated, more people of color and women are becoming infected. These changes necessitate a new awareness and sensitivity on the part of health care providers, counselors, and testers. In the case of women, an expanded array of symptoms and some difficult ethical and medical issues arise when an HIV positive woman becomes pregnant. In addressing the needs of people of color, a multitude of linguistic and other cultural barriers, such as ethnic groups where sex is not mentioned, must be overcome.

Neighbor Island Problems

The neighbor islands and their overworked HIV service organizations face special challenges in the 90's. Despite being categorized as "rural" by the Federal government, they experience problems common to both rural and urban America. They have injection drug users in increasing numbers. On Kauai and Lanai, where the physical and social dislocation of Hurricane Iniki and rapid resort development respectively have brought in large numbers of young construction workers from the mainland, drugs are now more readily available. As in small towns everywhere, there are problems ensuring confidentiality at testing sites and concerns about the reporting of AIDS cases to DOH.

For HIV-infected people who are symptomatic, specialized care involving certain technology or procedures is often unavailable on the neighbor islands. This can mean expensive, inconvenient, and exhausting travel to Honolulu with a time-consuming paper trail required to justify the expense. For pediatric patients, periodic trips to the state's Pediatric Immunology Clinic based at Kapiolani Medical Center for Women and Children in Honolulu are the only option.

Access Issues: Financing of Health Care

> I feel I am quite fortunate because I know how to access the system. I know all the "right" people. I know how it operates. I know what my rights are. And I know where to go for assistance, because I am part of the system professionally...But what about the people who don't have the ability to access the system due to social, economic or educational barriers? How do they access a hostile system, a system designed to discourage their use and participation? *(Andrew Ziegler, MHSA, testifying before the National Commission on AIDS, Washington, D.C., September 1990.)*

Some of the most complex unresolved issues in Hawai'i deal with health-care insurance coverage and HIV/AIDS. Many Medicaid recipients, especially on the neighbor islands, have difficulty finding a provider to care for them. Part of this is due to a reluctance among physicians to treat people with HIV disease, or the fact that the one "AIDS doctor" in a given community may be unwilling or unable to accept new patients. The inadequacy of Medicaid reimbursement to physicians and dentists coupled with the burdensome paperwork means that some of them refuse to see Medicaid patients. Although this problem has historically been worse among dentists, it is impossible to determine whether the refusal to treat Medicaid patients is just a convenient pretext for refusing to treat HIV-infected persons.

The second issue is what use insurance companies can legally make of the HIV test results of applicants or clients. The Insurance Commissioner has been under pressure to clarify these provisions, but both Robin Campaniano and his successors have been reluctant to promulgate rules. The Legislature for various reasons (such as the fact that key committee chairs work for insurance companies) has been unwilling to touch this hot potato. In the absence of specific rules, insurers can do what they like with test results. Luckily, since most insured persons in Hawai'i are in a group plan and not subject to health exams, the issue has not been a major problem thus far. A key lesson of the epidemic is that, as people with HIV disease stay healthy longer, it is both compassionate and cost-effective to keep them in the work force and not force them to "spend-down" until they qualify for Medicaid.

An ongoing issue in the financially straitened 90's is the allocation of funding for direct services for people with HIV disease versus funding for HIV education and prevention. This is one of those painful decisions that the Legislature forces on itself each session since the health and human service pie is continually shrinking, while the "pork pie" becomes ever fatter. All of these struggles are proceeding more or less invisibly since the media attention has moved on to newer and sexier issues. Sadly, it seems to take a Rock Hudson or a Magic Johnson to turn the press's attention back to the relentless killer in our midst.

Lessons of the HIV Epidemic in Hawai'i

If there is anything HIV advocates have learned from political struggles on the national and state level, it is that a unified approach is all important, especially when the most affected groups are historically marginalized and out of the mainstream. Although the message is slowly getting through that AIDS affects everyone, old stereotypes die hard. When dealing with a condition that can be devastating on so many levels, it is no wonder that there is a tendency to think of AIDS as happening to someone else.

With national health care reform high on the agenda for the remainder of Clinton's term, the AIDS experience in Hawai'i could play an important role. Just as Hawai'i's health care coverage, despite its shortcomings, became a model for the Clinton plan, Hawai'i's community-based, progressive approach to HIV disease could be a model: not only for dealing with HIV, but for any chronic disease.

Case management, home-based care, specialized housing, and the prominent role of non-governmental agencies have proven beneficial for people with HIV disease and for the community at large (by freeing up acute care beds, eliminating duplication, etc.) Most significantly, in the eyes of national health reform planners, these new modalities have proven to be cost-effective ways of dealing with an epidemic which is at the same time a chronic disease condition for hundreds of thousands of Americans.[9]

Of primary importance are community-based services and responsive multi-disciplinary government services and, above all, access to those services. Access must reach beyond availability of insurance, since each individual's situation includes multiple dimensions: social, legal, medical, psychological. Access includes case management (vitally important for PWAs with their multiple needs), culturally appropriate outreach and education, as well as assistance with transportation, housing and other non-medical needs. Access to care is unarguably better in Hawai'i than elsewhere in the U.S., and the innovations developed to address the HIV epidemic, such as the flexible financing of care via such mechanisms as the Medicaid waiver, are models that reformers in Washington could profitably examine as they re-think America's immensely complicated health care dilemmas.

References

1. "HIV/AIDS" or "HIV disease," rather than "AIDS," has become the preferred terminology since the latter represents only the last stage of this usually prolonged condition. In January, 1993, the Centers for Disease Control and Prevention (CDC) expanded the AIDS surveillance case definition of adolescents and adults to include all HIV-infected persons with severe immunosuppression, pulmonary tuberculosis, recurrent pneumonia or invasive cervical cancer. These changes had the effect of artificially inflating the numbers of official (reported) AIDS cases for at least one year. This expanded definition more quickly moves infected people into the "disability" category. More psychosocial support services will be needed for people who may feel "okay," but nonetheless have an AIDS diagnosis and may be experiencing the stresses associated with learning of it.

2. It is generally acknowledged that, due to concerns about confidentiality, particularly in rural areas, these "official" numbers represent an undercount of actual cases although no one can estimate the extent of unreported cases.

3. State-licensed labs report the numbers of HIV positive persons to the CDC cumulatively and anonymously. The numbers of AIDS cases reported are those which meet the CDC definition of AIDS. Persons with AIDS who were diagnosed in other states, but are now living in Hawai'i are not counted in the CDC tally. This becomes an important fiscal

issue since Federal AIDS funds are allocated to each state according to the number of reported cases there. Among conservative state legislators have speculated that scores of people with AIDS are "coming here to die" due to the purported generosity of Hawai'i's AIDS services. The data, however, do not bear out these concerns.

4. As in other health policy areas (notably abortion), terminology and rhetoric are critical in the AIDS arena. Many persons with AIDS have become highly politicized, and have made it clear that they do not wish to be characterized as "victims" nor as persons "suffering from" AIDS, but rather as people with AIDS (PWAs) or people "living with," not "dying from," AIDS (PLWAs).

5. Hawai'i Revised Statues (HRS) 325-16 (Informed Consent) and HRS 325-101 (Confidentiality) are the major HIV/AIDS related provisions. These have been amended virtually every year since their original enactment in 1987.

6. Renamed the Governor's Committee on HIV/AIDS (GCHA) in 1992 to reflect the reality that AIDS is only the end stage of the spectrum of HIV disease.

7. The New York City experience became the prototype. Despite the escalating death toll in the mid 1980's, the official public health response was weak and ineffectual. In this vacuum, the Gay Men's Health Crisis was founded and became the model for effective community organizing, education, prevention, and direct services.

8. Hawai'i was the first state to establish anonymous HIV test sites with this Federal money. It was also the first state to mandate HIV education in the schools. Prevention education though — like every other aspect of HIV/AIDS — is permeated with politics. Because there is no cure for AIDS, education plays an even more vital role than it does with other transmissible diseases.

9. According to a report done by Dr. Sumner La Croix for GCHA, the average lifetime medical cost of a person with AIDS in Hawai'i (from time of symptomatic HIV infection to death) is $93,158-$115,295. Dr. La Croix concludes that the management of HIV in Hawai'i is an excellent model for the management of other chronic diseases and that many of the state-subsidized programs such as HCOBRA and HSPAMM are highly cost-effective. The average person with AIDS is between 30-40 years old, and at their highest earning capacity. If they are able to stay in the work force with the assistance of subsidy programs, the cost-savings to the state can be substantial.

PART FIVE

Managed Care or Damaged Care?

CHAPTER FOURTEEN
What's It All About?
Implications of Medicaid
Managed Care for Hawai'i
KATHRYN SMITH-RIPPER

This chapter will examine the issue of Hawai'i's public-policy shift from fee-for-service, retrospective reimbursement to prospective reimbursement through managed care for health-care services delivered to low-income individuals and families. From its inception in early 1993 until its proposed start date of August 1, 1994, the Health QUEST (Quality care, Universal access, Efficient utilization, Stabilizing costs, Transforming provision of health care) proposal has provoked surprise, confusion, praise, controversy, and in 1994, limited legislative oversight. How these developments came about and their implications for the future are reviewed below.

Hawai'i's Medicaid program dates to the early days of the Federal War on Poverty program. Congress created Medicaid in 1965. Hawai'i implemented its state program in 1966, one of the first six states to do so. Hawai'i's program has been seen as a "Cadillac" version since its benefit package included virtually all optional services authorized by the Federal government. The state also has a generous welfare enrollment standard at 62.5 percent of the Federal poverty level (set higher for Alaska and Hawai'i). Most states' standards are set at or below 50 percent of the Federal poverty level (GAO, 1994). In addition, as Congress permitted states to add to their caseloads by setting higher percentages of poverty for pregnant women and young children in the 1980s, Hawai'i chose to implement those eligibility standards before they became Federal mandates.

Although Hawai'i's program covered more services than many other states and offered those services to more low-income families and individuals, the program suffered from many of the same problems encountered on the mainland. Providers complained about the amount of paperwork required by the state and the lack of compliance by Medicaid patients, particularly their no-show rates for appointments. Reimbursement rates were

so low that many health-care providers either would not accept
Medicaid patients into their practices or capped the number of
patients accepted. Advocates complained that Medicaid patients
consequently were denied access to necessary services, causing
inappropriate use of emergency rooms for primary care and
hospital admissions for sicker patients.

The main similarity to mainland Medicaid programs was
growing concern about general funding costs. The deepening
recession on the mainland and abroad had the ripple effect of
increasing Hawai'i's welfare rolls. Welfare recipients are auto-
matically eligible for Medicaid coverage. The state Department
of Human Services (DHS) asked the Legislature for emergency
appropriations of approximately $105 million as it faced fund-
ing shortfalls in fiscal years 1992 and 1993. Psychiatric and dental service benefits were capped. Advocates argued that such
benefit limitations were not cost effective in the long run since
recipients denied outpatient therapy and treatment would only
show up in the health care system in a more acute condition.
Some community advocates argued that rather than cut service
levels, state funding for potentially reimbursable services delivered by the Department of Health (DOH) needed to be seen as
sources of additional Federal match revenue, a process popularly known as "maximization of Medicaid funds."

Governor John Waihee signaled his administration's response to the Medicaid program's burgeoning budget in his 1993
State of the State address: he announced that a Federal waiver
would be sought for publicly subsidized health-care services.
Since Federal mandates govern Medicaid program operations,
a state must get approval to waive any key aspects of the program. However, no details followed and providers, the public,
and community advocates were largely unaware of immediate
developments.

The Waihee Administration made a decision to try to
capitalize on ties to the incoming Clinton Administration as well
as take advantage of relaxed waiver request reviews by the Federal government. A Medicaid waiver request was put on the
fast track without public notice. Two reasons were subsequently
given for the lack of public awareness and outside input: that
such input would have slowed the process irreparably and that
waiver requests needed to be submitted prior to the anticipated

release of First Lady Hillary Clinton's proposed health-care reform package in early May, 1993.

Word of impending change had just begun to leak into the community when the Governor hand-delivered the waiver request for the Health QUEST program to Washington, DC, in mid-April, 1993. However, it took some time for the news and comprehension of its implications to spread throughout Hawai'i. Rev. Frank Chong, Executive Director of the Waikiki Health Center, commented on the process and its aftermath: "What is most disturbing is that the entire program appears to have been politically driven and rather than a problem-solving format, we are continually second-guessing each other" (Chong, 1993).

What Is QUEST?

The QUEST program is a five-year demonstration project which converts the way in which Medicaid services are paid for from a fee-for-service reimbursement system to a managed care system. Fee-for-service reimbursement provides a strong incentive for utilization of services since the care providers are paid for services retrospectively on a claims submission basis. In other words, providers are paid according to the volume of services delivered. Under this reimbursement system, provider concerns regarding bureaucratic hassles associated with the Medicaid program became issues large enough to help inhibit some providers from active participation in the program. Fee-for-service medicine is based on the concept of "freedom of choice:" the patient chooses her/his own primary care provider(s), specialists, and hospitals.

However, the concept of managed care is based on linking a patient with a primary care provider (known as a "gatekeeper") who "manages" the care received by that patient. The primary care provider must authorize referrals to specialists for example, and is responsible for the continuing care of the patient. Under QUEST, managed care will be reimbursed on a prospective, capitated basis (calculated on a per member per month basis). Essentially, the fiscal incentives for providers are the opposite. Under a fee-for-service system, providers are paid only when services are delivered; under a managed-care system, they are paid in advance, usually on a monthly basis, and out of that amount must cover all services provided to patients.

Each reimbursement system contains incentives for consumers as well. The traditional fee-for-service system of private health insurance requires annual deductibles and patient sharing of charges for office visits and procedures, e.g., an 80/20 split between the insurance payer and the patient. Medicaid recipients do not have to satisfy a deductible and services are paid in full by the government. Although the Federal government permitted states to assess co-payments for services, Hawai'i did not do so. Although there should not be fiscal disincentives to obtaining care for recipients, as noted above many providers would not accept Medicaid patients and as a consequence, recipients used emergency rooms as primary-care providers.

Under the QUEST program, most recipients will be assessed nominal co-payments in line with private managed-care plans and, above certain income levels, share in the cost of premiums. Pregnant women and infants with incomes up to 185 percent and individuals with income up to 133 percent of the Federal poverty level will not be assessed co-payments for services or share the costs of premiums. Families will not be liable for co-payments for services to children up to the age of 19, but could incur premium cost sharing for those children depending upon income levels. The effect of Medicaid recipients' shift from no out-of-pocket payments to possible co-payments per visit and monthly premium payments, albeit on a sliding scale for income levels, is unknown. The Waihee Administration included co-payments in the program as a means to discourage inappropriate use of services and, along with the premium sharing, to raise revenues which will offset program costs and to discourage families from shifting from employer-based insurance to QUEST. However, many health and human service advocates fear that such changes will pose fiscal barriers to accessing care for a vulnerable population, even though each QUEST member will be assigned a primary-care provider.

Under the waiver, recipients of Aid for Families with Dependent Children (AFDC) and General Assistance (GA) payments will be combined with State Health Insurance Program (SHIP) participants into the pool of potential QUEST participants. This total is estimated at more than 100,000 persons, 10 percent of the state's population (due to rising unemployment, the size of the potential pool has grown since the waiver's submission). DHS will contract with private health-care plans to provide a standard benefit package of medical, dental and behavioral health services. Participants in the SHIP program who join QUEST will see a dramatic increase in covered benefits.

Precedents

The concept of applying managed care to Medicaid recipients is not new: as of February, 1993, 36 states were operating one or more managed-care programs (Newacheck, 1994). The QUEST program is unique, however, with the inclusion of the SHIP and GA eligible populations, since the Federal government would be matching expenses for previously state-subsidized groups. Under existing operations, the Federal government matches the amount of state dollars spent on services provided to Medicaid recipients in Hawai'i on a 50/50 basis. The QUEST program will expand the numbers of individuals eligible for such a Federal match. Yet cost containment is to be assured through budget neutrality at the end of the five-year period; the state has promised the Federal government that even with the addition of these two new populations, Federal expenditures will not be any greater than they would have been under the current Medicaid system.

Shock and confusion followed the QUEST waiver request announcement. Community agencies and DOH programs which had spent several years trying to bill Medicaid for services, and/ or trying to create the claims-processing infrastructure to bill Medicaid, now faced the disheartening prospect of providing services to QUEST recipients without reimbursement opportunities—unless the services were subcontracted to the QUEST health care plans—or of losing those clients altogether. Community health centers fought hard to obtain cost-based reimbursement in 1990 and yet faced the same prospect. Community advocates also voiced concerns about the adequacy and provision of culturally-sensitive case management and outreach services under a managed-care system.

QUEST Hearings

The state Legislature did not hold hearings on QUEST in 1993, due to the waiver's release so close to the end of session. Several round-table discussions were held by legislative leaders of the Health and Human Services Committees over the summer. These sessions served as forums for providers and representatives of the health and human services sectors to give feedback on the proposal to DHS. Fine-tuning of the proposed project's implementation occurred as a result; there was no serious attempt to completely derail the project by the legislators. Only in the 1994 session were hearings devoted to the program; state legislators did raise concerns about QUEST including the program's budget and the lack of legislative authorization for the program. However, the sense from the House and Senate hearings was that of a foregone conclusion. Yet there was one serious legislative attempt to impede the program's implementation. Senator Donna Ikeda, Chair of the Ways and Means Committee, killed the Administration bill which transferred the SHIP appropriations from the DOH to DHS. This provision was later reinstated by the budget bill conference committee.

Two issues addressed by the 1994 Legislature are of note. First, maximization of Medicaid monies, the topic of previous legislative action and repeated hearings, was not raised. On the one hand, this made sense as QUEST would eliminate much of the DOH's opportunity to bill Medicaid on a fee-for-service basis. Yet, the larger issue of QUEST's potential impact on DOH programs which serve Medicaid and SHIP clients was not reviewed extensively. Second, however, the related topic of a possible new "gap" group created by QUEST was taken up by legislators. Legislators agreed with community advocates that administrative barriers within QUEST could serve to create a new medically indigent population. As a consequence of this concern, the QUEST budget includes $1 million for services to the uninsured (this money will not be matched by the Federal government). This allocation stemmed from the SHIP program's previous funding of community health centers for services to the uninsured.

So what are the factors conducive to such a rapid and major public policy shift in the delivery and financing of health care for Hawai'i's disadvantaged populations and what are some of the preliminary results? Certainly the secrecy surrounding the QUEST program's development served its purpose as the work could be conducted without interruption or interference. However, what can be viewed as expediency by the Waihee Administration was seen by many in the community as confirmation of the inability to trust government agencies. The radical change in the Federal approach toward waiver requests for changes in a state's Medicaid program was critical to the quick and positive response given to Hawai'i's proposal. Waihee Administration proponents of QUEST saw the Clinton Administration's endorsement of "managed competition" as needed to achieve cost containment through a privatized delivery system. Another key factor contributing to the speed with which the program progressed was the lack of legislative scrutiny of the proposal: by the time informational hearings were held during the summer, 1993, the waiver had been submitted and approved.

An interesting result of the shift to managed care is the delivery system which will handle the program. Only one outside health-care plan entered the Hawai'i market, Denti-Care from California, despite predictions that mainland insurers with an eye on national health-care reform would see this as an opportunity to break into the local market. The most intriguing consequence of the QUEST proposal is the evolution and creation of AlohaCare, a plan based on the state's eight community health centers. A huge risk for the centers, incorporation of AlohaCare represents their chance at maintaining their patient base, estimated to include 30 percent of the projected QUEST population. As primary-care providers to all comers, it serves Hawai'i well to have the AlohaCare plan launched in order to preserve the integrity and existence of the state's community health centers.

A cornerstone of any managed-care program delivery system is the acceptance by the physician community of capitated reimbursement. QUEST has placed this issue squarely before Hawai'i's physicians in one fell swoop. Many in the physician community realized the fiscal implications of QUEST and mobilized for opposition in the 1994 legislative session. Sectors within the physician community advocated in the Legislature for mandated access by patients to specialists and for the dismissal of QUEST altogether. These efforts were partially successful as the bill authorizing the SHIP appropriations transfer was questioned as noted above and the bill mandating access to specialists progressed from the Senate to the House. Veteran legislative observers predict that legislative efforts to protect physician specialists' interests will emerge in next year's session as well. It is not clear how many and which physicians statewide will sign on with any or all of the five health care plans approved by DHS to provide QUEST medical services. If, as a hospital executive on the mainland has said, "Capitation isn't just a payment system; it's a different way of practicing medicine," (*Hospitals and Health Networks*, 1994), then QUEST will have gone far in changing the landscape of medical practice in Hawai'i.

Finally, the incoming governor and next three Legislatures will inherit the QUEST program's implementation and final budget costs to the state. Health-care plan administrators and community agency staff alike predict widespread confusion and chaos during the initial conversion and enrollment process. Yet the QUEST program ultimately will be evaluated by other measures: cost containment and access to and quality of care delivered. Community advocates' fears revolve around this relationship between cost containment and service delivery. A mainland commentator aptly summarizes these concerns as follows: "Consumers can't help but wonder whether they can trust a managed-care system that's so focused on cost that it may not pay enough attention to the quality of care that its providers are delivering." (Mendenhall, 1994)

Bibliography

Chong, Frank. (1993). "President's Message: the QUEST." *Ke Ola Kino*, Winter, 1993, p. 1.
General Accounting Office. (1994). "Health Care in Hawai'i: Implications for National Reform." Washington, D.C., p. 3.
General Accounting Office. (1993). "Medicaid: States Turn to Managed Care to Improve Access and Control Costs." Washington, D.C., p. 38.
Mendenhall, Mel E. (1994). "Managed Care Must do More to Truly Manage Specialty Care." *Modern Healthcare*, April 11, 1994, p. 40.
Montague, Jim. (1994). "Capitation and Physicians: Experienced providers say involvement is crucial to success." *Hospitals and Health Networks*, April 5, 1994, p. 30.
Newacheck, Paul W., Hughes, Dana C., Stoddard, Jeffrey J. & Halfon, Neal. (1994). "Children with Chronic Illness and Medicaid Managed Care." *Pediatrics*, Vol. 93, Issue 4, pp. 497-500.
Stano, Miron. (1994). "Outcomes Research: High Hopes, Low Yield?." *The Journal of American Health Policy*, 4, 2, p. 52.

CHAPTER FIFTEEN

Assuring Quality in Medicaid Managed Care
Protecting Hawai'i's Women and Children

GERI MARULLO AND CHENOA FARNSWORTH

This chapter will offer a sound argument for the continued development of Hawai'i's historical commitment to strong maternal and child health public policy and quality assurance mechanisms through the implementation of Hawai'i's new Medicaid managed care program, Health QUEST[1]. Of primary concern are the 56,579 children (Dayton, 1994) and their mothers living below 300 percent of poverty who will be part of this five-year managed care demonstration project.[2]

In light of the startling lack of evidence that managed care assures quality health care services and outcomes for poor mothers and children, Hawai'i's stakeholders have not yet committed themselves to negotiate and measure maternal and child health quality of care through creative delivery design and measurable outcomes. Considering that 1.29 billion state and Federal dollars will be invested in this demonstration project over the next five years, QUEST presents a unique opportunity to evaluate and monitor the effect of Hawai'i's managed care experiment on the maternal and child health population.

Essentially, we suggest a mandated and structured oversight committee for QUEST, independent of the state Department of Human Services (DHS), to watch over the quality of care for women and children in this new system. As the following literature review will show, an investment in solid research about the effects of managed care on our women and children is needed to guide future success of Hawai'i's health care.

Literature Review: Does Managed Care Help Women and Children?

Although managed care and managed competition are sometimes considered the cost-containment reform policy of the decade, both national and local health care policy-makers have neglected to address the true effect on quality of care. Hawai'i, like 37 other states, has embarked upon the revamping of its publicly-funded Medicaid benefit and gap-group insurance programs through "waiving" current Federal requirements and substituting partial or total managed care and privatization programs. Within the last year alone, the Federal government has granted comprehensive Medicaid waivers to five states: Tennessee, Oregon, Hawai'i, Rhode Island, and Kentucky.

Hawai'i, like most other states participating in Medicaid waiver programs, turned to managed care to control the runaway costs of subsidizing care to the Medicaid population. The $40 million Medicaid shortfall in 1991, the $64 million shortfall in 1992, and the projected $80 million shortfall for 1993, prompted quick action by the executive branch to develop an alternative program and to apply for a Medicaid managed-care waiver.[3]

To suggest that managed-care programs reduce overall health costs or increase the quality of care, especially for poor women and children, is purely an intuitive statement in most of the literature and discussions of this controversial issue. Of more than 200 articles surveyed, not one suggests a significant correlation between increased quality of care for women and children and either Medicaid or non-Medicaid managed-care programs. On the contrary, much has been written about the lack of conclusive evidence in this regard (Fox, McManus & Liebowitz, 1993).

No Evidence of Improved Quality

Authors Freund and Lewit (1993) suggest that available research does not support most claims of cost savings[4] and improved quality of care for children and pregnant women as a result of managed care. "It is difficult to prove that managed care reduces the total societal costs of health care for children and pregnant women or that it slows the rate of growth in these costs. About the only consistent finding is that managed care reduces emergency room use[5] by children enrolled in Medicaid and tends to concentrate their care among a smaller number of providers."[6]

Goldfarb, Hillman et al. (1991) examined the much acclaimed Philadelphia mandatory Medicaid case management program, HealthPASS, on the adequacy of prenatal care and birth outcomes among 217 enrollees. The conclusion: no significant differences were detected in the outcomes of the fee-for-service model versus the managed care model for Medicaid recipients. Since HealthPASS did not make it a goal to change provider or patient behavior with respect to obstetrical care, there was little surprise at the results. Carey, Weiss and Homer (1991) found the same results in their comparison of 2,339 in-patient and 823 prenatal care records of clients enrolled in both capitated and fee-for-service programs for AFDC (Aid to Families with Dependent Children) families. Valdez, Ware et al. (1989) found no significant differences in the health outcomes of 693 children in Seattle randomly assigned to either a staff model HMO or one of several fee-for-service insurance plans.

At a hearing during the 1994 Hawai'i legislative session, Gretchen Engquist, a mainland consultant, testified on behalf of DHS regarding the QUEST program: ". . .the quality of care is better under managed care programs in other states, especially for children."[7] Because of the lack of data in this area the Department of Health (DOH) asked for confirmation of her remarks. In response, two reports were sent. Prepared for HCFA (Health Care Financing Administration) review by Laguna Research Associates (1993) and SRI International (1989), both evaluated the Arizona managed care program, AHCCCS (Arizona Health Care Cost Containment System). The reports compared the health outcomes for Arizona under managed care with those for New Mexico under the traditional fee-for-service Medicaid system, and confirmed that there appeared to be slight or no difference between the two states in regards to real maternal and child health outcomes. Interestingly, in the 1994 *Kids Count Data Book*, a composite of health indicators ranks Arizona as 37th and New Mexico as 46th, indicating that neither state is doing well at providing health services to this vulnerable population. Hawai'i was ranked 18th in 1994.

Finally, in a comprehensive briefing report for the Child and Adolescent Health Policy Center, Fox and McManus (1992) conclude that little reliable evidence exists on the effect of managed care on the quality of care for children and adolescents. Freund and Lewit (1993) add that not only has the quality of care received by children and pregnant women in all care settings not been well studied, but even less attention has been paid to developing mechanisms to monitor and assure quality in the various managed-care plans currently being offered or developed.

Public Policy and QUEST: Who is Driving?

Although QUEST will provide care to one-tenth of Hawai'i's population (approximately 110,000 persons) and to those families and children most environmentally at risk, the program did not follow the state and national policy trends toward comprehensive planning, policy integration and outcome-based performance measurement. Despite this extensive movement, especially in Governor Waihee's sponsored initiatives[8], QUEST chose not to consider it a priority to integrate existing administrative policy initiatives into a comprehensive approach to maternal and child health service delivery and evaluation.

According to QUEST developers, the decision to fast-track development of the program eliminated the opportunity for inclusive health planning and policy development among MCH advocates and consumers. Such inclusiveness was not a priority for the granting Federal agency, HCFA. Due to its own run-away costs, HCFA has relaxed prior restrictions on the requirements and number of Medicaid waivers (Blankenau, 1993).

In retrospect, the speed of the waiver process has proven to be problematic in the attainment of a successful implementation in other states. As stated in the National Association of Public Hospital's critical review of Tenncare, Tennessee's Medicaid waiver project (1994), ". . .HCFA has tended to treat waiver requests almost as if they were proprietary trade secrets. This situation must stop if the waiver and demonstration process is to result in good public policy."

Lacking a more public and inclusive process, three major policy issues, developed internally by DHS, set a profound policy course with regard to maternal and child health for Hawai'i.

They were simply: 1) to make QUEST a purely medical or physi-ological model of service delivery with outreach and support services optional; 2) not to require linkages with existing core public services for this population as part of the RFP (Request for Proposal); and 3) not to include measurable outcome-based objectives as part of the short and long-term plan evaluation.

A Medical Model: Outreach and Support
Services Made Optional

The decision to make outreach and other support ser-vices optional for the plans symbolized a dramatic shift in pro-gressive maternal and child health policy in Hawai'i. Broader maternal and child health services, spear-headed by the state legislature, policy makers and advocates within government, community-based providers and consumers, had shifted in past years from traditional medical services to funding innovative programs and intensive outreach and community-based support services programs. The Perinatal Support Services program is an example of such an innovative community-based approach to health care. This state-wide program tracks high-risk moth-ers and does intensive follow-up to see that they receive timely and appropriate prenatal care, as well as such support services as counseling, referral to programs such as Healthy Start or BabySAFE,[9] and transportation. In 1992 the Perinatal Support program served 2,070 women statewide. About half of them did not have health insurance even though they were eligible,[10] and the majority ethnic group was Hawai'ian or part Hawai'ian. The most dramatic result for participating women was the drop in the prematurity rate to 5.0 per 1,000 live births, compared with 17.1 per 1,000 live births for the state. However, the developers of QUEST did not consider these program innovations a core value in development of their design.

These policy decisions run contrary to the primary rea-son for granting Medicaid waivers, which according to Sally Richardson (1994), the new Medicaid Director, includes "requir-ing that the state look at new concepts, new solutions to prob-lems and different ways of solving problems."

DHS's more traditional thinking included the decision to develop a back-up state-run outreach program for the Feder-ally required and narrowly defined, basic outreach. This program will be utilized by those participating plans not interested in incorporating outreach into their managed care design and capitated rate. Again, without engaging an inclusive planning process, DHS unilaterally decided to use a Federal and state funded welfare reform program, JOBS (Job Opportunities and Basic Skills) as the vehicle for this outreach. This program currently reaches about 4,500 women. The QUEST component of JOBS, called KeikiQUEST, will utilize a public health nursing model to monitor timely compliance of families to EPSDT (Early and Periodic Screening, Diagnosis and Treatment) schedules.[11] Currently the DOH is in discussion with DHS to negotiate the broader involvement of community-based providers in this KeikiQUEST effort.

The current EPSDT outreach plan, however, represents only the required denominator of what can be done to increase access and successful utilization of QUEST services. California, for example, is receiving millions of Federal dollars in Medicaid reimbursement through administrative claims for a broad range of services to the Medi-Cal population. These services include: outreach and intensive informing, case finding, facilitating Medi-Cal application, pre-screening and enrollment, skilled professional assessment and case planning and coordination, client assistance to access services, and interagency coordination (Medi-Cal Administrative Claiming, 1993). Hawai'i's MCH advocates will continue to pursue this type of outreach and support services expansion in the next legislative session if DHS needs additional policy direction and support in this area.

In addition to expansion of services such as those provided through Medi-Cal, several design options for delivering basic required outreach under QUEST were not explored among the maternal and child health stakeholders. Separating the outreach piece from the basic design created other options including: direct subcontracts between the plans and existing community outreach providers;[12] contracts between DHS and maternal and child health community-based providers; and development of an RFP, outside of state-run programs, requesting innovative proposals for community-based outreach.

In contrast, California's Medical Managed Care Program (Medi-Cal) decided not to carve out from managed-care plans the responsibility for providing essential target prevention and early intervention, including follow-up and case management. Medi-Cal has also mandated continued exploration and integration of programs including their maternal and child health branch to help develop guidelines and protocols for managed-care providers. For example, a signed interagency agreement between the California Department of Health and Department of Human Services will co-monitor children's mental-health services.

The direction presented by California has been replicated elsewhere and supported by numerous studies regarding outreach and its effectiveness on Medicaid programs. A recent study of Pennsylvania's 67 counties found that outreach programs significantly increased access for the medically needy and categorically needy populations[13] (Stine, 1991). Goodman (1993), on other studies, reached a similar conclusion stating that "to be truly effective, Medicaid managed-care programs must implement strong community outreach programs."

No Linkage Mandate With Core Public Health Providers

A substantial amount of support services and care are delivered outside the doctor's office, especially for targeted high-risk women and children with special health needs. Hawai'i's failure to require the involvement of other publicly-funded providers in their capitated managed care arrangements is unfortunately consistent in the 27 states reviewed by the Maternal and Child Health Public Research Center. The services reviewed included other Federal- and state-funded programs such as early intervention services for children with developmental delays, services for children with special health needs and multiple handicaps, maternity support services, children's mental services and school-based services. Moreover, the few states that have tried to require or promote linkages between managed care and other publicly-funded provider networks have addressed at most two services (Fox and Wicks, 1993).

According to Hughes (1993), Medicaid beneficiaries, because of their more stressful living circumstances, often have a greater need than the general population for services that affect health status but are not considered medical care. These include psycho-social support, counseling, and care coordination. The implication of these findings is that any plan effectively serving poor women and children should have available a comprehensive arrangement of services. Hughes' findings are supported by Goodman (1993) in his statement that Medicaid managed care programs "need to invest in social service programs that address the cultural and societal barriers to a healthy lifestyle."

The failure to mandate involvement with existing public health programs in the implementation of QUEST may prove very painful for the state as well as for the five plans in their longer term "societal" cost containment efforts. The lack of integration of public health services has been well documented with regard to the Arizona Medicaid managed care model. In fact, the ASTHO (Association of State and Territorial Health Officials) review of the Arizona program (1993) reports that the Arizona public health infrastructure and expertise was not utilized in either the planning or implementation of Arizona. ASTHO indicates in its report that the lack of integration and collaboration may responsible for the difficulties Arizona experienced during its implementation. The report concludes: "Only by collaborating will public health and health care delivery systems assure a full range of outreach, targeted and appropriate services delivery emphasizing preventative health services and including appropriate monitoring of quality and user satisfaction."

No Measurable Outcome-based Objectives

The most troubling decision made in the QUEST policy vacuum, was to exclude or at least phase outcome objectives into the QUEST quality assurance piece. These measure results, not inputs, and set goals, not minimum standards for achievement.[14] According to Benson (1992) there are several reasons to adopt measurable outcome objectives including: 1) prioritization of improvements; 2) consumer information; 3) effectiveness evaluation; and 4) goal setting.

QUEST designers chose not to follow this national trend towards outcomes development and turned to a generic model of basic input data collection, the Health Plan Employer Data and Information Set 2.0 (HEDIS 2.0) created by the National Committee for Quality Assurance (NCQA) as a quality assurance system. HEDIS 2.0 quality measurements include: immunization rates, cholesterol screening, mammography screening, and pap smear rates. These indicators measure services performed and, by inference, can track progress, and include some outcome indicators. However, no goals or benchmarks for these indicators are set to create strong incentives for the plans. For example, a goal that establishes a 10 percentage decrease of low birthweight babies for high risk mothers tends to encourage the development of alternative care strategies. Higher birthweights may result through strategies such as nutritional monitoring, smoking cessation programs and stressor management. Thoughtful primary preventive outreach may assure that mothers of previous low-birthweight babies receive first trimester prenatal care.

The maternal and child health population is one of the best targeted populations to assess because of direct correlations with other universal and established health status indicators collected by most states. The Association of Maternal and Child Health Programs (1993) strongly urge that managed care plans should be required to collect and report a uniform set of carefully developed data. The Association also advocates measuring not only by health status indicators but also by developmental and functional indicators.[15]

There are a number of outcome-based initiatives on the state and national level which QUEST officials could consider, which do focus on maternal and child health. These initiatives include real outcome objectives with benchmarks developed through an arduous process of community and consumer involvement.

At least five broad, outcome-based indicators development projects are currently underway in Hawai'i. Most of these projects include both state and local counterparts, and focus on the maternal and child health populations. Three of them emphasize health issues: 1) Governor's Family Policy Academy; 2) Healthy Hawai'i 2000; and 3) Hawai'i Kids' Count. Currently, these projects are dialoging under the guidance of the Hawai'i Chamber of Commerce to create a common set of goals and indicators for the state.

The Governor's Family Policy Academy includes appointed representatives from both the public and private sectors. After a two year process of discussion involving much community input, the academy developed seven goals ranging from housing to health to education and 36 indicators with benchmarks to measure the progress of families in Hawai'i.

The Healthy Hawai'i 2000 (HH 2000) project, spearheaded by DOH, is reviewing the 332 national objectives for Healthy People 2000 and creating a set of goals and indicators specific to Hawai'i's needs. Since June, 1993, HH 2000 has sponsored numerous conferences and workshops to promote its project and receive community input. Thus far, HH 2000 has identified nineteen areas for health indicators and is in the process of developing correlating benchmarks.

In January 1993, the Hawai'i Kids' Count project got underway with the selection of partners and an advisory council composed of both public and private advocates and constituents for maternal and child health. The Hawai'i Kids Count project will examine what data to collect for Hawai'i's children and will attempt to draw attention to these statistics in order to direct program and policy development for Hawai'i's youths.

The outcomes movement , combined with a need to justify state expenditures in these times of fiscal constraint, has fueled new interest in outcomes-based legislation. Senate Bill 3286 represents the boldest such legislation introduced in Hawai'i. Introduced by Senator Andrew Levin, the bill mandated both public and private adherence to "a common goal and a common set of performance standards for both public and private providers of maternal and child health services." Had the bill passed, it would have covered QUEST, and would have created a leveled playing field for all MCH providers. As West Hawai'i Family Support Services Program Director JoAnn Freed wrote:

> The State of Hawai'i has established many fine Maternal and Child Health programs which have begun to have a positive impact on the health outcomes put forth in this bill. My fear is that the emphasis on these outcomes may be lost in the transition from a public health to a managed health care perspective.

House Concurrent Resolution 454, introduced by Representative Dennis Arakaki, represented a similar attempt to incorporate outcomes-based objectives into state government.

Although, the outcome-based legislative proposals were unsuccessful in the 1994 Hawai'i State Legislature, similar initiatives have passed in other progressive health states. Oregon Benchmarks represents the foremost example of this type of legislation in the nation. In 1991, the Oregon legislature passed

Senate Bill 636, which designated certain benchmarks as the focus for public programs for the next five years. Accompanying legislation, House Bill 3310, required Oregon's Governor and Executive Department to budget according to the priorities established by the benchmarks.

Although the effectiveness of bold legislation such as Oregon's has not yet been analyzed, it is clearly the wave of the future. It increases accountability of state government, and sets funding priorities which, if implemented in Hawai'i, would include programs such as QUEST. The trend of outcome-based performance measurement as a basis for QUEST quality assurance has hopefully only been postponed until the next legislative session or the next amendment to the QUEST contracts.

Conclusion

Currently, there is no formal or informal mechanism for ongoing input to QUEST by the community-at-large, especially experts in the field of MCH and managed care. With the change of Administrations in December of 1994, it is critical to develop a strong transitional group that will oversee the development of a solid policy for MCH and improve health status outcomes in our troubled times.

As of now, the full evaluation component for QUEST will include an independent outside evaluation, as well as an internal evaluation, which may include a number of auditing and monitoring techniques (QUEST RFP, 1993). However, what we monitor over the next five years may not be (in retrospect) what we really want to know about the MCH population under managed care.

Standard quality assurance mechanisms may not monitor whether appropriate linkages and referrals were made to critical support services for high risk pregnancies, nor will it monitor the overall effect of the health status of low birthweight babies in relation to mitigating developmental delay. The data will not report the efficacy of family planning on the level of unplanned pregnancy, nor will it tell us the outcomes of pediatric patients treated for ear infections (otitis media) in relationship to ear tubes (laryngotomy). We need to measure the effectiveness of health care provided, rather than the level of service utilization. Without measurable outcomes the private sector plans have no policy direction for women and children except to cost contain and control utilization.

These dilemmas lead to the necessity for policy and law makers to consider establishing, through legislation, an oversight committee for the QUEST program with a focus on maternal and child health. Similar legislation in a different area was introduced and passed during the 1992 Hawai'i Legislative Session. Act 152 Relating to Infectious and Communicable Diseases created an oversight committee to monitor the progress of the experimental Hawai'i Needle Exchange Program. This could be used as a prototype for the QUEST surveillance.

Effective policy could be realized by an empowered oversight committee composed of health policy makers, consumers and community-based providers of MCH services (including prevention and early intervention services), DHS and the five plans contracted to deliver the managed-care services under QUEST. The committee would be given the authority and the appropriate resources to 1) negotiate common and overlapping measurable outcomes and objectives; 2) conduct surveys and research (in conjunction with the University and private foundations) on specific targeted populations such as native Hawai'ians; 3) recommend and enact necessary changes in health delivery structure when there is no evidence of managed care success; 4) review the level of coordination of public services with QUEST systems; and 5) survey "non-compliant" consumers, or high-risk families that have not been able to access care.

As current literature regarding maternal and child health under Medicaid managed care has shown, improvements for this population are not guaranteed: in fact, health status may decline. For Hawai'i, the universal Health State, this should be reason enough to broaden the commitment to make managed care work for more than just the agency implementing the waiver.

Ultimately, if we are to pay more than mere lip service to consumer empowerment, a yearly report card which would score the plans should be published. Negotiated categories could include a description of the managed care design of each plan, success rates in reaching their measurable goals, patient satisfaction, and any special features or programs that have been successful in addressing the needs of this population.

If we demand oversight, Hawai'i, in its five-year report

to HFCA, will not describe a lack of significant change in the quality of care to our maternal and child health population, as has been the pattern established in other states.

References
1.   QUEST: Quality care, Universal access, Efficient utilization, Stabilizing costs, and Transforming provision of health care
2.   A family of four at 300 percent of the Federal poverty level has a net income of $4,254 per month.
3.   According to DHS, the QUEST program is projected to save the state $150 million in deficit spending over the next five years.
4.   Recently a GAO report titled "States Who Turn to Managed Care to Improve Access and Control Costs" (March 17, 1993) reported that the various states were unable to prove whether cost savings resulted from the conversion of Medicaid to managed care.
5.   These findings are supported by the work of Hurley et al, which concluded that in a sample of four Medicaid managed care programs emergency room usage was reduced from 27 to 37 percent amongst children and from 30 to 45 percent amongst adult participants.
6.   The issue of reduced utilization is supported by the work of Manning, Leibowitz, Goldberg, et al. (1984) in which a 20 percent difference in hospital admission rates and close to a 40 percent reduction in hospital days were found among populations randomly assigned to a group HMO.
7.   Wednesday, March 30, 1994. House Committee on Finance. Information Briefing on Hawai'i QUEST.
8.   Initiatives include: Governor's Family Policy Academy, Healthy Hawaii 2000, Hawai'i Kids Count (through the Governor's Office of Children and Youth) and the Literacy Policy Academy.
9.   Healthy Start is a child abuse and neglect primary prevention program utilizing a risk assessment screening tool and paraprofessional home visitor follow-up. The BabySAFE program identifies mothers using drugs and/or alcohol and provides a range of support services including counseling and treatment.
10. The reportedly uninsured women were either unaware of their eligibility, unable to access the system due to lack of transportation and other socio-economic barriers, or unable to complete the complex application process without assistance.
11. EPSDT services include periodicity screens, and all medically necessary medical, dental and behavioral health diagnostic and treatment services. Federal requirements imposed by the EPSDT statutory provisions of the Omnibus Budget Reconciliation Act of 1989 (OBRA 89) mandates that 80 percent of EPSDT eligible children receive periodicity screens by 1995 (QUEST RFP, p.20).
12. The Department of Health, Personal Health Services Administration did produce a document in March, 1994, outlining and describing the various direct and contracted services in the community that could be available for contract under QUEST.

13.   The Federal government has categories of disease and ethnic group which are funded at a higher level than basic Medicaid benefits package.

14.   An outcome-based objective, for example, would measure and set a benchmarking goal for percentage of normal birth-weight babies. This indicator would provide information regarding the accessibility, timeliness, and quality of the prenatal care being offered by the plans. Another example would describe an input as the percentage of children fully immunized by age 2. An outcome is the percentage of children who should be free from vaccine-preventable disease by age 5, and by a certain time of year.

15.   Developmental indicators include assessments of milestones on the development of an infant. Functional indicators help to assess activities of daily living such as evaluation of speech skills for multiply handicapped children.

Bibliography

Annie E. Casey Foundation. (1994). *Kids Count Data Book.*

Association of Maternal and Child Health Programs. (1993). "Managed Care for Women, Children, Adolescents & Their Families: A Discussion Paper With Recommendations for Assuring Improved Health Outcomes and Roles for State MCH Programs," (March).

Association of State and Territorial Health Officials. (1993). "The Impact of Medicaid Managed Care On Public Health Systems in Arizona: A Case Study of Public Health and the Arizona Health Care Cost Containment System," (May).

Benson, Dale S. (1992). *Measuring Outcomes in Ambulatory Care,* American Hospital Publishing, Inc.

Blankenau, Renee. (1993). "Leeway for States; Revised Waiver Process May Encourage State Experiments." *Hospitals* (March 20), 44-48.

California Department of Health Services. (1993). "Expanding Medi-Cal Managed Care: Reforming the Health System; Protecting Vulnerable Populations," (March 31).

Carey, Timothy S., Weis, Kathi, & Homer, Charles. (1991). "Prepaid Versus Traditional Medicaid Plans: Lack of Effect on Pregnancy Outcomes and Prenatal Care," *Health Services Research,* **26,** 2 (June), 165-181.

Dayton, Kevin. (1994). "Users of Health QUEST Have Choice of Care Plan: 110,000 expected to join program in July," *The Honolulu Advertiser* (March 31), A-7.

Department of Human Services, State of Hawai'i. (1993). "KeikiQUEST Outreach Concept Paper." (May 10).

Fox, Harriette B., and McManus, Margaret A. (1992). "Medicaid Managed Care Arrangements and Their Impact on Children and Adolescents: A Briefing Report," Prepared for The Child and Adolescent Health Policy Center. (November).

Fox, Harriette, McManus, Margaret, & Leibowitz, Arleen. (1993). "What We Know About Managed Care for Children," Prepared for the Child Health Consortium (February).

Fox, Harriette B. and Wicks, Lori B. (1993). "State Efforts to Maintain a Role for Publicly Funded Providers in a Medicaid Managed Care Environment," Prepared for Maternal and Child Health Policy Research Center. (May).

Freed, JoAnn B. (1994). Testimony on Senate Bill 3286, Relating to Maternal and Child Health, (February 14).

Freund, Deborah A. and Lewit, Eugene M. (1993). "Managed Care for Children and Pregnant Women: Promises and Pitfalls," *The Future of Children—Health Care Reform*, **3**, 2 (Summer/Fall), 92-122.

General Accounting Office. (1993). "Medicaid: States Turn to Managed Care to Improve Access and Control Costs." Washington, DC (March 17).

Goldfarb, Neil I., Hillman, Alan L., Eisenberg, John M., Kelley, Mark A., Cohen, Arnold V., & Dellheim, Miriam. (1991). "Impact of a Mandatory Medicaid Case Management Program on Prenatal Care and Birth Outcomes: A Retrospective Analysis," Medical Care, **29**, 1 (Jan.), 64-71.

Goodman, James A. (1991). "Managed Care: Medicaid - A Special Case," *Journal of the National Medical Association*, **85**, 3, 173-176.

"Hawai'i Health QUEST: Request for Proposal for QUEST Health Plan." (1993). Prepared by the Department of Human Services, State of Hawai'i.

Hillman, Alan L., Greer, William R., & Goldfarb, Neil. (1993). "Safeguarding Quality in Managed Competition," *Health Affairs* (Supp.), 110-122.

Hughes, Dana C., Newacheck, Paul W., Stoddard, Jeffrey J., & Halfon, Neal. (1994 draft). "Medicaid Managed Care: Can it Work for Children?"

Hurley, Robert E., Freund, Deborah A., & Taylor, Donald E. (1989). "Emergency Room Use and Primary Care Case Management: Evidence from Four Medicaid Demonstration Programs," *American Journal of Public Health*, **79**, 7 (July), 843-846.

Laguna Research Associates. (1993). "Evaluation of Arizona's Health Care Cost Containment System Demonstration," Prepared for Health Care Financing Administration (April).

Medi-Cal Administrative Claiming. (1993). "DTS Function Listing," (July).

National Committee for Quality Assurance. (1993). News Release titled, "Newly Developed Health Plan Measurements Will Provide Meaningful, Standard Performance Data: HEDIS 2.0," (May 6).

National Association of Public Hospitals. (1994). "Assessing the Design and Implementation of Tenncare," Executive Summary (April 27).

Richardson, Sally. (1994). "Insider Commentary," *American Healthline*, **3**, 13 (April 1).

Rosenbaum, Sara, Hughes, Dana, Butler, Elizabeth, & Howard, Deborah. (1989). "Incantations in the Dark: Medicaid, Managed Care, and Maternity Care," *The Milbank Quarterly*, **66**, 4, 661-693.

SRI International. (1989). "Evaluation of the Arizona Health Care Costs Containment System; Final Report," Prepared for Health Care Financing Administration (January).

Stine, William F. (1991). "The Effect of Local Government Outreach Efforts on the Recipiency of Selected Medicaid Programs," *Inquiry*, **28** (Summer), 161-168.

Valdez, Burciaga R., Ware, John E., Manning, Willard G., Brook, Mark H., Rogers, William H., Goldberg, George A., & Newhouse, Joseph P. (1989). "Prepaid Group Practice Effects on the Utilization of Medical Services and Health Outcomes for Children: Results From a Controlled Trial," Pediatrics, **83**, 2 (February), 168-179.

Wallack, Stanley S. (1991). "Managed Care: Practice, Pitfalls, and Potential," *Health Care Financing Review* (Annual Supp.), 27-33.

CHAPTER SIXTEEN

It's A Wonderful Life
The Not-So-Secret Life
of An Executive Director

FRANK CHONG

The Waikiki Health Center has been providing health and social services to the community since 1967. During that time we have tried to find creative ways of addressing those that have little but need much: the frail elderly, runaways, the homeless, populations "at risk" for HIV/AIDS and other sexually-transmitted diseases, those without health insurance, and those who always seem to fall through the cracks.

As an Executive Director, one thing that I have found absolutely necessary is to keep "in touch" with the policy-makers and the people who carry out the policies. Decisions made today often have a cascading effect tomorrow. Asking the hard questions today can often avoid monumental problems tomorrow. The most important duty of an Executive Director is to stay current with today's issues in order to anticipate what tomorrow may bring.

To prepare for this chapter I took two days out of a week in November, 1993. I carried my pocket tape recorder with me and simply recorded items and events as the day went along.

November 16, 1993, 8:10 AM: In the car, leaving Kailua
It's Tuesday morning and I am on my way to True Value Hardware to pick up some supplies for the Waikiki Health Center—paint brushes, a door stop and other essentials. Then a quick stop at Longs Drug Store for a few other odds and ends.

As I think over the fall schedule it is quite obvious that the next six months will be a very interesting time for the Waikiki Health Center. The "external environment" is very unstable. The local political environment is as close to chaos as one can get.

Health Care Reform is on everyone's mind. Our major activity at the Waikiki Health Center is primary-care medical services, therefore, health-care reform, QUEST, the Legislature and the sudden downturn in the economy are all priority issues. Whenever things are tough economically we get busy. It is enough to give anyone nightmares.

Wonderful things to think about as one waits in traffic. Fortunately, it is late enough in the morning so most of the traffic is gone. The trip over the Pali won't be too bad. In fact, it might even be enjoyable. It is hard to believe how beautiful the Ko'olaus can be just about every day.

A quick trip into Waikiki, pick up messages, make a few calls, and then head for the State Office Tower for a picture-taking session with the Governor and 45 other AIDS service providers. I will probably spend all morning there, try to catch up with what is happening or not happening as the case may be.

10:00 AM, State Office Tower

December 1 is being proclaimed International AIDS Awareness Day. Stopping in at the Capitol today will just be the first of many trips there over the next six months.

Confusion is in the air. It is just part of the highly charged atmosphere. After the ouster of Jimmy Aki as Senate President by Norman Mizuguchi, it is not quite clear as to who is in charge. It is clear that everyone thinks that they are in charge.

Right now the key is to keep on top of everything but not get too involved because it will all change very fast, especially as the key positions change and the committee assignments change. Inevitably everything will have a ripple effect. How those ripples will affect the Waikiki Health Center is what I have to find out.

I did not stay too long after the picture-taking but decided to use the opportunity to visit with some legislators. Went down to Senator Bert Kobayashi's office. I have known Bert since college. He has chaired the Senate Health Committee a number of times, and there is not much that needs to be done to get up to speed with him. Will he still be the Chair of the Health Committee with the Senate Shake-Up? Policy issues affecting the people we serve are often decided in the Health Committee.

Who should be in Bert's office but Senator Tony Chang. We had a good chat about the Senate and the Legislature in general. We also had a good laugh about how so many things have changed. We decided that we are among the "senior citizens" when it comes to the legislature and legislative watching. After all, we both served on legislative staffs back in the early seventies. Tony was an aide to Sakai Takahashi, and I was an aide to Joe Kuroda, via the Hawai'i Council of Churches. But that is another story.

Staying in touch between sessions is helpful. You can take more time to explain the implications of different policy changes. Developing networks, reinforcing linkages or lobbying, whatever it is called: do it between sessions if at all possible.

Every year I write and edit the "Legislative Action Yellow Pages," an underground guide to the state legislature. It is geared for human-services types. It profiles each legislator and tries to give readers some insight on the decision-makers. It is helpful to know what their interests are and how to nurture them to see the world through the eyes of some of our clients.

After about 15 minutes, Bert walked in. I sat down and chatted with him for about 45 minutes. It is a log jam. Things have flip-flopped. Those that were once on the inside are now very much on the outside. The folks on the outside don't know how to be good losers, and those on the inside don't know how to accommodate those outside.

Curiously enough, Bert asked me how I thought things should go. I didn't have specifics, but did mention that it is apparent that the public may have more influence than it thought it did. When Mizuguchi appointed Milton Holt Chair of Ways and Means, the public outcry was loud, strong and swift. He quickly removed Holt and replaced him with Donna Ikeda. The negative responses of the public apparently made him move pretty quickly.

One of my other agenda items was to recruit celebrity volunteers to help serve Thanksgiving Dinner to the homeless at the Hard Rock Cafe. Bert thought he could help at the 11:00 AM serving. Bert represents the Waikiki area, and it is always nice to have him in touch with some of "our folks," both our clients and some of the good people who support us.

The old Kapahulu Health Center (548 Kapahulu Avenue) is about to be demolished. It would make an ideal site for a satellite clinic for the Waikiki Health Center. It might be affordable if we went into a joint venture with the state. Bert made some suggestions about parking and other design ideas. He will probably introduce a bill for us in the next session.

Then I went to see Representative Len Pepper, a psychologist by training and retired DOH employee. He was not in so I stopped in to see Representative Duke Bainum. Duke was fun to talk to. He had several items that he wanted to introduce this session and was testing them out with me. Some of them were environment-oriented, but his key health concern is "violence." I suggested he might look at "violence" as a public-health perspective rather than sell a criminal justice or medical issue. We also agreed that it was an important part of health-care reform since the cost of treating victims of violence can be astronomical. It was a good discussion.

It was also good to see Duke hit his own stride. I can remember back when he was an aide to Bert Kobayashi. Duke has always been one of our supporters and before he was elected he was a volunteer visitor to the elderly. He thought he would be able to help serve Thanksgiving Dinner at 11 AM at Hard Rock Cafe. I also talked to him about the property on Kapahulu for a joint venture with the DOH.

Then back to Pepper's to talk about getting some money for a psychiatrist to help provide mental-health services to the homeless. I think it will run about $100,000. His estimate was that a psychologist might cost about half that amount.

I was getting ready to leave and who should I run into at the elevator but Representative Jim Shon. He is still in political Siberia. He talked about long-term care issues not going very far this session. He is still happy to write letters and continues to be the champion of under-represented causes.

We talked until 11:45 AM. I then went back to my car parked in the DOH parking lot. I thought that since I was there I should at least stop in and see Calvin Masaki, Deputy Director of Health. He was not in so I left a message with his secretary. I wanted to talk to him about 548 Kapahulu.

It was a very helpful morning as I reconnected with some good people who will be making some important decisions in a few months.

12:00 Noon

I then headed over to Kalihi-Palama Health Center for an AlohaCare meeting. The primary care centers have banded together and formed a new corporation which will be one of the bidders for Health QUEST, the State of Hawai'i's response to the Medicaid crisis. We have started to work on the by-laws. Going was slow but we made good progress. I stayed until 1:30 PM then headed back to the Waikiki for another meeting. Looks like AlohaCare will be working with Managed Care Solutions from Arizona. Everything is beginning to fall together for Health QUEST.

2:00 PM

Got back to Waikiki Health Center about 2 PM. Just in time to meet with "Tint," an MD from Burma at the School of Public Health looking for a way to stay in Hawai'i after his degree program is over. Needless to say it is very complicated. I chatted with him for half an hour.

Then I met with Mary Spadaro, Director of Development at Waikiki Health Center, for about a half hour. We went over a bunch of fund-raising issues like direct mail, other fund development programs and some grant proposals that are due in December.

I made a couple more calls for Thanksgiving Dinner. We are still looking for help at Hard Rock Cafe.

Jean Paty called to set up a February meeting with the Central Union Church Youth Group at the Youth Outreach (YO) Project. The youth group wants to learn more about our program for runaway youth in Waikiki. It is a collaborative effort with Hale Kipa. We both do outreach to teens in Waikiki. Hale Kipa does the case management, and we do the health and medical care. There is a real need for outreach services to this group, because so many of them end up in Waikiki and often end up in real trouble.

Then at 5 PM it is up to UH for a pre-meeting for the Public Administration program. I teach a one session on the state budget to a group in the public administration program. I will be teaching it with Ed Rogoff tonight.

As far as "a day in the life of an Executive Director," it has been busy, will continue to be busy, and won't let up until late tonight. Finally, I had about ten minutes to prepare for class and headed up to UH for a quick bite and a pre-class meeting.

4:50 PM On my way to UH

Class went very well! Ed and I split the responsibilities. I took the dull part and talked about how the budget is supposed to be put together and how the Program Planning Budgeting System (PPBS) is supposed to work. He talked about how the budget is "really put together." He talked about the underside of how state budgets are put together. Our general emphasis was on the political nature of the budget process and how the political process often conflicts with the budget process.

A major policy change such as the move from "fee for service" in the Medicaid program to QUEST and "managed care" is so dramatic that if it is done for political reasons it creates total confusion, because the fiscal and programmatic infrastructure is not present. The political appointee often makes the decision, but the civil servant then has to carry out the policy.

We had a very good discussion on the role of the civil servant versus the political appointee. The most interesting discussion was on how to restore integrity to the Civil Service System. I then gave Ed a ride home to Waikiki.

About 9:30 PM, on H-1 on the way from Waikiki to Kailua

I am finally getting to the end of a long day. Left home

over 13 hours ago and if I am lucky, I'll be home about 10:15 and in bed by 11 PM. What a day!

11:30 PM

I got home to find a message on my answering machine from Sharon Sutter about one of our Family Planning Contracts. She wanted me to return her call regardless of how late it might be so I did. The day started before 8:00 AM and finally got done at 11:30 PM.

Wednesday, November 17

I spent the morning downtown. Got to DOH about 9 AM and had a very good discussion with Calvin regarding the possible uses of the old Kapahulu Health Center. The options at this time are viable and wide open. There have been some very preliminary studies done but no commitments have been made. A satellite clinic is definitely a possibility.

The original intent was to demolish the current structure and replace it with a three or four story building. More recently the talk has been about a three story building. The major problem is parking. The cost will go up significantly if it has underground parking.

My idea is to have shared use of the building with multiple funding sources using a condominium concept. Bert Kobayashi suggested parking on the other side of the water station. Who knows what will happen? If you don't ask, you don't get.

Then I talked to Masaru Oshiro, Deputy Director of Behavioral Health Services, about a Grant-In-Aid request that we will be submitting to the legislature. I told him we need a psychiatrist to work with the homeless. No surprises for the bureaucrats. They like that. At least they are warned early enough to know something is coming. We will be requesting $110,000 from the Legislature.

Then I met Jack Lewin, the Director of Health, in the hallway. We chatted about the critical need for adolescent mental health. He was concerned about getting some solid numbers. This is a problem especially when the kids are not in school or are runaways. I suggested contacting our Youth Outreach Project as a source.

Then I went to the Alliance for Health and Human Services meeting at the YWCA. It ran from 10:00 AM-noon. We talked mostly about strategies for the next legislative session.

Some of us want to revise the law that sets the procedures for state funds being allocated to non-profits (Chapter 42D).

After all this, I got a sandwich and sat under a tree on the Capitol grounds and just enjoyed watching people. After all, one must stop to smell the flowers once in awhile. Then it was back to Waikiki Health Center about 1 PM.

Riverside Travel was on the phone when I got back. They received a call from Kaua'i Mental Health Center to help get a patient from Kauai to the mainland. They had arranged for transportation but Riverside Travel needed some money up front to lock in the reservations. I agreed to advance them the money out of our Ohana Funds. No one else was around, so I got back in the car and ran the money downtown to them. I don't mind helping when people really go out of their way to make something work.

When I finally got back to my office I spent most of the afternoon opening mail, doing paper work and answering phone calls. At 6 PM I went to the Neighborhood Justice Center Annual meeting at the Ala Wai Club House. Just 3 minutes away so I didn't mind.

By chance I started to talk to Peter Lewis, one of the VPs at Hawai'i Electric, about our need for more space. HECO has some property across the street from our building on Ohua Avenue and there are no plans for it at the moment. I'll call Peter in the morning to find out about HECO's plans and if they would be interested in a joint venture or something.

All it takes is a little asking around. It may never get anywhere but who knows, if you don't ask you will never find out. What a Life! Or maybe I should get a life!

Some End Notes:

•A Bill was introduced at the 1994 Session to explore the future use of 548 Kapahulu Avenue. It also put emphasis on possible joint use and health care. The bill made it through all the committees until it reached House Finance. There it was changed from "health related purposes" to "elderly housing." The Department of Accounting and General Services then gave an estimate of $82,000 for the cost of demolition, because it is filled with asbestos. The bill died.

•At the end of the session Bert Kobayashi announced that he would not run for re-election after serving 16 years in public office.

• The Grant-In-Aid for psychiatric services for the Homeless was submitted with a request for $110,000. It came out, $80,000.

• All bills relating to Chapter 42D died.

• The individual from Kaua'i was reunited with his family on the mainland.

• The HECO property on Ohua is still empty. Apparently HECO wants to keep it empty for a small substation or booster station sometime in the future.

• A group of parents, individual children, and community organizations filed a class action suit against the State of Hawai'i for not providing mental-health services to children and adolescents as required by law. The suit is to go to Federal court sometime in 1994.

• The 11th Edition of the Legislative Action Yellow Pages went through major revisions and updates and, as scheduled, came out ten days after the session opened.

• And The Hard Rock Cafe provided Thanksgiving Dinner to almost 400 homeless and elderly people on Thanksgiving Day as their gift to the community with or without our celebrity servers.

Conclusions

Part I: Background for Reform

Bob Grossmann

Three lessons from the February, 1994 U.S. General Accounting Office (GAO) February 1994 report, *HEALTH CARE IN HAWAI'I: Implications for National Reform (HEHS-94-68, pp. 16-17)*, set the stage for reforming Hawai'i and bear implications for the rest of the nation. The GAO found that: 1) "an employer mandate by itself will not necessarily result in universal access to health care," and "other publicly sponsored programs are necessary" to meet the residual gap group; 2) although near-universal access has resulted in lower health insurance premiums, the Prepaid Health Care Act (PHCA) "did not have explicit cost-control provisions, and Hawai'i's costs have risen at a rate similar to the national average; and 3) Hawai'i's employer mandate "has not created large dislocations in the small business sector," but "factors unique to Hawai'i may have contributed to this outcome." In addition to these findings, the inherent policy contradictions exposed in *The Unfinished Health Agenda* must be dealt with "head on" and with a sense of urgency. Otherwise, our comparative advantages will continue to diminish rapidly.

The GAO report uses a big-picture analysis with broad policy brush strokes to compare Hawai'i with national trends. However, for Hawai'i to see the day-to-day detail, its own policy analysis has to get more nitty-gritty. The various chapters from *The Unfinished Health Agenda* confront the myth that insurance can do the job alone. The book challenges policy makers to get back to the details and to be politically open to exploring the underlying health-care policy contradictions.

Most chapters call for health-care budgets tied to other social needs such as social injustice to Native Hawai'ians, violence, substance abuse, housing, child care, long-term care, or education. Hawai'i, because of its diversity in culture, may be less able than some to directly confront these social pressures that will result in a continued increase in both physical and mental health services. The inability and, perhaps, even the unwillingness of some state administrative and legislative leaders to effectively plan for those who will continue to be without health insurance in the transition into managed-care programs like Health QUEST is a good example or what needs to change and what is often at stake.

Any new major health insurance policy is going to cause some dislocations, because of new rules and administrative barriers. Even with an employer mandate and an expanded Medicaid program, some of Hawai'i's residents will never participate in any insurance program. Factors such as behavioral health problems, not having a social security number, inability to turn in a complete application in English, or inability to pay one's "fair share" of monthly premium payments may result in many not accessing health insurance. This gap group will also be "fluid," in the sense that the individuals uninsured will change significantly from year to year or even by month.

Fully understanding the many reasons for being uninsured will force the state or Federal government to more fully expose the problems and inequities that plague us. Solutions are complex, costly, and usually avoided in policy debates.

The Hawai'i State Primary Care Association attempted to raise this contradiction associated with the Health QUEST program in the 1994 Legislature. The Association's testimony exposed the basic arguments as to why a gap group would remain and why services would probably diminish for those who continue to be uninsured.

The first contradiction was the fact that SHIP funds and staff were being transferred to Health QUEST without analysis by the state of those who would continue to be both poor and without health insurance. Yet, the SHIP program, as enacted in 1989, was to creatively use funds to provide services to this residual gap group through non-insurance mechanisms. For instance, SHIP would pay community health centers a voucher payment per visit (less than cost) to treat those medically-indigent prior to Health QUEST.

Initially, the community health centers received a letter from the SHIP Administrator saying that the voucher program would end the day that Health QUEST was initially scheduled to begin. The loss of this dedicated funding to the residual gap group was not seen as a necessary part of the overall health-care reform efforts in Hawai'i. The Hawai'i State Primary Care Association fought to assure that at least $1 million was set aside from the Medicaid budget to help pay for those medically-indigent in the years to come.

The Association's Board also introduced legislation to mandate that the state continue to provide cost-based reimbursement for enabling service (e.g., to assure effective outreach and follow-up) to this expected gap group. Ironically, in a state as culturally diverse as Hawai'i, an amendment to the Health QUEST Request For Proposals allowed bidders to make language and cultural services optional. Again, without some dedicated funds to this vital part of care, the services to this residual gap group would likely diminish to charity care only. The state's policy, which grew out of the National Governors' Association, was to eliminate all cost-based reimbursements—specifically to Federally Qualified Health Centers—in an effort to shift policy toward managed care. The myth that managed care would bring health insurance to all and the need to politically "fast-track" the program kept solid policies from being developed.

The Unfinished Health Agenda exposes many of these gaps in policy and funding. As stated by Jon Martell in his chapter, "Those who need medical insurance most may have the hardest time getting it." The homeless are dying in Hawai'i and elsewhere at rates higher than many under-developed countries. With 40 percent of the homeless population seriously mentally ill, learning disabled or demented, it is not surprising that many will never avail themselves of the Health QUEST program.

DHS did not effectively evaluate the cost of not serving these individuals, especially when a large number of Hawai'i's uninsured live on islands other than O'ahu, and will avail themselves of emergency rooms at state-run hospitals. DHS and their outside consultants were focused on the major goal to reduce Medicaid costs; costs that will be shifted to other state programs were not effectively evaluated nor did the Health Care Financing Administration (HCFA) require such evaluation.

Furthermore, with some 70 percent of Hawai'i's homeless still uninsured, even with the SHIP program in operation since 1989, the reasons why the majority of homeless do not have health insurance was not included in the Health QUEST vision. Given the complexity of problems faced by Hawai'i's homeless, managed care—based on a financing driven by monthly per

capita rates—is not likely to provide adequate contact for successful holistic treatment to individuals with multiple problems
(e.g., mental health and substance abuse). The lesson here is
that health policy analysis for large social programs must be comprehensive and based on reality, where treatment can be delivered in a social context.

At the heart of many chapters in this book is the notion
that more community-delivered care is needed versus further
government-controlled care. Although the Department of Health
was strongly advocating for alignment with the Institute of Medicine (IOM) recommendations that state government should involve itself more with assessment, policy, and assurance functions, the era of management care has seen yet another reversal.

Even the issue of *who* is community for given issues will
play itself out as new interests emerge when higher stakes are
played on the health-care industry "game board." Truly, hundreds of millions are at stake! For example, an issue over the
establishment of a family practice residency program in Hilo,
although benign in theory, has raised significant controversy in
several communities.

At issue is whether the University of Hawai'i Medical
School's residency program should be used to set up ambulatory care centers that compete directly with community health
centers giving primary care, and whether a holistic model is
achieved or just a subtle variation of the medical model.

Also, given the proposed structure of national health-care
reform, a key policy question needs to be asked: Are ambulatory centers being created as the *only* Academic Health Centers
that would capture Hawai'i's share of funds set aside for the
training of practitioners in non-hospital settings?

This is precisely the policy level at which Hawai'i needs
to assess what is going on, because the implementation of this
plan would have tremendous effect on meaningful reform in
Hawai'i. Health-care reform in Hawai'i and nationally must assure that any new huge piece of the puzzle adequately supports
the basic principles of prevention and primary care by a *team* of
practitioners involving not only physicians, but those from the
Schools of Social Work, Nursing and Public Health. Furthermore, such new initiatives should be in concert with those who
have struggled to deliver primary care in communities for years
to those who, for the most part, no one else really wanted to

treat. Otherwise, the reform will be a zero sum game. The pieces will be moved around, the costs will continue to escalate faster than the average rate of inflation for other goods and services, and quality of enabling services is likely to further diminish as dollars for basic public health functions, outreach, and language services become the territory for cost savings. This is so, because other less meaningful factors will be linked to "quality control" and "utilization'" that will be politically more in line with self-serving health care agendas. It is also highly possible that the era of managed care will result in an even further concentration of ownership and control of more and more of the health dollars nation-wide.

The fundamental goal—to provide health care to the tens of millions who go without—is the heart of health-care reform. What will continue to be at issue is: how will this inclusion of access to health insurance be financed? In other words, how is it going to be paid for, and what is everyone's fair share? An agreeable notion of everyone's fair share may be difficult to achieve politically, because the playing fields for major social and economic factors are so uneven. Health care is very personal and critically linked to the quality of life.

Part II: Just What Part of 'All' Don't You Understand?

JIM SHON

In December, 1994, representatives from 15 states met to hammer out certain principles they wanted incorporated into any Federal health-care reform. Their idea was to be partners in reform by noting state and regional differences, thus giving a sense of ownership to the implementation of a national plan.

The states were enthusiastic about their own experiments, often reflecting differences in their demographic and economic profiles, politics, urban-rural ratios, immigrants, and their existing health systems. Hawai'i has its employer mandate, using the private sector to finance insurance; Alabama depends heavily on county health departments; Florida must respect its citizens' commitment to free enterprise; Vermont embraces government regulation; Minnesota and Washington like employer mandates, and Oregon believes in a rational prioritization of benefits.

Among their tasks as they met just outside of Washington, D.C., was to clarify what was meant by "universal" in health- care reform. It is clear that "universal access" has sometimes been used to mean "you can have it if you can find it and pay for it." "Access" is often associated with health insurance rather than the actual receipt of health-care services.

The product of their discussions over access is a useful standard to measure whether or not the *Unfinished Health Agenda* has been incorporated into health-care reform.

In many ways, these chapters have sought to expand upon what happens when this comprehensive standard of universal access and coverage is not met. (See Figure 1.)

In the spring of 1993 a legislator wrote to urge the Department of Justice to take over Hawai'i's mental-health system and force the state government to do the right thing with respect to child and adolescent mental-health services. A dialogue was initiated that for the first time brought Department of Health (DOH) representatives in direct collaboration with a variety of mental-health advocacy groups and service providers. Together they forged a document that set out in detail the needs for child and adolescent mental health in Hawai'i.

Months passed and the state seemed unable to respond except defensively. Finally, a coalition of groups brought a class action suit against the state. They won their case! A comprehensive remedy was approved. Apparently mental-health advocates in other states are very excited about this victory, as the suit was the largest class action group ever to win a settlement under that particular Federal statute.

This was an instructive lesson both for Hawai'i and the nation. Leadership need not wait for state government initiatives, or even Congressional action. Universal access can be sought by applying existing Federal laws, as well as state and Federal constitutional protections. This is one example of Hawai'i's commitment to health care, but in this case it is the community itself that forced the issue, not government.

As government becomes less and less the preferred agent of change, having lost to some extent public confidence that it can be competent and fair at all times, perhaps other citizen initiatives will be necessary in partnership with government to ensure that the *Unfinished Agenda* is addressed.

FIGURE 1

Universal Access/Coverage

By (specific date) each state shall assure that every citizen is identified and enrolled in a universally-accessible health-care delivery system. A universally-accessible system includes services that:

- are affordable (and without deterrents to appropriate care) . . . timely, reflect community values and are portable;
- are culturally appropriate for all populations, including minorities, whose who speak foreign languages, disabled, homeless, teens, etc.;
- meet community standards of appropriate quality of care;
- are coordinated with other relevant social and wellness services that may or may not be part of the benefit packages;
- are periodically measured by objective criteria related to actual receipt of services;
- provide consumer and technical evaluation of the correspondence between delivery of services and outcomes and client needs;
- engage states and communities in a discussion of values and their needs;
- assure, measure, evaluate and train to establish and maintain a cadre of needed health professionals;
- provide consumer education and outreach.

MILBANK MEMORIAL FUND CONFERENCE, DECEMBER, 1993

The growth of the private, non-profit service sector, often receiving significant subsidies and contracts from government, is one symptom. This sector has grown in part not as a competitor of public service, but as a complementary addition of services that government has been unable or unwilling to fund completely "in-house."

The big buzz word in the politically-correct *reinvention of government* jargon is "partnership." One is tempted to view this as a cop-out on government's part, or a faddish phrase with little lasting meaning. Yet it is hard to point to a purely governmental victory in extending access to the indigent. So often, it is the community of health-care workers and providers themselves that are providing both leadership and solutions.

The Unfinished Health Agenda wishes to emphasize that it is not only the substance of health care that must be broadened, but also the process for affecting change. Institutions of all sorts, governmental or private, may need a political or legal kick in the pants. Leadership and creativity are not the exclusive attributes of those institutions.

In reflecting on Section 1 of the U.S. Constitution's Fourteenth Amendment, we note that *all* citizens are entitled to the same privileges or immunities, due process and equal protection of the laws. We might pose the question to those who currently control health care: Just what part of "all" don't you understand?

> *Sec. 1: All persons born or naturalized in the United States, and subject to the jurisdiction thereof, are citizens of the United States and of the State wherein they reside. No State shall make or enforce any law which shall abridge the privileges or immunities of citizens of the United States; nor shall any State deprive any person of life, liberty, or property, without due process of law; nor deny to any person within its jurisdiction the equal protection of the laws.*

The Unfinished Agenda demands that we take the Fourteenth Amendment seriously. It is a principle that should permeate all our health-care efforts. To follow our Constitution, we must be truly inclusive and universal.

Bibliography

COMPILED BY VIRGINIA SHICHIDA TANJI, LIBRARIAN
UNIVERSITY OF HAWAI'I SCHOOL OF PUBLIC HEALTH

Baumgartner, Eric T., Grossmann, Bob, Fuddy, Loretta. (1993) Hawai'i's near-universal health insurance—lessons learned. *Journal of Health Care for the Poor and Underserved.* 4(3):194-202.

Blaisdell, Richard Kekuni(1993). Health status of Kanaka Maoli (Indigenous Hawai'ians). *Asian American and Pacific Islander Journal of Health* 1 (2): 116-160.

Burke, Marybeth. Hawai'i's health-care plan stirs Capitol Hill debate over access. *Hospitals.* 66(8):32-26, Apr. 20, 1992.

de Lafuente, Della. Cost of paradise. Critics say Hawai'i's much-touted health plan has an expensive price tag. *Modern Healthcare* 24(4):30-34, Jan 24, 1994.

Dukakis, Michael S.(1992). The States and Health-Care Reform *New England Journal of Medicine* 327(15):1090-1092.

Friedman, Emily (1993). The Aloha Way: Health Care Structure and Finance in Hawai'i. Honolulu: Hawai'i Medical Service Association Foundation.

Gilbert, Fred I. Jr., Nordyke, Robert A. (1993). The case for restructuring health care in the United States: the Hawai'i paradigm. *Journal of Medical Systems* 17:283-288.

Hawai'i. Department of Health. Anuual report statistical supplement, 1971- . Honolulu: the Department.

Health Trends in Hawai'i: a Statistical Chartbook for Policy Makers and Planners (1994). Honolulu: HMSA Foundation.

Health Care in Hawai'i: Implications for National Reform (1994). Washington, D.C.: U.S. General Accounting Office.

Holoweiko, Mark. Health-care reform: what does Hawai'i have to teach? *Medical Economics* 69(3):158-164,171-173,174.

Kim, Howard. Life after mandatory insurance: Hawai'i providers ride a new wave. *Modern Healthcare* 21(7):21-25.

Lewin, John C., Sybinsky, Peter A. (1993). Hawai'i's employer mandate and its contribution to universal access. *JAMA* 269(19):2538-2543.

Neubauer, Deane. State model: Hawai'i. A pioneer in health system reform (1993). *Health Affairs* 12 (2): 31-39.

Schmitz, Anthony. Say aloha to health reform. *Health* 7(4): 6272, July/August 1993.

Wegener, Eldon L. (1989) The health of Native Hawai'ians: a selective report on health status and health care in the 1980's. *Social Process in Hawai'i* 32.

About the Contributors

Susan Chandler, PhD, is a professor in the School of Social Work, University of Hawai'i at Manoa (hf. UHM), and a research associate with the University's Center of Youth Research. She teaches in the areas of social welfare policy, community practice, and mental health. A past president of the Mental Health Association of Hawai'i, she serves as an Associate board member.

Frank A. Chong, MSW, has been the Executive Director of the Waikiki Health Center since March, 1977. Before that he was the Associate Minister of the Community Church of Honolulu. He has a Masters in Social Work degree (1968) and a Certificate in Public Administration (1985) from UHM. He received his Masters in Divinity degree from Union Theological Seminary, New York City, in 1971. He has been writing and editing the Legislative Action Yellow Pages every year since 1983.

Daniel Domizio, MPH, PA-C, is a certified Physician Assistant practicing on the Wai'anae Coast of rural O'ahu, and Vice President of the Hawai'i Association of Physician Assistants. His career includes service as Clinical Training Coordinator at Duke University, community medicine on Native American reservations in the American Southwest, and international health experience. In cooperation with the School of Public Health at UHM, he has been helping to develop a physician assistant training program.

Chenoa Farnsworth, BA, is special assistant to Geri Marullo at the state Department of Health. She previously worked as an aide to state Senator Andrew Levin. She holds a bachelor's degree in political science from the University of California, Santa Cruz.

Henry A. Foley, PhD, currently is Director of Ke Ola O Hawai'i, a Kellogg Foundation-funded multidisciplinary approach to community health care. Formerly Deputy Director of Health, for Hawai'i's Behavioral Health Administration, he served under President Carter as the Administrator of the Health Resources Administration.

Bob Grossmann, PhD, Executive Director of the non-profit Hawai'i State Primary Care Association, is an Assistant Clinical Professor for the School of Public Health at UHM. He has worked for eight years as Special Assistant to the Director of Health and as staff to the House Health Committee of the Hawai'i State Legislature. He has also been an analyst for the U.S. Congressional Office of Technology Assessment, the Food and Agricultural Organization of the United Nations, and the East-West Center.

Robert V. Hollison Jr., MD, is a native hapa-haole, a practicing family physician and internist with a broad background in primary-care practice, medical executive leadership roles, academic teaching and program development, and more than ten years of medical managed care experience. He has served as Managed Care Medical Director of The Queen's Health Care Plan and has been directly involved with the strategic implementation and development of a Hawai'i State-wide Primary Care Physician network of the Queen's Health Systems.

Joyce Ingram-Chinn, MEd, is the former Hawai'i State Chief of the Alcohol and Drug Abuse Branch, Department of Health. She is currently Project Manager for the Hawai'i Emergency Event Data Project (HEED), President and CEO of her own consulting firm. She has a Master's degree in Educational Psychology and is working on her doctorate in Social Welfare at UHM. She has frequently represented Hawai'i on national and regional substance-abuse policy groups.

Pamela G. Lichty, MPH, has been involved with HIV issues in Hawai'i since obtaining her MPH from UHM in 1987. She served as Committee Clerk for the House Committee on Health during the 1988 and 1989 sessions. Following this, she was planner for the Governor's Committee on HIV/AIDS for two and a half years. In this capacity she served as Legislative Liaison and was instrumental in the establishment of Hawai'i's Sterile Needle Exchange Program. Since leaving GCHA, she has worked as a consultant on health policy issues. She is currently an Assistant Researcher at the Social Science Research Institute at UHM, working on drug policy issues with an emphasis on harm reduction.

Gregory P. Loos, EdD, MPH, MS, is an Assistant Professor in the Department of Community Health Development, School of Public Health, at UHM. He has served with the Hawai'i Department of Health, Department of Education, and with the Kamehameha Schools. He has been instrumental in the development of a physician-assistant training program to prepare mid-level health-care practitioners for Hawai'i and the Pacific Basin.

Jon Martell, MD, is an Assistant Professor of Medicine at UHM's John A. Burns School of Medicine. He has worked with the medically-under-served in Hawai'i since 1984, at the Kalihi-Palama Health Clinic, the Wai'anae Coast Comprehensive Health Center, and the Queen Emma Clinics successively over the ensuing ten years. Dr. Martell began working with the homeless population in 1985 at Kalihi-Palama, and helped to organize its Health Clinic Health Care for the Homeless project in 1988 and sustain it since. Currently he spends most of his time on medical education but continues with the homeless project as their medical assistant.

Geri Marullo, RN, MS, has been the Deputy Director of the Hawai'i State Department of Health since 1989, responsible for administering over $70 million of outreach and community-based services to families in need. She also serves on the Board of Directors of the American Nurses' Association and on national advisory committees on health-care reform.

Nancy McGuckin-Smith, MPH, RN, currently is Executive Director of the Hawai'i Nurses' Association. A graduate of UHM, Schools of Nursing and Public Health, with major emphasis in the area of health policy and planning, she is a member of the Hawai'i Statewide Health Coordinating Council of the State Health Planning and Development Agency, Aloha United Way, and the Hawai'i Community Services Council.

Deane Neubauer, PhD, is Professor of Political Science at UHM, having been an undergraduate at the University of California, Riverside, and a graduate student at Yale University. He has taught public policy since his arrival at UH 24 years ago, and for the past 12 years has worked on issues of food and health policy as well as the dynamics of the international political economy. His recent work focuses on health-care policy, budgeting, and the role of the bureaucracy in Hawai'i. With Professor Albert Robillard of the Department of Sociology at UHM, he is currently at work on a book of post modernist interpretations of Hawai'i.

Mark O'Donnell, MPH, is the Executive Director of the Mental Health Association of Hawai'i. A former Peace Corps volunteer in Niger, he has worked in the human-service field as an advocate and program director throughout his career.

M. Jan Pryor, DO, MPH, is an Assistant Professor in the Department of Public Health Sciences, School of Public Health, at UHM. Before coming to Hawai'i, he served as faculty with the John A. Burns School of Medicine's Pacific Basin Medical Officers Training Program located in Pohnpei, Federated States of Micronesia, and is a collaborator with Dr. Loos and Mr. Domizio in developing a physician-assistant training program combining public health and clinical care personnel to help meet the state's health care needs.

Marilyn Seely, MPH, since 1986 has been a planner with the Executive Office on Aging, Office of the Governor. She is an assistant clinical professor at UHM, School of Public Health.

Representative Jim Shon, who has completed five terms in the Hawai'i State Legislature, was a Peace Corps teacher/trainer in Korea during 1970-1973. He did his graduate work at UHM in Asian History, and was elected as a Delegate to the 1978 Constitutional Convention. He is the author of the 1980 State Plan for Marine and Aquatic Education. He worked at the University's Curriculum Research and Development Center, specializing in science, social studies, and Hawai'ian History. He became Chair of the House Committee on Health in 1987, a position he held for six years, and in which he authored many laws dealing with smoking, mental health, primary care, and AIDS.

Kathryn Smith-Ripper, MA, received her undergraduate training at Allegheny College in Pennsylvania and her graduate degree from The Ohio State University. She has worked for the state legislature in Ohio, the Ohio Health Department, and state and national hospital associations. In Hawai'i, she has worked for the Departments of Health and Human Services and the March of Dimes Birth Defects Foundation Chapter of the Pacific.

Jeanette Takamura, PhD, director, Executive Office on Aging, Office of the Governor, State of Hawai'i. She has served as joint faculty with the Schools of Social Work at UHM.

Donald Topping, PhD, has been at UHM since 1962. He is a Professor of Linguistics and, since 1974, Director of the Social Science Research Institute. In addition to his descriptive linguistics work on Pacific languages, he has written on social change in Pacific Island nations, telecommunications, and drug-policy issues.

Scott Whitney, MA, is an ethnographer, free-lance writer, and staff researcher for Birch and Davis Health Management, Hawai'i. He was for five years the substance-abuse consultant and Assistant Chief of Social Services for the Territory of American Samoa. His master's degree is in Pacific Island Studies from UHM, and he has published frequently in the area of substance abuse and culture.